REVIEWS FOR OTHER BOOKS BY TROY TAYLOR

"SEASON OF THE WITCH is the best documented and most definitive work of the Bell Witch to date! Mr. Taylor has outdone himself in researching and collecting the material necessary to thoroughly examined and address this most mysterious tale ... I highly recommend this book to anyone interested in the full story of the Bell Witch!"
Dale Kaczmarek, author of "Windy City Ghosts"

Troy Taylor has brought a new level of professionalism to the field with THE GHOST HUNTERS GUIDEBOOK, which stands as the best and most authoritative book written to date on ghost investigation. Both beginners and experienced investigators alike should make this book their bible it gives the straight savvy the material is grounded, practical and informative. It comes as no surprise that Taylor s book has received international praise!
Rosemary Ellen Guiley, author of Encyclopedia of Ghosts & Spirits

Troy Taylor has done it yet again. In HAUNTED ILLINOIS the author has hit that rare (and delightful) middle ground between fascinating paranormal research and compelling storytelling. His stories will put you on the edge of your seat and his insights into the supernatural will keep you there....a must-read from one of the best ghost authors writing today.
Mark Marimen, author of the Haunted Indiana Series

Troy Taylor s HAUNTED ILLINOIS manages to capture the spookiest aspects of life on the prairie in a way that no other book has done. For those who believe that Illinois is merely corn fields and forests, he only needs to read this book to realize that strange things are lurking on the midwestern plains.
DAVE GOODWIN, author of MILITARY GHOSTS & Others

GHOSTBOOKS BY TROY TAYLOR

HAUNTED ILLINOIS BOOKS

Haunted Illinois (1999 / 2001 / 2004)
Haunted Decatur (1995)
More Haunted Decatur (1996)
Ghosts of Millikin (1996 / 2001)
Where the Dead Walk (1997 / 2002)
Dark Harvest (1997)
Haunted Decatur Revisited (2000)
Flickering Images (2001)
Haunted Decatur: 13th Anniversary Edition (2006)
Haunted Alton (2000 / 2003)
Haunted Chicago (2003)
The Haunted President (2005)
Mysterious Illinois (2005)
Dead Men Do Tell Tales: Bloody Chicago (2006)
Resurrection Mary (2007)

HAUNTED FIELD GUIDE BOOKS

The Ghost Hunters Guidebook
(1997/ 1999 / 2001/ 2004)
Confessions of a Ghost Hunter (2002 / 2007)
Field Guide to Haunted Graveyards (2003)
Ghosts on Film (2005)
So, There I Was (with Len Adams) (2006)

HISTORY & HAUNTINGS SERIES

The Haunting of America (2001)
Into the Shadows (2002)
Down in the Darkness (2003)
Out Past the Campfire Light (2004)
Ghosts by Gaslight (2007)

OTHER GHOSTLY TITLES

Spirits of the Civil War (1999)
Season of the Witch (1999/ 2002)
Haunted New Orleans (2000)
Beyond the Grave (2001)
No Rest for the Wicked (2001)
Haunted St. Louis (2002)
The Devil Came to St. Louis (2006)

BARNES & NOBLE PRESS TITLES

Weird U.S. (Co-Author with Mark
Moran & Mark Scuerman) (2004)
Weird Illinois (2005)
Haunting of America (2006)
Spirits of the Civil War (2007)
Into the Shadows (2007)

THE GHOST HUNTERS GUIDEBOOK COMPANION

CONFESSIONS OF A GHOSTHUNTER

Adventures & Misadventures in Ghost Research

BY TROY TAYLOR

- A Whitechapel Press Title from Dark Haven Entertainment -

This book goes out with much appreciation to all of the ghost researchers and investigators who have worked so hard in this strange and often disconcerting field. To all of you who have made great strides and have weathered the barbs of debunkers and perhaps more damaging, the bickering and fighting that goes on with other enthusiasts in the field --- this one is for you!

The title of this book , *Confessions of a Ghost Hunter,* is a blatant homage to Harry Price, the first ghost hunter who understood that to educate, also meant to entertain. My own research can never compare to that of the original!

Illustrations in this book include Gilbert James illustration for the Bat Ball (1922) and James McBryde s chilling illustration for M.R. James story, Oh, Whistle and I ll Come to You My Lad (1904)

Original Cover Artwork Designed by
© Copyright 2007 by Michael Schwab & Troy Taylor
Visit M & S Graphics at www.manyhorses.com

This Book is Published by:
Whitechapel Press
A Divsion of Dark Haven Entertainment, Inc.
15 Forest Knolls Estates - Decatur, Illinois -62521
(217) 422-1002 / 1-888-GHOSTLY
Visit us on the Internet at http://www.prairieghosts.com

Second Edition - April 2007
ISBN: 1-892523-28-0

Printed in the United States of America

The Ghost Story must have a setting that it fairly familiar and the majority of the characters and their talk such as you meet or hear any day. A ghost story of which the scene is laid in the twelfth or thirteenth century may succeed in being romantic or poetical; it will never put the reader into the position of saying to himself, If I'm not careful, something of this kind may happen to me!
Author M. R. James (1911)

I first discovered the ghost stories of this author in grade school and the illustration above gave me nightmares for weeks after (read the story and you will feel the same way!) but I never imagined at the time that I would someday be hoping that something of this kind may happen to me!

TABLE OF CONTENTS

PREFACE TO THE NEW SECOND EDITION OF "CONFESSIONS OF A GHOST HUNTER"

I never imagined how much would change after I published the first edition of this book in 2002. I didn't imagine that within five years I would be living in a different city, would be operating seven tour companies in Illinois, would have written dozens of other books (including a sequel to this volume called "So, There I Was..." with my friend Len Adams), or that the American Ghost Society would have grown to become one of the largest ghost research groups in the country.

All of these changes made me take a second look at the original text of "Confessions of a Ghost Hunter" and I wanted to update the book with some of the new adventures --- and misadventures -- that could not be included in the first edition. In making these changes, I also removed some of the "how-to" information from the book and moved it over to the "Ghost Hunter's Guidebook", where it fits a little better. In place of that material, I have added new (and old) personal encounters and experiences with ghost research. I think you'll enjoy the changes, updates and new material.

So, read on and be sure to leave a light burning as you explore these pages --- you just never know what might be sneaking up on you!

TROY TAYLOR

INTRODUCTION

Confessions of a Ghost Hunter

Sometimes when you write about the things that I do, I often tell people, you become a part of the story, whether you want to become a part of it or not. Essentially, that's what this book is about --- becoming a part of the story. In my case, that story is a ghost story. But writing about becoming a part of the story is what makes this book so hard to write. You see, as a writer, I am not supposed to be a part of the story. I am supposed to tell you --- the reader --- the story and to let you judge the authenticity of its outcome for yourself. The writer is not supposed to offer commentary on the truth (or in some cases, the fiction) of the tale. Such things, I believe, are up to the reader to decide.

That was the reason why I was dragged into writing this book kicking and screaming, so to speak. It was not so much that I did not want to share my own stories and my own encounters with those elusive "somethings" that we call ghosts. It was simply that it went against everything that I believed in as a writer to become a part of the tale.

Now some of you may be reading this and may be thinking --- wait a minute, didn't he share some of his own experiences in the *Ghost Hunter's Guidebook*? If that's what you're thinking, you would be right, I did. However, one of the biggest complaints that I have ever received about my books is that I do not share enough of my own personal stories within the pages of them. In my defense, I felt that I did this quite a bit in the most recent edition of the *Guidebook*, but it was apparently not enough --- because some people wanted more. A friend of mine, who has been an investigator for the American Ghost Society for quite some time, has been bothering me about doing a book like this one for close to three years now. Despite his persistence though, I have declined until now.

Truthfully, writing an autobiography would never be my style, so I have stayed away from that with this volume, except for where the story really called for it. I was hard to convince (and perhaps am not yet convinced) that I have experienced enough in my years as a researcher to warrant an entire book on the subject. I have always fancied myself writing a book of that sort when I am old and gray, perhaps ensconced in my library with a pipe and slippers, looking back over decades of research into hauntings. However, my friend reminded me that I have been involved in literally hundreds of investigations over the years and surely this alone would warrant a look back. Perhaps it would, I explained, but the vast majority of those outings were totally uneventful, turned out to be misidentifications or even outright hoaxes. Who would want to read a book about all of the things that did *not* happen?

Keeping that in mind, I realized that this book could not be a catalog of every single investigation that I ever became involved with. A list like that would make very boring reading, let me assure you! As almost every ghost researcher knows, the majority of your cases have nothing to do with ghosts. What I would need to do is to highlight the cases, the anecdotes and the stories where I believe that I encountered something that could not be explained. Ghosts? Perhaps, but I will have to leave something for the reader to decide for himself.

In addition to this criteria for the book, I had others as well. Tossing out the idea that this could be a retrospective of my life or filled with hair-raising adventures around every corner, I settled into the idea that it could still serve a purpose for other ghost hunters. Why not tell about the investigations that I have been involved in where things happen that I could not explain? And also, why not relate the stories of investigations that went horribly wrong and what lessons I learned to make it possible for me to write a volume like the *Ghost Hunter's Guidebook*?

As I stated a number of times in that book, there are no "experts" when it comes to ghosts and ghost hunting. Ghost researchers do not uniformly agree on what makes a place become haunted, or even about what ghosts actually are. Everyone has his or her own ideas on the subject and mine are certainly not meant to be the final word. My ideas and theories about ghosts and ghost hunting came about from my own past experiences. I often started out with certain ideas about how to do things, only to find those ideas thrown aside in light of new events and happenings. What I wanted to do with this book was to show the reader how those new ideas and events shaped my theories and ghost hunting techniques.

I have been involved with many locations where things fell apart or ended up badly. There have been times when things went horribly wrong but I often found that these investigations were almost as useful to me as the ones that went well. Because of them, I learned valuable lessons that enabled me to create new plans and outlines for future research.

You see, I wanted this book to serve a dual purpose. I wanted it to not only entertain the reader with my own adventures, and misadventures, in ghost research but I also wanted it to serve as something useful, as well. Perhaps the reader --- and would-be ghost hunter --- could learn from the myriad of mistakes that I have made over the years. These mistakes would hopefully serve as a manual on what *not* to do!

Just remember though, no matter what I might include here, this book is not meant to be the final word on the subject of ghosts and ghost hunting. My goal with this volume, just as it is with the *Ghost Hunter's Guidebook*, is to present information that the reader can use, pick apart and revise to best suit the individual's needs. If you get nothing out of this book but a little entertainment from the stories that I have included, I will be disappointed, but satisfied. If however, you come across some ideas and theories that spark your interest and spur you to devise your own theories, I will be even happier. There are a lot of years, a lot of research, and a lot of mistakes contained within these covers and if you even take away one small thing, then the book has served its purpose.

Enjoy the book. Even though I have spent a lot of time trying to convince you that I didn't want to write it, I actually had a lot of fun looking back and recounting these stories. I hope that you get as much enjoyment out of reading it.

Happy Hauntings!
Troy Taylor
Summer 2002
& Spring 2007

Ghost Hunter Harry Price, whose work inspired this book and inspired me
To pursue ghosts at an early age. Although often maligned today, most ghost hunters
Follow in Price s footsteps, whether they know it or not!

I. THE BEGINNING OF A GHOST HUNTER

More years ago than I would care to admit to now, I happened upon an old, abandoned house in the woods. Such unusual finds were not uncommon for me. I grew up on a farm in a rural part of Illinois and during the summer months, I would often explore the back roads, cemeteries and stretches of forest near my parent's home. This particular house turned out to be a little more unusual than most, though, and actually marked a pivotal event that likely changed my life forever. This discovery, combined with a paperback book that I discovered at the age of 13, set me on the road to my present career.

I found the old house in a dark stand of woods and it did not appear that anyone had lived in it for many years. There was no path left through the woods that would have provided access to the surrounding roadways. Only a shallow track remained and it had long since been covered with brush and decades of fallen leaves. Remarkably though, the structure remained in fairly good condition. I crossed the sagging porch, pushing open the leaning front door, and entered the shadowy interior hallway behind it.

Strangely, all of the furniture had been left behind in the structure, even to the point that there were photographs still hanging on the walls and coats in a closet that had a door standing open. Yes, there was evidence of animals passing through and the weathering of years passing by, but all in all, the place had been eerily preserved.

This was all strange enough to a young boy, but it was the kitchen that would unsettle me the most. It was here that I found the last real vestiges of human occupancy in the house. There were still plates and silverware resting on the table and pots and pans still sitting on the cold, metal stove. It was as if the family that had once lived here had suddenly just gotten up and walked away one day --- never to return.

What could have happened to cause someone to leave a house and to simply leave everything they owned behind, abandoning their lives and likely disappearing without a trace?

The house has long since been destroyed and the answer to my personal mystery has never been solved. I returned many times to that house over the next several years, until I finally grew up and moved away from home. As time has passed, I have never forgotten this place and the questions that were created on the day that I first found it remain with me even now. I searched many times for some clue as to where the former occupants had vanished to, but I never found anything. I have since come to realize that this puzzle will never be solved.

But I do think that at the moment I walked into that house, I crossed a line that I could never turn back from. It was at that moment that the unsolved and the unexplained became an obsession and consuming passion for me. It was at this moment that I truly began to believe in ghosts....

It was also at that time that I made a wonderful discovery in a local bookstore. It was a discovery that would not only reinforce my thirst for the unexplained, but it would also set me on the road to the career that I now have.

Don't get me wrong though, I had always been interested in ghosts, for as long as I can remember. One of the most disappointing answers that I have to give to people (mostly reporters) when they ask me about my interest in ghosts and how it came about is that it is simply a lifelong passion. I have often joked that these interviewers want me to say that my mother died when I was child and came back to haunt me, but this is not the case. It's a boring admission to make for a ghost hunter, but there was no single event that caused me to become fascinated with ghosts and hauntings. I can say though that it was a combination of a number of things, from my stumbling across that inexplicably abandoned house to the books that I discovered around the same age.

Books have had the greatest impact on me in my life. I wanted to be a writer all of my life, from the time that I began scribbling out stories in battered notebooks as a child. I was also one of those kids (everyone seems to know at least one) who could always be found with his nose buried in a book. I didn't really care what I was reading, as long as it could transport me somewhere else and, preferably, give me a good scare or two along the way.

You see, in addition to being an avid reader, I was also the kid at my school who was obsessed with monsters, ghosts, horror movies and anything else that was sure to creep out my friends or incur the wrath of my teachers. I can't count the number of times when my monster magazines were confiscated by some well-meaning (but very misguided) educator or the number of disapproving glances that I received while poring over an already dog-eared copy of a new horror novel.

I also discovered sometimes truth can be stranger than fiction. I had always been interested in the realm of ghosts and the supernatural. As far back as my grade school years, I can recall reading books with titles like "True Ghost Stories", but no book made an impression on me like the one that I bought when I was 13.

I was in a local bookstore one day when I ran across a paperback book with a vivid blue house on the cover. The gothic-looking mansion had one window glowing eerily on an upper floor and you had no need to read the title of the book to know the subject of the book was a spooky one. The name of this particular book though was *Haunted Houses.* It had been written by Richard Winer and Nancy Osborn. I remember picking it up and reading the back of the book and despite the catchy descriptive text, there was one section of it that really got my attention ---- *Every tour of the unexplainable in this book is based on documented investigation.*

This was no recounting of legends or ghost stories, I realized, this was the real thing. I flipped open the book and looked over the contents and the photographs inside. I made a quick decision that I needed to own this book and immediately paid for it. I spent the rest of the family shopping trip sitting in the car, already devouring my latest find.

In the weeks that followed, I read and re-read the book several times. I couldn't get enough of it. The horror novels that had so previously fascinated me could not compare with the investigations of Mr. Winer and Ms. Osborn. They weren't just talking about ghosts, they were actually going out and finding them. Was such a thing possible ---- could someone could actually do this for a living?

I can't remember how many times I must have read that book during the summer months that followed but it literally changed my life. After that, I became determined to not only become a writer, but a writer about ghosts. In my way of thinking, Richard Winer made his living traveling all over the country, writing about haunted houses. I would, I told my likely skeptical mother, do the same thing. In 1995, that vow became true and I published my first book. At the time, I had not yet traveled all over America in search of ghosts --- but I was beginning my journey.

My reputation for strangeness continued throughout my school years and although I was still interested in a good, frightening read, my real interests took a darker turn. I was now seeking out "true" stories of terror, haunting used bookstores and ordering books from the back of magazines with whatever allowance money I could spare. I began delving into authors like Hans Holzer, Daniel Cohen, Susy Smith and whoever else I could find in those days before ghost books could be easily found at your local bookstore. True ghost stories were not plentiful at that time, but where there was a will, I discovered, there was also a way.

Unfortunately, not everyone appreciated my taste in books and some of the same caliber of teachers who had confiscated my monster magazines a few years before were now hauling me into the principal's office to talk about the "devil". Now keep in mind, this was the early 1980s and fundamentalists, worried educators and police officers were seeing "Satanists" around every corner. It was the era of what has since been dubbed "satanic panic". Thanks to books like *Michelle Remembers* and accounts of "repressed memories", anything that ran toward the dark side was immediately suspect. I can assure you that I was never involved in anything of the sort but I can understand why some of my reading and interests might have raised a few eyebrows.

But not all of my teachers were so concerned. I was not always a great student in school, but if a subject (like history) caught my interest, I was hooked. For that reason, many of them didn't worry about what I was reading --- they were just happy that I was reading at all. In a class where so many students couldn't finish a single volume for a book report that was due in three weeks, I would have read a dozen or more books by that time! My interest in my studies seemed to fuel some of my teacher's interests in the things that I was so fascinated with.

It was not uncommon for some of my teachers to bring in magazine articles and newspaper clippings that dealt with ghosts or the unexplained. In March 1984, during my senior year in high school, one of my teachers brought me a stack of newspaper clippings about the so-called "Columbus Poltergeist" case, which was then occurring. I was enthralled by the case at the time and have written about it since. Because of it, I have remained intrigued by poltergeist-like phenomena (as you will see in the pages to follow).

The Tina Resch case, if you are not familiar with it, involved a young girl in Columbus, Ohio who was apparently unconsciously manifesting psychokinetic activity in her parent's home. It has since become a famous and very controversial case. And in spite of the claims of the debunkers, a number of eminent researchers have come to believe this was a case of genuine activity ---- at least for a time.

The Columbus Poltergeist

In March 1984, the John and Joan Resch family included their son, Craig, their adopted daughter, Tina, and four foster children. That month, their 14-year old daughter Tina had become the focus for a strange and very frightening series of events.

On a Saturday morning in March 1984, all of the lights in the Resch home suddenly went on all at once, even though no one had touched a switch. John and Joan assumed the incident had been triggered by a power surge and they telephoned the local utility company. It was suggested that they call an electrician, which they did. An electrical contractor named Bruce Claggett came to the house and he assumed, as did John and Joan, that it was simply a problem with the circuit breaker. However, he soon learned differently. He was unable to make the lights stay off and even went as far as taping the switches in the off position. As fast as he could tape them however, the lights would turn back on. Closet lights that operated with a pull string would be turned out, but seconds later, the bulbs would be glowing again. Claggett finally gave up, unable to explain what was going on.

By evening, stranger things were being reported like lamps, brass candlesticks and clocks flying through the air; wine glasses shattering; the shower running on its own; eggs rising out of the carton by themselves and then smashing against the ceiling; knives were flying from drawers; and more. A rattling wall picture was placed behind the couch, only to slide back out again three different times.

As the weekend wore on, a pattern began to develop. The intensity and focus of the activity seemed to be Tina, who was even struck by a number of the objects. A chair was seen tumbling across the floor in Tina's direction and it was only stopped from hitting her because it became wedged in a doorway. Family members, neighbors and unrelated witnesses actually saw Tina being hit and smacked by flying objects, which came from opposite sides of the room from where she was standing.

Near midnight on Saturday, the Columbus police were summoned to the house but there was nothing they could do. The only respite from the strange events came on Sunday, when Tina left the house for church and then again in the afternoon when she went out to visit a friend.

By Monday morning, the house was a wreck and literally dozens of reliable witnesses, including reporters, police officers, church officials and neighbors, had reported unexplained phenomena in the Resch home. Desperate for help, the family turned to the news media for an explanation. When reporters for the Columbus Dispatch arrived, they also witnessed the strange happenings but one of the reporters, Mike Harden, knew of Dr. William G. Roll's work on similar cases and suggested to Mrs. Resch that she contact him immediately.

Dr. Roll arrived in Columbus on March 11. As the Project Director of the Psychical Research Foundation in Chapel Hill, North Carolina, he had long been considered the country's leading expert on poltergeist phenomena. Roll was born in Bremen, Germany in 1926, where his father was the American vice-counsel. He graduated from Berkeley in 1949, where he studied philosophy and psychology, the closest fields he could find to psychical research. In 1950, he went to England to study at Oxford and with support of the Society for Psychical Research and Eileen Garrett, he set up a small research laboratory, where he worked from 1952 to 1957.

While at Oxford, Roll got in touch with J.B. Rhine at Duke University in North Carolina. In 1957, he invited Roll to come to Duke and a year later, he was sent, along with fellow parapsychologist J.G. Pratt to investigate a poltergeist at Seaford, Long Island. Their report concluded that the disturbances were most likely the result of unconscious manipulations by a young boy in the family. Roll and Pratt coined the term "recurrent spontaneous psychokinesis" (RSPK) to explain these types of cases. It is in general use today as another name for poltergeist activity.

Since that time, Roll had investigated well over 100 cases of poltergeists, both modern and historical. From his reports and personal observations, Roll determined that there were patterns of RSPK effects in the reportedly "haunted" locations. These inexplicable, spontaneous physical effects repeatedly occurred when a particular person was present. He believed that the activities were expressions of unconscious PK carried out by the individual acting as the agent.

His past research certainly made him qualified to study the events in Columbus but even so, he had little idea of what to expect from the case. He had come at the direct invitation of Joan Resch, after seeing the case widely reported in the newspapers. He ended up spending a week in the house and while the poltergeist activity seemed to calm just after he and his assistant arrived, it made a noisy return by the end of the week.

The most impressive events occurred on March 15, when Roll observed a brief flurry of activity first hand. The incidents that he witnessed took place when he and Tina were alone on the second floor of the house. As things began to happen, Roll stayed very close to her and left his tape recorder running so that he would have an accurate account of the events. A slamming sound came from the bathroom as what Roll believed to be a bar of soap was thrown from a dish on the sink. He and Tina walked into the bathroom and then emerged again. As they did so, a picture on the wall to their left suddenly fell to the floor. Roll had the girl under observation the entire time and saw no movement on her part.

However, Tina did become upset because the picture was one of her mother's favorites. Fortunately, it was not broken, but the nail had been ripped out of the wall. Roll offered to nail it back up again and began to do so when the poltergeist once again began to react.

"I was keeping Tina under close watch throughout this period," Roll later reported. "So when I hammered in the nail, she was standing right next to me and I was very aware of her exact position and what she was doing. Before I proceeded, I placed my tape recorder on the dresser, which was behind us and to our left. As I was hammering in the nail, we heard a sound like something falling to the floor. We turned around and my tape recorder was on the ground." The recorder had somehow managed to travel about nine feet, seemingly without assistance. Roll could see no way that Tina could have touched it.

Roll had been hammering the nail back in with a pair of tongs that he had found on the dresser. When he was finished, he had laid them back down again. During the few moments that his attention was focused on the traveling tape recorder, the tongs had also been flung from the top of the dresser and had landed about six feet away. Tina had been nowhere near them at the time.

Not surprisingly, as the case made national news, cries of fraud and hoax began to be raised by the debunking community. Three representatives of the Committee for the Scientific Investigation of Claims of the Paranormal showed up at the Resch house unannounced on March 13, while Roll was still investigating. One of the group members was the debunker and magician James Randi, who had already publicly attacked the case in the press. The CSICOP investigators became more skeptical when the Reschs refused to allow Randi into the house. They had no objection to the other two investigators, both scientists, but would have nothing to do with Randi. Because of this, the entire team decided to withdraw (for reasons that remain unclear) and began to issue negative statements about the case, even though they had never actually investigated it.

But it would be the sensational photograph that was taken in the house that would galvanize people all over the country.

When John and Joan Resch contacted the news media about the strange events in their home, one of the reporters who responded was Mike Harden, who wrote for the *Columbus Dispatch*. It would be Harden who would suggest to the Resch family that they contact Dr. William Roll. Harden also got in touch with a professional photographer named Fred Shannon, who had worked for the *Columbus Dispatch* for 30 years. These two veteran newsmen would make national news themselves with their involvement in the case and would release a series of photographs that would shock the world.

Shannon received the first call from Harden on March 5, 1984. He phoned him directly from the Resch home, a pleasant, two-story, stucco house in a nice part of the city. Harden asked him to come to the house immediately and Shannon packed up his gear to leave, never realizing that he was about to embark on one of the most bizarre assignments in his career. Even the words of warning from Harden over the telephone did not prepare him for what he was about to experience. His experiences in the Resch home would be brief, but his later testimony about what he saw would become compelling evidence of the paranormal.

Shannon was met at the door by Mike Harden when he arrived. He was introduced to the Reschs and they began to explain to him about the strange happenings that had been taking place. The "force", as they were calling it, was hurling household objects all about the place and the majority of the disturbances seemed to be aimed at their daughter, Tina. They began to show him about the house, starting in the dining room, where the chandelier had been damaged by flying wine glasses, as well as by other objects that had been hurled from the walls and had crashed into it. The force had almost completely destroyed the long-stemmed glasses that the Reschs kept in the room. When Shannon arrived, only one glass remained on the portable bar in the corner.

After looking over the damage for a few minutes, John and Joan Resch went into the adjoining kitchen, leaving the photographer alone in the dining room with Mike Harden and Tina. Moments later, they followed the girl's parents into the other room and, within seconds, they heard the sound of glass shattering in the dining room. "Uh-oh," Joan Resch groaned, "there goes the last wineglass." They raced back into the dining room and found the splintered remains of the glass in the opposite corner from where it had been.

The now perplexed photographer followed the rest of the group back into the kitchen a few minutes later and to his surprise, found that the force again chose that moment to react again. A tremendous clatter was heard in the dining room and when they returned, they found that six metal coasters (which had also been sitting on the portable bar) had sailed through the air in the same direction as the last wineglass. They now lay in a scattered pile near the broken pieces of glass.

According to Shannon, they soon entered the kitchen uninterrupted and the Reschs told him about all of the things that had happened in the room. For example, "all hell broke loose" whenever Tina opened the door to the refrigerator. Eggs would fly out and burst on the ceiling, jars would overturn, containers of leftovers would burst open and expel their contents onto the floor. On one occasion, a stick of butter had erupted from the icebox and had sailed across the room to become lodged between two cabinet doors. Instead of slowly sliding to the floor though, the butter inexplicably began moving upwards toward the ceiling.

The Reschs then took Shannon into the living room. They explained about the time that a large, overstuffed chair chased Tina out of the room, cart-wheeling until it slammed into the wall and dislodged a picture. Shannon was intrigued by the story, so he decided to take a photo of the chair and the picture, the whole frame of which was still intact although the glass was shattered. He asked Tina to pose next to the chair and to hold the picture so that he could see it through the lens.

At that same instant, when he shot the photo and the flash went off, Shannon heard a loud crash. Tina claimed that something knocked the picture out of her hand. Shannon was thinking that she had just dropped the picture and the crash when it hit the floor was what had startled him --- but he soon had second thoughts about this. He quickly noticed that she was still holding the corner of the picture in her hands, as if something had struck the picture with force and had knocked it out of her hands, leaving her holding one small corner of it.

Unnerved and upset, Tina sat down on a couch in the family room on the opposite side of the kitchen. As Shannon and Harden turned to go back into the kitchen, they heard a tremendous booming sound! Without thinking, Shannon immediately turned and snapped a photo. The developed image would later show Tina covering her head --- the lamp on the stand next to her had crashed to the floor.

Since his eye was not on her at the time, Shannon was unable to say for sure whether or not Tina knocked over the lamp herself, but he was confident that she had not. "I had swung around so rapidly," he later said, "that I don't see how she would have had time to knock over the lamp and so completely cover her head. She was covering her head because she had been attacked by so many various objects. She was a badly frightened girl and her fear never left her all during the time these things were going on. At this point, I had been in the house for 15 minutes!"

Tina sat down on the arm of a chair across the room from the couch where she had been sitting. Shannon took up a position in the doorway near a love seat, with his back to the kitchen. Suddenly, the love seat that was close to him began to move towards Tina. It pivoted on one leg and shuffled toward her about 18 inches! Needless to say, the skeptical photographer was startled --- but not so much so that he was unable to snap a photo of the shocked expression on Tina's face. "I knew the photo wouldn't mean much to someone who wasn't there, as I was, to see what had happened", Shannon explained. "Anybody who chose to think that way would say it was just a setup. So I was looking for other things to happen. I didn't have long to wait."

Shannon and Harden decided to observe the girl more closely and took a seat on the couch, with Tina on the loveseat, facing them. On the floor in front of her was a colorful afghan, which Joan Resch had earlier explained had once rose off the floor and had covered Tina. Within a few moments of the journalists sitting down, they saw this repeated and Shannon took a photo of her with the afghan draped over her body. He had no explanation for how it could have lifted from the floor and could find no method as to how Tina could have accomplished this on her own.

Later, the three of them went into the kitchen and were talking with John and Joan, when they all heard a loud sound in the unoccupied family room. Shannon stated that it sounded "like a cannon had gone off --- it had that much force." They went to investigate and learned that a heavy bronze candlestick (which had been on the floor to the immediate left of the loveseat and near the back door) had taken flight a short distance and had banged into the door. That door, which was made of metal, was hit with such force that two dents were left on it. The Reschs had taken to placing heavy objects like this on the floor because it seemed that items left on walls and tables had a habit of flying in Tina's direction. Once, a wrought-iron clock had flown from the wall and had hit her in the back of the head, leaving a lump.

A few moments after the first, another bronze candlestick took flight from the other side of the loveseat, near the kitchen. Tina was sitting in a chair in the family room and Shannon and Harden were watching her from a couch across the room. No one was anywhere near the candle holder and yet somehow, it moved! It all happened so fast, and the thing moved with such speed, that Shannon never even saw it start to go! According to Tina, who had been at an angle to see the candlestick, it had flown four of five feet into the kitchen before making a 90-degree turn and shooting down the hallway. She said that it had been turning end over end through the air.

Shannon admitted that he had not seen the candlestick, but he had certainly heard it. As it propelled itself, the object made a roaring sound, an incredible noise that he said sounded "something like a locomotive".

Everyone was shocked and when they recovered, they all got to their feet and hurried into the hallway. The first thing they saw was the hanging lamp at the entrance of the doorway. The lamp was swinging back and forth quite rapidly from what Shannon believed was wind left behind by the fast moving candlestick. The lamp, he later reported, was swinging as if it were in a hurricane.

The incident with the candlestick was only one of the strange things that happened while Harden and Shannon were watching Tina in the family room. Most of the other incidents involved telephones that were located on a stand next to Tina's chair. Many people have wondered why the Reschs had more than one phone on the stand. The reason for this was that when the outbreak began, the house was plagued with all sorts of electrical problems, including malfunctions with the telephone in the family room. Because of this, the Reschs bought a second, cheap phone and installed it next to the sturdier, original phone. Both sat on the stand next to the chair in the family room but it was the second phone that was most affected by the "force" in the house.

According to Fred Shannon, he was present on seven different occasions when one or the other of the phones flew in Tina's direction. The first two times, they hit her on the left side and fell next to her on the couch. During the other incidents, the phones flew over Tina's lap in the direction of the loveseat. The events occurred unexpectedly, usually minutes apart, but happened in seconds. This made it nearly impossible for Shannon to get a photograph of the events. At one point, he sat for more than 20 minutes with the camera up to his eye, waiting for something to happen - but nothing did. Finally, each time that he would lower the camera so that he wasn't immediately ready to take a photo --- the phone would go flying through the air!

That caused him to wonder if he was dealing with a blind force after all. Could it be aware of his presence? If this was true, he decided to devise a

The famous photograph that was taken by Fred Shannon at the Resch house. It was later picked up By the Associated Press and appeared in newspapers all over the country. Skeptics attempted to debunk the photo, even go as far as to smear Shannons outstanding reputation, in order to prove their point. (photo Associated Press / Columbus Dispatch)

strategy. He brought the camera to his eye, his finger poised on the trigger, and waited, watching Tina for about five minutes. Then, without taking his eyes off her, he lowered the camera to the level of his waist, still keeping it pointed in her direction and his finger on the shutter. As he did this, he turned his head in the direction of the kitchen, where the Reschs were talking with some visitors. He waited patiently for something to happen, pretending that his attention was somewhere else.

A few seconds later, he saw a white blur out of the corner of his eye and by the time that he pressed the shutter of the camera, a phone had streaked through the air and had sailed all the way across the chair in which Tina was sitting! The resulting photo captured not only the flying telephone but also the frightened expression on Tina's face as she jerked backwards to keep from being hit. In all, Shannon was able to get three different photos of the telephone in flight but this first one was the one that got the most attention. The day after it appeared in the local newspaper, it was picked up by the Associated Press and made front pages all over the country.

The photo was immediately attacked by the debunkers, who began savaging the entire case, but Shannon was adamant about what he had seen. He emphasized in writing: "I am damned sure that she did not throw those phones. From what Mike and I observed, I would say that she couldn't possibly have thrown them - absolutely no way. We were sitting in a well-lighted room; we were looking right at her. When one of us was looking away for a moment, the other had his eyes on Tina all the time. And of course, there were some objects that took flight while she was nowhere near them --- the candlesticks, for example."

Shannon also witnessed an incident with the telephones that did not involve Tina. It occurred just a few minutes after Shannon took the astounding photo of the phone in flight. A Franklin County Children Services caseworker and an associate arrived at the house on business and the caseworker sat down in the loveseat. Shannon warned her not to sit there as he knew that she would be in a direct path of the telephone. She didn't take him seriously and made several comments to assure him that she thought the whole thing was a joke, but humored him anyway by moving to the other cushion on the loveseat. She stood up, shuffled sideways and sat back down again. Just as she was lowering herself to the seat, the phone shot through the air and landed hard on the cushion where she had been sitting. If she had not moved, the phone would have struck her in the chest! The incident startled her so much that she made no more light of it and she and her co-worker quickly finished their business and left.

A little while later, Harden, Shannon and Tina were standing in the middle of the family room when a box of tissues (which was also on the phone table) suddenly leapt into the air. It zipped past Shannon's leg and landed on a small table next to the couch. When it hit the table, it did not skip or bounce even though it had been moving at tremendous speed. Instead, it stopped in place as if it had been caught by a magnet or glued into position.

This was the last activity that Shannon witnessed in the family room but his experiences at the Resch house were not yet over. He decided to take some photos in the kitchen and hoped that if he got Tina to open the refrigerator door, something would fly out of it, as had been allegedly happening over the last few days. The kitchen was already a mess from these past incidents and in fact, the Reschs had been cleaning the room during most of the time that Shannon and Harden had been in the house.

Tina waited in the kitchen as he set up his camera in the corner, directly across the room from the refrigerator. Shannon ducked low to avoid being hit by any flying food and asked Tina to open the door --- but nothing happened. She repeated it three times but everything inside remained where it was. Tina decided to use the moments of inactivity to make a sandwich and Harden and Shannon decided to pack up and leave, having spent nearly four hours in the house.

As soon as the story of the Resch house, and Shannon's accompanying photo, began to appear in newspapers, the self-appointed critics of the paranormal immediately began an attack on the reality of the events that were being reported. In spite of the fact that none of them had investigated the case, nor had been to Columbus, they were convinced that the whole thing was a hoax. It was simply a matter of "if I don't believe it, then there is no way that it can be true".

The debunkers managed to obtain the negatives of the photos that Fred Shannon had shot at the house. Because there were three photos of a phone in the air above Tina's lap (not just the one that appeared in AP wire stories), Shannon was immediately accused of faking the photos and having Tina throw the phone so that he could photograph it. Although Shannon explained how he managed to capture three photos, he was dismissed as a fraud. This was done without investigation of the scene, assessment of the evidence and with no regard to Shannon's 30-year career and outstanding reputation.

The debunkers also dismissed the entire case based on the fact that Dr. Roll admitted that he believed that Tina had faked some of the less impressive activity in the house. However, he did believe that genuine activity was taking place in the case, even when conceding there was some limited fraud involved as well. "It is certain that Tina threw a lamp down on one occasion," he said. "That's obvious. She told me that she did the same thing on two other occasions. So there's no doubt there were some fraudulent occurrences."

Roll stated that it was not uncommon for victims of poltergeists to get into the act themselves as part of the mischief-making. He had been able to formulate many of the poltergeist patterns into a profile through his research. Usually at the center of the activity was a child or teenager who possessed a great deal of internal anger, usually caused by a stressful situation in the household or a mental disturbance. The PK was an unconscious, and unknowing, way of venting that hostility without fear of punishment. Because of the mental states of the agents in many of his cases, genuine phenomena and trickery often go hand in hand.

In such cases, the PK effects of the unstable person will actually cause genuine phenomena to occur. However, as the events are recorded and gain the attention of others in the household (and sometimes even the authorities and media), the agent in the case begins to receive the much-needed attention they desired. As this begins to occur, the phenomena will cease. To continue the attention, the agent will often fake the phenomena. Unfortunately, as the agent is often caught in the act of doing this, debunkers will claim the entire case was a hoax and are able to discredit any research material gathered in the early stages of the case. Because of this, many authentic cases are never brought to public record.

Roll felt that the minor episodes that occurred did not discredit the Resch case. "I can only say that when I was present, I couldn't find any ordinary explanation for the incidents I witnessed," he stated. "In my opinion, it is very unlikely that they were caused normally. And of course there are a number of witnesses we interviewed in Columbus who had seen things under conditions where no family members could have caused them."

Later that month, Roll took Tina back to North Carolina where he and other scientists conducted computer-based ESP and PK tests on her. The results of the test were in no way striking, leading most to believe that she did not possess any long-term psychic abilities. As in other poltergeist cases, the mysterious happenings seemed to be confined to a short period of time. And while there were some poltergeist incidents in the home of Dr. Roll and at the home of a counselor where Tina was staying, the researchers believed that her aggressive manipulations were short-lived.

What caused the manifestations? No one knows for sure and the story behind the Columbus poltergeist remains a mystery. Poltergeists in general tend to focus on disturbed children who are suppressing hostility and anger. The displacement of energy acts as a safety valve for the pent-up emotions. In

Tina's case, there had been recent problems at home over the fact that Tina, against the wishes of John and Joan, had recently been searching for her natural parents. Also, Tina's best friend of two years had ended their friendship just two days before the events began. To make matters worse, the Reschs had recently taken Tina out of school because she was having trouble getting along with other students. She was apparently unpopular with most of her classmates and was having difficulty with one of her teachers. Because of this, she was being tutored at home and was seemingly "cut off" from the outside world. All of this apparently combined to create an outward transference of energy.

Eventually, the activity ended and after Tina's return from North Carolina, only a few minor incidents were reported in the home. Dr. Roll was never sure of the cause of the cause of the case, but his studies pointed to the theory that poltergeist agents seemed to suffer from disturbances in the central nervous system. This may have been the case with Tina Resch, for even though the bizarre incidents ended in her home, her story was not quite over.

Many poltergeist agents have been documented to be in poor mental health, which deteriorated further in stressful situations. This might explain the findings of many standard psychologists and mental health professionals. They often discover that patients with unresolved emotional issues are associated with, or have lived in, houses where poltergeist activity has been reported. In addition, while studying the personalities of those thought to be poltergeist agents, psychologists have found anxiety issues, phobias, mania, obsessions, disassociative disorders and even schizophrenia. In some cases, psychotherapy may eliminate the poltergeist phenomena but apparently, not in all of them.

For despite counseling, Tina Resch went from being an unhappy child to being a disturbed adult. She went from one disastrous situation to another, finally to two marriages and two divorces and then finally to a sentence of life in prison for the torture murder of her own daughter. Although she claimed to be innocent of the crime, she was sent to a Georgia prison in 1994 and remains there today.

My First Paranormal Experience

Not surprisingly, this case, and the elements of the investigation that surrounded it, left a lasting impression on me. It was at about this time that I got involved in something else that would also have a lasting effect. It was not only some of the teachers who had a sympathetic view toward my interests, but also many of my friends and fellow students, as well. One Halloween night, I came up with what I thought was an interesting and original idea --- I would take a group of my friends on a "tour" of all of the allegedly haunted places near the small town where we attended school. We would explore the old cemeteries, the old houses where ghosts were said to linger, the bridge where a ghostly woman was supposed to weep and end up at a stretch of haunted woods for a wiener roast.

This would by my first ever "ghost tour" and I continued them for the next several years. Then, in 1994, I started doing them for a living and have been doing them ever since. It was only supposed to be a lark back then, who knew what it would turn into?

I started my first "ghost tours" in high school but it was also at this time that I had my first encounter with something that I have never been able to explain other than as something paranormal. I have never forgotten this experience, which stemmed from a night at a place alleged to be one of the most haunted spots in the area where I grew up. I have recounted this story often but it never fails to give me a fresh batch of goosebumps every time that I tell it.

The weird happening took place at a spot called Peck Cemetery, located in a remote section of Central Illinois. The cemetery was an isolated place, enclosed by a rusted iron fence, and hidden from the road by thick woods. It was surrounded by heavy forest and trees loomed over the grounds. In addition, the graveyard was accessible only by way of a rutted dirt road and through a metal gate, which was usually kept locked. Trespassers were not welcome here.

The reason for this is because since the 1970s, Peck Cemetery had been a popular place for teenagers to go and have parties and attempt to scare themselves silly. If this were the end of it, that would not be a problem. Unfortunately, a small minority of these teenagers also felt the need to vandalize the cemetery. The burial ground was in deplorable condition by the time that I was in high school since the majority of the stones had been toppled and broken, had been turned over and had been sprayed with bright paint. There were very few of the monuments standing upright when I first came here and many of those lean dangerously to the side, thanks to digging that had been done around their bases.

Vandalism was not the only thing that added to the reputation of the cemetery either. It was also believed to be a haven for occult groups who were trying to tap into the negative energy of the place. And while I think (and thought then) that most alleged "Satanists" are little more than disturbed teenagers and that most "devil worshipping cults" are simply the fevered imaginings of fundamentalist religious groups trying to scare the general public, there are some pretty scary people out there. There are people who do take the occult very seriously and I have it on pretty good authority that some of them used to gravitate to Peck Cemetery. While the stories may have grown a little larger than life over the years, some pretty strange and bizarre things have taken place here.

Satanic cultists aside, though, stories had been told for a number of years that suggested that something lurked in this cemetery. There were many tales told about the place and witnesses and late night visitors to the cemetery had come forward to claim a number of strange happenings and to recall many frightening events. Such stories included apparitions in the graveyard, inexplicable cries, whispers and voices, hooded figures, eerie lights, and even the sound of a woman's scream that seemed to come from nowhere!

These were just a few of the stories that I was hearing from other students at my school and thanks to my interest in the subject, I managed to collect some other strange tales from students at other area schools as well. I was determined to see this place, no matter how hard it apparently was to find.

Because of its remote location, I needed to track down someone who had already been there and soon found a couple of acquaintances who had made the trip --- and returned! I was informed that it was a matter of bravery for visitors to the cemetery to go there late at night and to park their cars at the gates to the graveyard with their headlights pointed inside. As the gate was located at one corner of Peck Cemetery, they could literally angle their car so that the headlights would shine back to the farthest corner. The visitor's courage came into question when they left the car and walked all the way to this dark corner and then turned and walked back. It doesn't sound like much to the reader, I'm sure, but take my word for it --- it was not a pleasant prospect when you actually arrived at the old burial ground.

According to my friends, they knew of a student at another school (of course!) who had gone to Peck Cemetery one night and was completing the challenge when a ghost actually came up out of the ground in front of him! Needless to say, he ran from the graveyard and never went back.

After hearing this, I wanted to see the place more than ever and made arrangements with my friends for them to take me out there on the following Saturday night. Even then, I was more than a little bit of a skeptic when it came to other people's encounters but I figured that since there were so many stories told about this one location, at least a few of them had to be true. Right?

A few nights later, we made the trip out to Peck Cemetery. It was (believe it or not) a dark and stormy night and as we turned off the hard road and onto the gravel lane that ran back to the woods and the cemetery, everyone in the car grew quiet. We traveled along the rutted lane and followed it as it dipped down into a low area that was filled with a spooky --- and very unnerving --- fog. After we reached the top of the hill on the other side of the ravine, we turned the car sharply to the left so that the nose of it was up to the cemetery gates. The headlights stretched out in front of us and illuminated the jumble of broken stones and the glistening raindrops on the overhanging tree branches. Unfortunately, it was what the lights did not illuminate that had me bothered --- namely the far corner of the cemetery, which we planned to walk to in just a few moments.

My friend turned off the ignition of his vintage Camaro and we sat there for a moment with no one speaking. There was absolutely no sound but the drip of water on the roof of the automobile. I think that, at this point, we had managed to spook ourselves so badly that if one of us had suggested that we leave and go home, we likely all would have agreed. As it was though, no one did and we quietly got out of the car. Once outside, I think that we finally realized how nervous we had been making ourselves and we started to relax. Joking and laughing, we started off across the cemetery, following the twin beams of light that pointed off into the darkness.

As we walked further and further away from the car, the laughter ended and we began to pick up the pace a little bit. I know that I simply wanted to get to the other side of the cemetery and then get back to the car again. I can't really explain what made me feel this way (and I am sure my friends shared the feeling) but if you ever get the chance to visit Peck Cemetery, you will understand it. There is just a bad feeling here, a coldness that seeps into your bones and leaves you with an uncomfortable sensation that you just can't put your finger on.

Within a few minutes, we had reached the farthest corner of the graveyard and we turned to start back towards the car. We must have breathed a small sigh of relief, as well. Nothing had occurred on the trip over --- no lights, no ghosts and not even a single sound, save for the rain that was dripping off the trees and the crunch of the damp leaves under our feet. Feeling much bolder, we began walking back to the car, wandering to look at some of the vandalized tombstones as we made our way back. We were convinced by this time that nothing out of the ordinary was going to occur.

We were wrong.

We had reached the halfway point on our return trip when suddenly, the headlights on the car that we had left in the cemetery gates snapped out. The graveyard was plunged into darkness! Needless to say, we froze where we were standing. We now had a major predicament on our hands --- the question was whether to run back to the car, and possibly meet whatever had turned out the headlights, or to simply stay where we were, in a cemetery that we now had started to believe just might be haunted after all? We argued both points for a few moments, mostly concerned about the fact that the doors to the car had been locked. How had the lights been turned out?

We decided to compromise. We agreed that we would return to the car, but we would do so very, very cautiously. You see, those tales of ax-wielding Satanists in black robes didn't seem quite so silly anymore! The four of us managed to get all of the way back across the cemetery and we crept up on the silent, and now darkened, automobile. After peering under the car and into the shadowy backseat, we determined that no one was hiding nearby. However, we had not solved the mystery of how the headlights had turned out. Could the battery have gone dead? Were we going to be stranded out here until someone came along to help us?

Concerned, the driver quickly unlocked the door and started to get inside. He was about halfway into the car when he stopped and his face turned white. His eyes were big when he looked over at the rest of us and he hurriedly climbed back out of the car again, stumbling a few feet away from the vehicle.

We asked him what was wrong and he simply told us that we needed to come and see how the lights had been turned out. Keep in mind, this was a 1960s era automobile and there were no fancy switches or time delays to control the headlights. The lights turned on and off by way of a knob that was fitted into the dash --- a knob that you pulled out to turn the lights on and pushed in to turn them off. My friend had left the knob pulled out when we had exited the car and started across the cemetery. Short of this knob, the only way that the headlights could have been turned out would have been to have the battery die during the few minutes when we were walking in the graveyard.

The battery was not dead. Somehow, through the locked doors and rolled tight windows, a hand had physically reached in and had punched the headlight knob to the "off" position. There was no way that anyone could have done this --- no way that anyone who was still among the living anyway!

And that was the end of the evening for us. I did not return again to Peck

Cemetery for almost 10 years...

After my school career ended, I traveled extensively and then ended up in the book business. At this point, I was a frustrated writer, pounding out manuscripts and then locking them away in a closet to never see the light of day. I figured that selling books would be about as close to writing them as I would ever get, so I settled for this next best thing. But being in the book business only fueled my desire to write professionally and it also began adding to my collection of ghostly titles. One day, while buying books at an estate sale, I ran across a book with an interesting title. It was called *The Most Haunted House in England* and it had been written by an author named Harry Price. I blew some dust off the book and packed it away to take with me, never realizing that the next step to my becoming a ghost hunter had just fallen into my hands.

I decided to give the book a try and I was hooked by the first chapter. Harry Price was a fascinating character, a real-life ghost hunter who made a name for himself by conducting a year-long investigation of Borley Rectory, the "most haunted house" of the book's title. During these investigations, Price literally invented the first "ghost hunter's guidebook" for examining the house and the first "ghost hunter's tool kit" as an example of what might be needed for the research. I would later try to expand on both of his ideas in my own work. Price was also the first ghost hunter to recognize the fact that to educate the general public about ghosts and hauntings, you had to entertain them as well. This would be something else that I would also attempt to emulate in the years to come.

Reading about Price's investigations got me interested in perhaps conducting my own. I had long been hearing, and collecting, stories about haunted places in Central Illinois, where I grew up. There were many ghost stories about the cities of Decatur and Springfield and also about the small towns and the isolated spots like Williamsburg Hill and the Chesterville Cemetery. It's interesting to see that many places from the region, like Greenwood Cemetery, have become very familiar names over time. Back then however, people seldom mentioned them. When they did though, they always found a listener with me. I quickly discovered that the best way to track down leads to ghostly spots was to simply listen to people recount their stories and their recollections. And if the events they recalled did not happen to them, then they must have happened to a friend or relative, for I found that everyone seemed to have had an experience they simply cannot explain --- or they knew someone who had!

Another great way to find the stories was just to drive around and ask about them. One summer, I took several trips to southern Illinois and stopped in gas stations, diners and roadside stands, asking about "anything strange" that the employees might have heard about in the area. I was treated to tales that involved everything from ghosts to Bigfoot sightings to glowing tombstones! I also returned to a place that I had visited a few times as a small child, the Old Slave House, which is likely the most famous haunted place in southern Illinois. By simply being a good listener, I was able to become personally acquainted with the owner of the house at the time and to visit there on many occasions, right up until the day that it closed down to tourists. Unfortunately, years later (as of this writing), it is still closed down. However, if it had not been for my searching for ghost stories, I would have never had the opportunity to visit the place and to spend as much time there as I did.

My First Psychical Investigation

My trips around Central and Southern Illinois --- and later, the Chicago area --- introduced me to many ghosts and haunted places that I might not have known about otherwise and it also got me started in "official" investigations. My first real investigation started with a telephone call from a friend of a friend who happened to believe that her house was haunted. Our mutual friend and I had attended school together and she recalled that I was always interested in ghosts and strange things, so she recommended that her friend get in touch with me.

After I got the call, and the circumstances were explained to me, I agreed to drive out to her house and take a look around. To be honest, I was not really sure what I would find. My entire repertoire of conducting ghost investigations had been gleaned from Harry Price and I certainly did not have an entire staff of researchers to assist me. In addition, this was not long after ghost "busting" had become a well known term, thanks to what remains one of my favorite films. I had no fancy equipment or gadgets to take with me to the house and I certainly had no uniform or sporty car to make me look like a professional. However, I had recently found a book by a real "ghostbuster" named Loyd Auerbach called *ESP, Hauntings and Poltergeists* and began cramming information out of it into my head. I had finally realized that I was about to conduct my first genuine ghost investigation and I wanted to be ready!

The investigation began late on a Saturday afternoon in September. The woman who contacted me (who we'll call "Jill" for the sake of the narrative) lived in east central Illinois in an old farm house that was later learned to have been built around 1890. It was located on a large lot with trees along the western side. Two sides of the yard melted into corn fields and the fourth opened to driveway that led from the hard road back to the house. The rest of the property was mostly open, save for some smaller trees, some bushes and two older outbuildings. One of them had been converted into a garage and the other had been left to decay at the edge of the yard.

At the center of the lot was the house, a large and rambling two-story affair with a wide front porch and a back door that led in from a mud room. Basically, it was just like hundreds of other old farm houses that you'll find scattered all over Illinois. As I turned into the driveway and parked in the shade of the woods on the western side, I received no feelings of foreboding or impending doom. I always wondered if I might be able to sense when ghosts were near or that a house was haunted --- but I was soon to find that I was out of luck on those accounts. In the years that have passed, I have discovered that I am about as psychic as a fence post!

When I went up to the door, I took with me what turned out to be my first "ghost hunter's kit". I had stuck a number of items into a canvas bag, including a notebook and a pen; a sketch pad with some colored pencils; a tape recorder; a tape measurer; a flashlight; and, of course, a camera and some extra film.

The reader should remember that most of the items that we take for granted today were simply not in common use to ghost hunters at that time. I couldn't afford a video camera, which was very large and bulky at that time anyway, and EMF detectors were not only very expensive but had not really been adapted for use in the paranormal field yet. Even if I had owned one, I wouldn't have had a clue as to what to do with it.

After I introduced myself to Jill, she and her husband and I sat down and they began to tell me about some of the strange goings-on they had experienced since moving into the house a few months before. They had taken up residence in the house back in May of that year. Both of them worked high pressure jobs in Champaign, Illinois and had wanted to find a place in the country where they could relax in the evenings and on weekends. However, the short time they had been living in the place had been anything but restful!

Not long after they had moved in, they first heard the strange sounds. They were lying in bed late one night, talking and likely feeling quite lucky about having purchased a country house, when they heard footsteps on the staircase outside their bedroom door. The older house had all of the bedrooms on the second floor and Jill and her husband had taken the largest one as their own. The staircase from the main floor came up into the middle of a second floor landing. Doors opened to a total of three bedrooms and a bathroom off the landing. The master bedroom was the closest to the top of the stairs. The heavy thud of boots broke the stillness of the night as they walked to the top of the steps and then came to a thudding halt outside of the door.

Jill's husband (let's call him John) jumped out of bed and hurried to the door. He twisted the knob and pulled it open, anxious to confront the intruder who had managed to get through the locked doors and into the house. When he opened the door, he saw no one on the other side of it. The second floor landing was empty!

In the nights to come, this eerie event would repeat itself many times. John told me that he became so obsessed with trying to find out what was going on that when he heard the footsteps, he would creep to the door and peer through the keyhole, trying to see who was there. Finally, he decided to remain outside of the bedroom throughout the night. He moved a chair into the darkest corner on the landing, which was out of sight of anyone coming up the stairs. There, he waited for several hours and eventually drifted off to sleep. However, the sound of the heavy boots awakened him in the still hours of the morning. They plodded up the wooden staircase and then turned and came to a halt outside the master bedroom door. But who was there? Even though it was quite dark on the landing, John could see well enough by the light spilling in from the window to know that no one was standing there! The landing was impossibly empty!

It was at this point where Jill and John began to suspect that their house might have a ghost.

The strange events did not end there, however, and in fact, after John's vigil in the hallway, they actually seemed to multiply. Soon, footsteps and unsettling knocking sounds began to be heard all over the house, and at all hours of the day. They paced through the kitchen during breakfast and through the living room while John was watching television. The knocking sounds could be heard coming from inside of the walls, under the floor (seemingly from the basement, although no one was there) and often on the front door. Both John and Jill also noticed that both footsteps and knocking sounds were often heard on the front porch. Even some friends who came to visit heard the sounds, making the couple breathe a little easier. They were afraid their newfound isolation in the country was making them susceptible to imaginations gone berserk. With confirmations from an outside source that they were not losing their minds, they decided to get in touch with me and see what I thought about the possibility of a resident haunt.

The first afternoon that I spent at the house involved a lot of talking and a lot of walking around to see the areas that seemed most affected by the knocking and the mysterious footsteps. And while I heard nothing out of the ordinary while I was there, I saw no reason to think that Jill and John were not telling the truth. They seemed like reasonable people, with steady, responsible jobs and people who had no interest in the idea of ghosts or haunted houses, prior to their own personal experiences. These were not people who were looking for attention or who were willing to believe anything. They truly wanted an answer to what was going on, whether it involved an actual ghost or another, more logical explanation.

It was now up to me to drag out everything in my limited experience to see if I could find some answers for them. We combed through the house, literally knocking on walls, doors and every available space we could find, hoping to duplicate the sounds that had been heard. We searched for loose floorboards and weak areas that might create the sounds of footsteps. We even tried standing in different parts of the second floor so that we could try and create a sound like someone walking up the stairs. It was no use, though, because even though we found plenty of loose boards in the nearly century-old house, we found nothing that could be mistaken for a man's heavy boots.

I left that afternoon and promised to return the next day. Thoroughly puzzled, I drove into the nearest town with the idea of searching for some records and history for the house. Perhaps they might provide some answers as to what was going on. My first stop was the public library and I spoke to a sympathetic librarian, who allowed me to look back through some directories and some local history books.

After an hour or so, I found what little information there was about the original owner of the place. The house had been constructed in 1888 by George Duncan, a farmer from Ohio who had settled in the area with his wife and two sons. The family had owned the property until 1946 when the Duncan heirs had sold it to a couple from Mattoon. The records only showed one additional owner after that and offered no real information.

The librarian made some copies of the records for me and also made a call to a friend who worked at the local newspaper (ah, small towns!), who promised to check and see if any other information was available. After getting something to eat, I stopped by the newspaper office, which was actually closed on Saturdays. However, the librarian's friend had gathered what little he could find on the house and what he did discover may have turned out to be the answer to the entire mystery.

One of the few snippets of interest that he had on the house, and the Duncan family, was that George's oldest son, Robert, had been killed in Cuba during the Spanish-American War. A large gathering of local farmers and townspeople had turned out to greet the funeral train when the body was returned and a service was held at the Methodist Church. There was no record of where Robert was buried. Unfortunately, that was all there was and I made a copy of it and drove back home for the night. I planned to return to the house the following day.

I was back to Jill's house by noon on Sunday and I told the couple of my small discoveries from the day before. When I mentioned Robert Duncan's name, a strange look passed over John's face. I asked him what was wrong and he insisted that he had to show me something. He rushed me out the front door and led me over to the side of the porch. He moved aside a section of the wooden slats on the edge of the porch revealed a dark opening to the area beneath it.

He explained: "I was working out here this summer, replacing some of the boards on top of the porch. A few of them had rotted out and I crawled underneath here to pop the boards out from the bottom. That's when I found this..."

John got down and crawled under the porch and I followed him. The area was cool and dark and the dirt beneath our hands and knees was loose and smelled faintly of rotten leaves. We scooted over a short distance and I saw that John was dusting off a white stone that had been tossed there. He looked at me: "I found it lying face down and I saw this when I turned it over."

I looked over his shoulder and saw a narrow white stone with a curved top partially buried in the dirt. Raised letters on the stone read "Robert Duncan". It was a military tombstone that had been thrown haphazardly under the porch!

And this was not all that John wanted to show me. We climbed out from under the porch and he took me into the backyard. There was a gloomy spot in the back corner of the yard that was nestled under the trees. John took me there and asked me if I noticed anything strange about it. At first, I didn't, but as I continued to look, I saw a sloped mound that was located in the center of the small area of the yard. It looked exactly like a grave in the cemetery! John explained that he had noticed the area when he mowed the yard for the first time but never thought anything of it. Yes, it did look like a grave but he was sure that it was just a natural anomaly, but now he had to wonder --- and so did I!

Together, John, Jill and I came up with a plan. We heaved the tombstone out from under the porch and using a wheelbarrow, we managed to get it back to the far corner of the yard. With shovels and a spade, we placed the stone in the ground at the head of the unusual mound. We didn't really have any idea if this was the grave of Robert Duncan or not, but it certainly seemed possible. It was not at all uncommon in those days (and occasionally even in some states today) for people to bury their loved ones at home. We imagined a scenario where a later occupant of the house decided that the tombstone in the backyard was morbid and pitched it under the porch, leaving the slain soldier's grave unmarked. Could this have been the case?

It may or may not have been, but I will pass along to the reader that the strange knocking sounds and the footsteps were no longer heard in the house. I spoke to Jill and John several times in the months to come and the noises never returned. Had we actually put a ghost to rest? Was Robert Duncan attempting to make his presence known and to convince someone to honor his grave once again?

After all of these years, I have never really known if my first paranormal investigation involved a ghost or not. I would like to think that it did and that my efforts resulted in a spirit being able to rest in peace. I don't know if this house ever became haunted again or not. Five years later, Jill and her husband moved away but they left instructions with the new owners that the tombstone in the backyard should stay just where it was. I don't know the folks who moved into the house but I have driven past there since and I can say that Robert's stone still stands in that corner of the lot. I would say that it's the only house with a cemetery in the back yard in all of central Illinois!

Ghost Business

Other investigations followed this one, but few were as promising at first. Still though, spooky new stories began to come in and I began to contemplate the idea of compiling all of these stories into some sort of book about central Illinois and its ghosts. It seemed to me that the stories, whether true or folklore, needed to be written down and collected. They should be preserved, if you will, for future generations to enjoy and perhaps to get a chill from. I am sure that I was inflating my importance to think that if I didn't write them down, then no one would but nevertheless, I turned out to be the first to do so.

In 1993, I started a small publishing company called Whitechapel Productions Press. At that time, we were printing a small journal called the "Whitechapel Gazette" that focused on the history of the Victorian era, mysteries of the time, ghost stories and their authors. I decided that this company would make the perfect imprint for my book of true ghost stories and so I set to work on it. At this same time, two related events occurred that would make the book possible.

The first was a small newspaper article that talked about my intentions of doing the book and explained that I was looking for further information, true stories and first-hand accounts of ghosts. The newspaper article led to television interviews on all of the local stations and more media attention than I knew what to do with at the time. Soon, stories were coming in from all over the place and many of the local radio stations began expressing an interest to have me do shows about local haunts for the upcoming Halloween season.

But the article was just the tip of the iceberg. I was just about to find out how many people in central Illinois, and specifically Decatur, were interested in ghosts!

The idea for the book had gone ahead thanks to a discussion that took place between myself and a friend, Skip Huston, in August 1994. I had been thinking about a compilation of local ghost stories and mentioned the idea to him one day while I was over at his house. He immediately told me that he thought the idea would work and pledged to help me to get the material together if possible. We also came up with another idea --- if we could get a good response for the book idea, what if we organized some sort of tour to take people around to see the various haunted places?

At that time, Skip was hosting a music show for a local radio station and he took the idea of a "Haunted Decatur Tour" to the station manager --- who quickly rejected it as ridiculous. No one, he insisted, would want to buy tickets to drive around town on a tour and look at places that were supposed to be haunted! But Skip persisted and finally after a week or two of begging (and because Skip's show was quite popular), the manager agreed that the station would sponsor the tour but since no one would buy the tickets, he was convinced, they would be given away on the air.

As you can imagine, we were a little disheartened by the lack of support for the tour but figured that it would be good publicity for the book, even if it was only with the people who called in for the free tickets. When the morning came for the tickets to become available, we expected the worst. Even though a large article appeared in the newspaper touting the tour and giving me a full page to preview the book, the station manager insisted that we would be lucky to get the required 50 people to fill the bus. The on-air people announced the tickets and we waited for something to happen. The first call came in to claim tickets, followed by another, then another, and another --- ending up with over 600 calls altogether! Finally, when the bus was filled, the deejay suggested that those who were unable to get on the bus, but were still interested, should come down to the place the bus was leaving from and hope that something opened up. Again, we were assured the interest in the tickets was a fluke and that no one would come to be on a waiting list. Another 400 people showed up that night!

And the "Haunted Decatur Tour" was born. That was the first year and we were again assured that it would never last. Sure, lots of people came for free tickets but wait until we tried to sell them the next year --- it would never happen. Well, for those who don't know, the "Haunted Decatur Tour" is still going as of this writing!

Thanks for the tour and the media publicity that I received through the newspaper and television stations, there were a number of people anticipating the release of what became my first book, *Haunted Decatur*. To be completely honest, I had no idea what I was doing when that book was put out and to look back at those original copies makes me cringe. The book looked as though I had printed it in my garage but strangely, no one seemed to care. It was released to good reviews in May 1995 and as bad as that book looked, it sold an amazing 48,000 copies before going out of print in 1997.

The original *Haunted Decatur* book was followed by three sequels, *More*

Haunted Decatur, Ghosts of Millikin and *Where the Dead Walk.* In 1997, it was replaced by a new edition called *Dark Harvest,* which was in turn replaced by an expanded and updated book called *Haunted Decatur Revisited* in 2000 and *Haunted Decatur: The 13th Anniversary Edition* six years later.

In addition, new editions of *Ghosts of Millikin* and *Where the Dead Walk* were produced in 2001 and 2002 respectively. Another book in the series, *Flickering Images,* about the haunted Avon Theatre, was also released in 2001. I moved away from Decatur in 1998 (but returned in 2005) and during that time, this haunted city was never far from my mind. I wrote about it often and as you'll see, it appears often within the pages of this book.

In addition to finally starting me down the career path that I had long dreamed about, the books also served another purpose, as well. As the first volumes began to make the rounds, the phone calls began to come in from the people who believed their homes were haunted. Many were exciting, many were silly and most had nothing to do with ghosts --- but they still came in, giving me many more opportunities to conduct investigations and research.

And not only was my list of investigations starting to grow, so was my list of equipment. As I continued to read and research, I began to meet other ghost hunters and to be introduced to new ideas and theories about the paranormal. One of these theories was that ghosts, or at least paranormal energy, could be detected using electronic devices. At first, I bought a number of cheap, garbage meters before being introduced (by my friend and experienced researcher Dale Kaczmarek) to the TriField Natural EM Meter. I began using this meter in 1996 and I am still using it today.

If you are not familiar with the use of Electromagnetic Field (EMF) Meters, they are likely the most commonly used devices for modern ghost hunters. For the most part, they are the most reliable devices that can be used as well. Electronic devices had recently been adapted for use in the paranormal field to detect energy that cannot be seen with the naked eye. Researchers believe that ghosts (or paranormal energy) are electromagnetic in origin. The energy that a ghost gives off (or uses) causes a disruption in the magnetic field of the location and thus, becomes detectable using measuring devices.

The devices not only give the researcher credibility but also provide a form of evidence that can be presented to witnesses and observers. By using such technology, along with cameras and recorders, the ghost hunter is able to collect real evidence that will be useful once the investigation is over. Learning to use such equipment can sometimes be a trial, though, and since they were not originally designed to be used in psychical research, they usually pick up things that have nothing to do with ghosts. They can be hard to use and mistakes are often made. Even so, I have become convinced that these meters can be very useful tools.

In spite of all of the excitement with the new investigations and research that I was getting involved in, ghost hunting was turning out to be a lonely business. In later years, I would often instruct people to not conduct investigations by themselves. Occasionally, I still act as a single investigator (despite my admonitions to others) but this is normally in cases that involve strict confidentiality or because a case comes up suddenly and I have no time to contact other researchers for assistance. In the early days, though, I did every investigation alone. I was starting to find out that this was perhaps not the best plan. It made it nearly impossible to keep track of everything that needed to be done in an investigation because no one person can be everywhere at once.

My days of lone investigating were quickly coming to an end, though. As many other researchers around the country had done, I conceived of the idea of a research group that would help to expand my investigations beyond central Illinois. In 1996, I began expanding the book company that had started a few years before and a few months later, in early 1997, I launched the *Ghosts of the Prairie* website (www.prairieghosts.com), which would start searching for people beyond Decatur and central Illinois who were looking for hauntings to investigate.

Around Halloween 1996, though, I decided to launch the research group for ghost enthusiasts in the Decatur area. I began spreading the word by way of flyers and word of mouth and in November, we held out very first meeting at the haunted Lincoln Theater.

That night was my first realization of how some people's interests frequently change and how some people will remain with you to the end. That first open meeting found us with nearly 100 people, all claiming to be interested in ghosts and in taking part in serious investigations of the paranormal. Keep in mind that not a single one of them had ever been involved in the field before and most were simply people who had taken my ghost tours that season and thought that being a "ghostbuster" might be fun. They had no idea of the hundreds of rolls of film they would be required to use, the hours that had to be spent looking over video tapes, the drudgery of sitting around a house waiting for something to happen --- none of it.

With that in mind, I started my lecture that night with these words: "Take a look at the person that you see on either side of you tonight. The next time that we have one of these meetings, two of you will not be here." And then I went on to explain to them why that would be and all of the reasons why real ghost research was nothing like what you see on television or at the movies. I was right with my prediction too ---- the next time we had a meeting, we had pared our local group, now dubbed the Ghost Research Society of Central Illinois, down to about 40 members.

In 1997, all that would change. In April of that year, I launched the *Ghosts of the Prairie* website and began researching areas of the country outside of Illinois, starting with the Midwest. As we began to attract more visitors to the website, we started to gain dozens of new members in the ghost society each week. Finally, I decided to expand the group and the small local research group became the American Ghost Society. In the years since then, we have grown to over 650 members (as of this writing) in the United States and Canada.

It was also in 1997 that I held the first of our national ghost conferences at the Lincoln Theater in Decatur. I certainly did not invent the idea of a ghost conference, but we were the first in recent times to present one and are still presenting them today. It's been a pleasure to see how many of them, in the wake of our first event in 1997, are now popping up all over the country. Such events give ghost enthusiasts in different areas the chance to get together and talk about a subject that just might get them looked at with sympathy in other kinds of company.

In 1998, I moved away from Decatur to Alton, Illinois, which is located just across the Mississippi River from St. Louis. In Alton, I expanded the company once again and opened the History & Hauntings Book Co. In 1999, I launched the History & Hauntings Tours (now the Alton Hauntings Tours) and also began offering tours in nearby Grafton, St. Charles and St. Louis, as well. These new tours shifted from outings aboard a trolley to walking tours, which made them even more successful than we could have imagined. The walking tours now visit many of the most haunted places in Alton, a town that we have put on the map as "one of the most haunted small towns in America."

In 2000, the tour business took another turn with the founding of the American Hauntings Tours, which began offering haunted overnights and excursions to spots in Illinois and Missouri. Eventually, we expanded to include sites all over the country. In past years, I had hosted an annual Halloween event where people had the chance to spend the night at a haunted place. With the American Hauntings Tours, we decided to offer such a chance on a regular basis and began setting up locations all over America.

We continued to grow and things changed again. I moved back to Decatur in 2005 and a year later, took back over the management of the Haunted Decatur Tours, which Skip had been handling while I was living in Alton. That same year, I also help start ghost tours in Springfield, Illinois and started the Weird Chicago Tours with my friends Ken Berg and Adam Selzer. These new tours were based on my book *Weird Illinois*, as well as on the experience that all three of us had with hauntings (and strange stuff) in the Windy City. With those guys, along with assistance from Len Adams, Luke Naliborski, John Winterbauer and my wife, Haven, what were once several different tour companies were placed beneath one banner ---the Illinois Hauntings Tours. Soon, we added more tours in Lebanon and Jacksonville, Illinois and, along with the American Hauntings Tours, have placed a lot of "ghost stuff" on our proverbial plates.

What started out as just a hobby has now become a profession and while I focus much of my working time on writing books, speaking, and hosting tours and events --- my investigations into the unknown continue as well. In the pages ahead, I will be recounting investigations, ideas and theories that have been compiled over nearly a decade and a half of tracking down ghosts and hauntings. This is merely a sampling of the cases that I have been involved in, both good and bad, and while they have not always gone well, they have always been interesting.

And another thing's for sure --- they have never been boring!

2. NIGHTS IN HAUNTED HOUSES

Delving into the Spirit World

In the chapter ahead, I will be taking the reader along for a look back at a number of the different outings, excursions and adventures that I took part in during my early years of investigations. Looking back, it seems that almost every one of them was a learning experience in one way or another. Usually, my lessons were learned the hard way (which you will see in the last chapter of the book) but each bit of bungling, or mishap, left me looking for a way to do things better the next time. Other investigations actually went smoothly and were often uneventful, which is why you have not seen them chronicled within these pages.

The accounts in this chapter span a number of years and delve into a variety of different types of investigations. Some were strange, some encountered ghosts, and some didn't. I recount the first investigation where I learned the importance of "corresponding evidence", tales of "accidentally" finding haunted houses and finally, the first time that I ever saw a ghost!

I hope you enjoy the pages that follow but be sure not to laugh too hard when you read about the silly things that I sometimes did --- my disasters may have just provided the information that kept a lot of people from making the same mistakes themselves!

Haunted History

During the years that I have been involved with ghost hunting, one question is constantly brought up to me in regards to my investigations. That question always seems to be "how can we prove that ghosts actually exist?" My answer to that is, scientifically, I am not sure that we can.

By definition, a ghost is a disembodied personality and, at this time, we have absolutely no physical evidence that the human personality even exists. Science will not admit that such a thing is present inside of the body while it is still functioning, so we are far from scientifically proving that it exists outside of the body (as a ghost) after death. We can only infer this by observation.

It's unlikely that mainstream scientists will ever accept paranormal research as a legitimate science. This is not really because it is fraudulent, but because they cannot understand it. To be able to prove something scientifically, it has to be duplicated over and over again under strict conditions. As we all know, the supernatural does not work in such a way. We can measure, document and record, but ghosts do not perform on command. This is what science demands and psychical research is unable to offer this.

But can we prove that ghosts exist in another manner? The answer to that is "yes"! While we cannot prove them scientifically, we can prove their existence historically. What do I mean by this? Let me give you an example that I used in the *Ghost Hunter's Guidebook*:

One Tuesday afternoon, a robbery takes place at a small store on a side street of a large city. The robbery is recorded and documented by a reporter who receives a phone call and travels to the scene. He later writes about the crime in the newspaper that employs him. You purchase this newspaper and read about the robbery. While you believe this has occurred, there exists no actual "proof" of the crime. For there to be proof, the crime would have to be duplicated. In other words, it would have to occur over and over again.

However, there is "historical evidence" that the crime took place in that it was experienced by the reporter and the witnesses who were on the scene. The police officers who came to the store documented the event by collecting eyewitness testimony and evidence that the crime occurred. In this way, they have "proven" that the robbery took place.

Ghost research is not really that different. We can provide historical evidence of hauntings by gathering witness testimony and details about a ghost that may be present in a location. We can then research that gathered information and match it to the alleged ghost when it was still a living person. Better yet, we can collect testimony of events that occurred in the house by residents in the past and then match that evidence to current events that are now taking place. Having independent witnesses, of different time periods, with matching experiences makes for some very convincing evidence. Technically, we have "historically proven" that the house is haunted and that ghosts exist.

I can give you a better example of this with a case that has been taken right out of my files. It involved a house in Illinois that a young couple moved into a few years ago. Shortly after taking up residence, the young woman started to get strange feelings and sensations of being watched in the house. A short time later, she actually got her first glimpse of the ghost. He was described as being a middle-aged man, who would often appear in the master bedroom of the house. He would stand silently, watching the other occupants of the room. He was most often seen in the bedroom at night, standing near a window that looked out onto the street outside. As the man continued to appear, the young woman decided to try and found out what she could about the history of the house. Eventually, she contacted me about it and we began to search for information.

One of the first things that was done was a check through the old city directories, which revealed one name to be connected to the house for a longer period of time than any others, from 1922 to 1951. After that, it became a matter of checking through other records, including newspapers, obituaries and eventually (thanks to a former classmate who was a police officer) even criminal files. It turned out that the longest running occupant of the house had been involved in a local scandal almost 70 years before and it had been featured in the newspaper over the course of several days.

In 1925, the man had been an official at a prominent city bank. Prior to that, he had been a circuit clerk and had been involved in a number of businesses. In the fall of 1925, he began suffering from financial problems and bank examiners who conducted an audit at his place of work discovered that over $200,000 in bonds were missing. Two days later, the former owner of the house vanished. The following morning, his body was discovered on his summer farm with a bullet to the head. His death was ruled a suicide by the coroner, despite the fact that his alleged suicide note was never found, there were no powder burns on his hands or head, and the gun that killed him was found in another location than where his body was discovered.

The bank was never able to recover from the loss of the funds, or from the scandal, and the establishment closed down a short time later. Whispers began to circulate around town about the missing money. Some claimed that the owner of the house had been tied to organized crime. Perhaps they had backed an investment for him and he never paid up, so he stole the bonds to repay the loan. It was theorized that when the bank learned of the missing funds, he got nervous and threatened to make a deal with investigators. This led to his death a short time later. We'll never know if this is true. After all of these years, the case remains open and unsolved.

But was the house haunted? If so, was it haunted by this man's ghost?

After tracking down the information about the house's most infamous resident, I printed out copies of the man's photograph from the old newspaper files. Curious to investigate the case further, I also printed out five other photos of men who were about the same age and whose photos also appeared during the same time period in the newspaper. All of these photos were then pasted onto a single sheet, in no particular order.

Then, using the information that I discovered while searching for past occupants of the house, I started contacting those who had lived in the house over the last few decades. I had heard rumors that some of the previous residents were also aware of the ghost, but I wanted to hear this directly from them. The reader can only imagine the strange telephone calls that I was forced to make in order to get in touch with folks --- and to determine if they believed their former house had been haunted!

However, after assuring them that I was not crazy, I was able to learn that in four instances out of five, each of the families who had lived in the house prior to the current occupants believed the house to be haunted. In all of these instances, the witnesses that I spoke with described the ghost of a middle-aged man who often lurked in the master bedroom. Intrigued and excited, I made arrangements to meet with the families and when I did, I offered them the sheet of photographs that I had put together and asked them to pick out the person who looked most familiar. I also went back to the current owner of the house and asked her to do the same thing.

They pointed out the original occupant of the house --- our mysterious "suicide" --- every single time!

In my opinion, this experiment *proved* (at least historically) that the house was haunted. There was no other way that all of these independent witnesses, each of whom did not know one another and who also lived in the house during completely different time periods, could have identified the original occupant of the place by sheer luck. Every one of these people identified a man they believed to be the ghost, never having any idea who this man was or that anyone else had identified him in the same manner. Could this have been simply a coincidence? That would be very unlikely and I think we can rest assured that none of the witnesses were drunk, confused or crazy --- as debunkers would have you believe.

I simply don't have another explanation for how these people could have each identified the same man as a ghost who haunted their house other than that they were telling the truth. Ghosts do exist and I believe this case proves it!

But not all of the cases that I have been involved with have been so cut and dried. I have decided to devote this chapter to cases of merit that I have found myself involved with over the years. This is not a travel guide of every single location that I have ever visited that was alleged to be haunted. Tossing aside thick stacks of files, notes and writings about places that I have traveled to, but have not actually *investigated*, I was forced to leave out some of my favorite ghostly spots like the Winchester Mansion and Mammoth Cave. However, I do think the accounts ahead will provide the reader with a glimpse inside of psychical research as I came to know it.

Spirits of the Speakeasy

Growing up in the Decatur area, I knew that the city was no stranger to crime. The criminal element came to Decatur less than 30 years after the city was founded when a small settlement called Dantown (but nicknamed "Hell's Half Acre") opened along the outskirts. It was made up of a few hastily constructed houses, a whiskey distillery, gambling parlors, saloons, a racetrack and several brothels. It lasted until the Civil War, when a high tax on whiskey closed down the distillery. The women, the gamblers and thieves departed with the alcohol.

During the early part of the last century, Decatur was a famous city in the Midwest. It was known as a good place to hide out from the law and as a city where many different types of vice would be tolerated. The city had a number of gambling houses, wide open drinking establishments during Prohibition and one of the largest "Red Light Districts" south of Chicago, as well.

The heyday of crime in Decatur began around 1910, at the same time that my great-grandfather began working as a policeman in the city. In those days though, even the cops were crooked and some of the stories that have been told about these days don't exactly put my relatives in a favorable light, I can assure you. But while this period began the heyday of crime, there was nothing that had a greater impact on the criminal element of the city than Prohibition. And once it was repealed, the floodgates opened and crime, corruption and gambling rushed into the city.

When the 18th Amendment to the Constitution, which abolished the sale and distribution of alcohol, took effect on January 16, 1920, many believed that it would cure the social ills of America. Little did they know at the time, but it would actually do just the opposite. America's great thirst for the forbidden liquor bred corruption in every corner. Across the country, over 200,000 "speakeasys" opened. These drinking establishments were so named because many of them were located behind, above or below legitimate businesses and patrons often drank in silence. Huge bootlegging operations sprang into operation to supply the speakeasys and those who chose to ignore the new law.

Prohibition was widely considered to be doomed by 1928, but it hung on for another five years before being repealed in 1933. By then, it had taken its toll, leaving law enforcement in disarray and making crime organizations so powerful they were able to move onto other pursuits, like legalized gambling, with wide public approval.

Prohibition in Decatur, as in most American cities, was a complete failure. The popular outlook on Prohibition in Decatur wavered between completely ignoring the law and taking an occasional drink. Lawbreakers and suppliers were occasionally caught but enforcement of the law was lackluster at best. Local bootleggers found that by spreading a few dollars in the right direction, they could insure their booze shipments and guard against arrest at the same time. A number of speakeasys opened in Decatur, many of them operating quite openly. Others were accessed through secret doors and back stairways, hidden away behind perfectly law-abiding stores and shops.

But law breaking during Prohibition was only the tip of the iceberg in Decatur. Over the course of the next few years, crime ran rampant in the city --- earning Decatur a reputation that still haunts the city today.

Bell's Jewelry Store is located in the 100 block of East Prairie Street in Decatur. The building in which the store operates was built in 1865 and has undergone a number of changes over the years, including housing a number of other stores and shops.

Located on the third floor of the building is a double set of rooms that are divided by a wide doorway. The south room has three large windows that once looked out toward Merchant Street, but have long since been sealed over. Years ago, these rooms saw people, activity, life, and perhaps even death. Today, they stand empty and abandoned. Or are they perhaps not empty at all?

In the 1920s and early 1930s, these rooms marked the location of one of the downtown area's most popular speakeasys and gambling parlors. According to old reports, the speakeasy sold homemade beer and whiskey through the Prohibition era. Afterward, it served as a gambling parlor and brothel until 1936 or 1937, when it was closed down for good. Access to the speakeasy was gained by a stairway from the street and then customers had to enter a secret door (in the form of a sliding panel) to get into the rooms themselves. The room outside, where the door was located, was once a legitimate sporting goods shop that acted as a "front" for the speakeasy. It was apparently not a prosperous shop, however, as many older men that I have spoken with recall coming to the shop as children. They would be left to look around for a few minutes while their father vanished into the speakeasy. Those who recalled the sporting goods shop remembered the merchandise was always dusty and never seemed to sell.

After prohibition was repealed, the speakeasy owners looked for other enticements for their customers and interest was sold to gambler Harry Stewart, who proceeded to set up card and gaming tables in the north room. The owners also contracted the south room as a brothel until the place closed down. The end came during the late 1930s when the place became a victim of changing times and of a crackdown on vice in the city.

For more than two decades after that, the rooms stood empty and sealed off with the original door still in place. The door was finally removed in the 1950s, when some remodeling was done on the old sporting goods store. This room was turned into a frame shop for one of the jewelry stores in the building.

The speakeasy itself was never used and remains empty today. The rooms seem trapped in time, looking much as they did years ago. This is due to the fact that they remained untouched for so long --- and because few dared venture into them, as stories were recalled about the history of the place. The walls of both rooms are still plastered with pin-up photos clipped from film and "girlie" magazines of the early 1930s. Most of the tattered pictures still remain, although now they are faded and yellowed with age.

While I did not become involved in the strange events that were taking place in the building until 1996, weird happenings were already being reported at least two years prior to that. This was at about the same time that the interiors and front facades of the historic buildings on the block were being renovated. This seems to be especially important in this case as the renovations seem to have "awakened" something in the building. Whether there are "memories" of the past or actual spirits is unknown. However, such an event is not uncommon when it comes to old buildings. Many older structures suddenly "become haunted" during repairs and renovations as the ghosts, or residual energy, in the building are disturbed.

In this case, the first reported activity seems to have occurred in 1994 when an employee from the local utility company was making his monthly rounds reading the power meters. He was working in the upstairs of the building adjacent to the gambling rooms and noticed that odd sounds could be heard coming through the wall. He later reported to me that the sounds were of a number of people talking and laughing, music being played and something that sounded like a marble spinning on a roulette wheel. At that time, he had no idea that the rooms next to where he had been that day had once contained a gambling parlor, nor that the rooms were abandoned at the time he claimed to hear the sounds.

In early summer 1996, the employees at Bell's Jewelry store started to notice that strange things were occurring on the upper floors of the building. Three employees of the store individually reported hearing sounds like heavy objects falling and footsteps on the third floor. When they went upstairs to investigate, they found nothing. At one point, they even called in an exterminator, thinking that a rodent problem might account for the odd noises. The pest control company was unable to find any openings where animals could get access to the rooms.

All along, store employees had reported feeling uncomfortable in the old gambling rooms when they had any occasion to go inside of them. In fact, they had largely avoided them before the noises had started. One of the employees recalled the weird feelings that she would get inside of the rooms: "The first time that I went up there, I felt afraid. I knew instantly that I didn't like it up there.... A year later, curiosity got the best of me because I wanted to see the old magazine pictures that were supposed to be on the walls. I had my niece go up there with me and it seemed like the room was very cold... I got the feeling something was in that room. There were cold spots in there and it gave me a bone cold feeling. My hair actually raised on my neck."

The inexplicable noises continued over a span of several months and then other things started to happen, like items in the store downstairs going missing. Tools, cases and small pieces started to vanish without a trace. Some of these items would turn up again in other places, while most things, like a mostly full bottle of Jim Beam whiskey, were never seen again. They also reported that on one occasion, all of the jewelry cases in the store were somehow unlocked and opened during the night --- even though the elaborate alarm system was never triggered.

These strange events were more than enough to convince the staff that they should contact someone who was more familiar with this type of activity. They called me in the fall of 1996 about the weird goings-on and I came to the store with a friend one warm afternoon to see the gambling rooms. We were taken upstairs by Doug Bell, the owner of the store, who was intrigued, but skeptical, about the reported phenomena. Over time, he would become convinced that there was more to the building than he first thought!

Doug led the way up to the third floor and we all three noticed there was a sharp chill to the air. It was odd that on the third floor of an old building, on a very warm afternoon, that it would be cooler than on the lower floors.

After gaining access to the speakeasy, I took a look around and made plans to come back and spend some time in the place after dark. As I walked around, I wandered into the southwest corner of the north room (where the gambling tables were located) and suddenly felt as if I had walked into a freezer! The air around me was very cold and almost electrified. I could feel a chilly, tingling sensation and all three of us saw the hair on my arms literally stand on end as though I was experiencing a mild electric shock. Then, as suddenly as the sensation had come, it vanished and did not come back. I could find no explanation for the bizarre incident, although I would later learn that, according to legend, a man had died in that same corner in the 1930s.

I believed this to be my first encounter with one of the spirits of the speakeasy --- but it would not be my last.

The strange noises continued through the fall of 1996 and additional items disappeared from the store. The rooms were kept locked during the daytime hours and were largely avoided by the building staff. One afternoon, a store employee was locking the door to the speakeasy and as she reached for the door handle, she saw a bright light in the far north corner of the room. She would later claim that she saw the outline of a person in the light. There was no one in the room at the time and there is no explanation for what this light could have been. Strangely, a visitor to the rooms (who knew nothing of this report) also claimed to see a light in the same location a short time later. He stated that it had dropped down from the ceiling to a height of about four feet and then vanished.

Other visitors to the room reported their own unusual encounters. It was common for people to report unknown noises, phantom footsteps, and even the soft sound of music being played in the rooms. Unaware of phenomena that had already been reported, they also told of cold chills and electric-like sensations in certain areas of the room. Much of the strangeness was centered on the same corner of the room where I had experienced my own brush with whatever was there.

I returned to the former speakeasy have my own encounters, as well. One afternoon, I stopped by the store and went upstairs to the gambling rooms. I climbed the first flight of steps from the lower level and distinctly heard the sound of someone following me up. Assuming that one of the staff was going to accompany me upstairs, I paused on the landing to wait for them. After a few moments, no one appeared, so I looked to see who was on the stairwell. There was no one there! I quickly learned that the employees had been with customers at the time and no one had been near the stairs.

During another visit, I was inside of the rooms and left for a few minutes. I returned a short time later and discovered two vintage playing cards had mysteriously appeared on a small table. They had not been there previously. I still could have written the whole thing off to coincidence if not for the fact that I discovered them in the same corner of the room where I had felt the "presence". It made me wonder --- if a man had really been killed in that corner, just what cards he had been holding in his hand?

During the winter of 1996-1997, I brought members of the American Ghost Society to the location and we began conducting investigations inside of the gambling rooms. We were hoping to record some of the strange activity taking place there and in many instances, were not disappointed. A number of photographs were taken that appeared to show anomalous activity and during one outing, we used two separate video cameras to record the proceedings.

The cameras were set up in the empty rooms and were left to film anything strange that might happen. Both cameras managed to record unexplainable sounds on their audio tracks. At one point on the recording is the sound of a heavy wooden door being slammed (although there is no door to slam) and at another point, the sounds of several people walking around and stomping their feet could be heard. This was impossible because the room was locked and empty, as is plainly visible from the visual portion of the tape. In addition, all of the investigators present were on the bottom floor of the building at the time. There was no one else in the building.

Another investigation took place in the spring of 1997. We were given access to the rooms and we set up another controlled experiment using audio and video recorders, along with stationary sensors to pick up movement and the presence of any unexplained energy fields. Not surprisingly, the audio recordings managed to pick up the same sounds as before, including footsteps and the sounds of doors opening and closing. After the investigation was all over, five members of the group would report an identical occurrence, not realizing that anyone else had reported it. Three members first reported they had felt a "cold wind" blow past them and later, two other members also said they felt the same "wind" seconds later. They experienced it a short distance away from the original three members.

And that wasn't all that was reported on this same evening. At one point during the investigation, three different cameras recorded what appeared to be a shimmering light at the same location in the room. All three of the photos were taken just seconds apart. If only one camera had captured the odd image, it would be easy to dismiss the light as a film flaw, or lens flare. However, the fact that three different cameras picked it up makes a logical explanation rather hard to believe.

The investigations of the speakeasy continued into 1998 and up until the time that I moved away from Decatur. The reports of strange phenomena continued too, with various people claiming to encounter everything from eerie cold spots to witnessing balls of light that flew about the rooms in the darkness. On my last evening at the speakeasy, I spent some time in the company of a friend who had no idea of the history of the building. At one point, as we sat there in the inky darkness, he leaned over and nudged me.

"Do you hear that?", he whispered.

"Hear what?" I asked him.

"Music... it sounds like one of these old crank-up record players," he replied. And maybe, just maybe, it was!

Since that time, several years have passed and the haunting of the old speakeasy continues, although the rooms are closed to visitors today. I remain convinced that this location is truly haunted. There have been too many strange things that have happened here, involving too many reliable witnesses, for me to not realize there is more to this place than meets the eye. Whether you believe in ghosts or not, it is a fascinating time capsule from a period in history that most of us know little about. If you are a believer in ghosts, and you ever get the chance to see this spot, the history of the place just enhances your experience.

And while I do believe the location is genuinely haunted, I have to confess that not everything that occurred here during our investigations could be considered ghostly. Because of the sheer number of investigations that I was able to arrange at this location, we were able to experiment with many things. We tried analytical and detailed, scientific investigations and we also attempted old-fashioned séances as well, using Ouija boards and dark room sessions. The séances turned out to be the least successful of the investigations that we attempted. However, it was one investigation that we tried, which combined the elements of both types of research, that caused me to learn that EVP cannot always be trusted!

The practice of attempting to record ghosts is called Electronic Voice Phenomena (EVP). The sounds that make up EVP are apparently sonic events of unknown origin, which can be heard, and sometimes captured in recordings, on various types of electronic apparatus, including tape recorders and even radio equipment. The messages that are recorded are rarely simple but often are fragments and sounds that require hours of listening to understand. This often opens the research up to criticism, but most ghost researchers have stopped short at totally condemning the practice. I don't condemn EVP completely, but I do have my reservations about it.

I have long believed that there is a natural human inclination to project meaning onto otherwise innocent phenomena. Many tend to do this with EVP. It is an attempt to make the messages simpler, or to appear more mysterious, than they really are. The human imagination will try to impose meaning on what appear to be intelligent sounds on the tapes. If no sense can be made of them, then an idea will be invented, and/or introduced, to support what we want to hear. The human mind has a tendency to "fill in the blanks", which is the main problem with EVP. It has been suggested that if you listen to something enough times, you can hear anything that you want to hear. This problem is most apparent when the researcher announces to anyone who will be listening to his recordings, just what they should be listening for. The power of suggestion can easily take over and destroy whatever credibility this experiment may have had.

Another problem (I have since learned) is that EVP cannot stand alone as evidence of the paranormal. The reason for this is that it is almost impossible to authenticate. There is no way that a researcher can absolutely prove that the sounds recorded on his tape are not the result of a hoax, or a result of some natural interference. All that a non-believer (or a debunker) has in the way of evidence is the word of the researcher and unfortunately, that's not enough to make it qualify as real evidence.

Of course, I learned all this the hard way, after what seemed to be a productive investigation at the speakeasy above Bell's Jewelry Store. We had gathered on this evening to try and attempt a combination investigation, meaning that we would try and conduct a séance, while recording the event with high-tech gear, recorders and cameras. While I do think this does make for an interesting approach to investigation, one event occurred that evening that caused me to lose a lot of faith in EVP recording!

The first portion of our evening was spent setting up cameras and recorders that would monitor the events that we hoped would take place. Once we had everything prepared, we shut down the lights and took up positions in a circle of chairs. One of the team members stayed outside of the circle to monitor the cameras and to take photos of the proceedings. The rest of the group was seated and then one of the members began to try and make contact with the spirits in the room. Whether or not this was successful is open to debate, especially in light of what later happened. Anyway, nearly a hour passed with the one team member speaking aloud, hoping that the ghosts in the room might do something to let us know they were present. At the end of this period, we called the séance to a halt and began to review the tapes and video that we had obtained.

A short time later, one of the group members became very excited about what he heard on the large, reel-to-reel recorder that we had been using. As he played back the tape, he heard an eerie exchange and I have to admit that when I listened to it, I also felt the hair on the back of my neck stand on end! He played the tape again for me:

"Can anyone hear us?" the voice of the group member who had been presiding over the séance intoned on the tape. "Is anyone there? Will you make some sign so that we know you are with us?"
<silence>
"Are there spirits present in this room?"
<silence --- then the sound of someone shifting in their chair>
<more silence>
"Is anyone here with us?"
Another voice then cuts into the conversation, although it was definitely no one in the room and none of us heard the voice during the séance. It spoke with a very eerie, moaning sort of sound.
"Hellooooo", the voice groaned.

After that, the voice of the group member continued on but the playback of the tape got the attention of everyone in the room. All of the investigators abandoned their tasks and came over to hear the recording again. It seemed that we had actual evidence of ghosts in the speakeasy --- captured on tape! We marked the spot on the recording and then played the rest of the reel but there was nothing else out of the ordinary on it.

In the weeks that followed, we played the recording over again over again. I listened to it carefully, speeding it up and slowing it down. I knew that no one had spoken during this moment of the séance because there had been nothing on the video recordings of the event. I watched the videos closely and heard absolutely nothing. The only explanation for the absence of sounds on the video was that we had been using a very sensitive microphone with the audio recorder. Could this have picked up something that nothing else did?

After all of this, I could find nothing to dispute the fact that we had captured the sound of a ghost, or at least had captured something paranormal, on the tape. I played the tape for dozens of researchers and ghost enthusiasts and even announced its existence at a meeting and played it for an assembled group of about 50 people. Imagine my embarrassment the next day when I discovered that the "ghost" on the tape was likely nothing more than a bowl of chili!

Let me explain... After the meeting that night, one of the team members who had been present at the investigation came over and explained that he needed to talk to me. He felt terrible about something and hadn't known how to tell me about it. What he could tell me though was that the sound on the tape was definitely *not* a ghost! According to this team member, he had eaten dinner just before the investigation and by the time that the séance began, his stomach was starting to bother him. At the point in the recording, where the "voice" was allegedly taped, his stomach had gurgled and churned, emitting a sound that (on the tape) sounded just like someone moaning the word "hello". It happened that he had been sitting very close to the sensitive microphone and the quiet sound had somehow been picked up on tape, even though none of us present had heard it and neither had the microphones on the video cameras.

Boy, was my face red! The team member felt terrible (although apparently not terrible enough to come forward with his explanation a little sooner) and I quickly began explaining to people that the recording was not exactly as it seemed to be. It was an embarrassing lesson to learn but I was glad that I learned it when I did.

Hauntings at the Lincoln Theater

Looking back now, I can't really remember my first visit to the Lincoln Theater in Decatur. I must have been young though because during my childhood years, the theater was always open. There was no place else in the city quite like the Lincoln. Of the two downtown theaters, the Lincoln and the Avon, you could always perhaps count on a better show at the Avon, but the atmosphere of the sprawling, old Lincoln was a place of wonder for a child of my interests. The huge auditorium always seemed to be cast with shadows, whether the house lights were on or not.

You could wander the mezzanine, perhaps slip into the balcony or even vanish behind the curtains where only darkness, hanging ropes and discarded scene props seemed to wait.

Journeying down into the basement to find the bathrooms was a journey all its own and one that was guaranteed to send chills down the spine. And why was this? Because the Lincoln Theater, the stories always said, was filled with ghosts!

Growing up, my family visited the theater often. This was in the days when the grand old theaters were still showplaces, albeit fading ones. The cracker box cinemas at the shopping malls were still in the future and the best way to see a film was still on the big screen. On Saturdays, we frequently attended the show at the Lincoln. By 1980 though, this afternoon ritual came to an end when the Lincoln closed its doors and went dark. Sadly, except for a few music events, plays and even an occasional film, it has remained that way ever since.

In spite of this, I have never lost my love for this old theater. I have been fortunate to visit it many times over the years and have been involved in fund-raising events and shows that have managed to keep the lights on the marquee flickering for just a little while longer. And I have also been here in search of the theater's ghosts...

I can say with all honesty that I have had more encounters that I believe to be supernatural in nature at the Lincoln Theater than at anywhere else in Decatur combined! Many of these encounters have been chance happenings when ghosts were the furthest things from my mind. Ghostly footsteps, inexplicable sounds and even icy cold chills that appear and disappear without explanation have been incidents of my Lincoln Theater experience. I have been both alone and with others when strange things have occurred and in some cases, photographs and videotape have managed to capture the elusive presences that have been previously part of my subjective encounters.

There are ghosts at the Lincoln Theater, have no doubt about that. The spirits of the building were created by the history that has passed through its doors and has managed to take root within its walls. The Lincoln is a glorious place and the ghosts who dwell here are glorious in their own right, from a stagehand who died here to the restless phantoms of those whose lives ended on this spot before the theater ever existed. The building is truly a place where the history "comes alive"!

The Lincoln Theater, located on North Main Street in downtown Decatur, is one of only two of the city's grand theaters that remain standing today. It opened in 1916 with a large seating capacity and a sprawling stage. It was a labyrinth, and remains so today, with its mezzanine, high balcony, basements and sub-cellars. The theater holds many secrets, and according to some, many ghosts.

The theater was not the first building to stand on the site that it now occupies in downtown Decatur. Aside from frontier construction by the early settlers, the first real building on the site was the Priest Hotel. W.S. Crissey opened it on the northwest corner of the Old Square in 1860, although it was completed and operated for many years by Franklin Priest. In 1880, Riley Deming took over the establishment and changed its name to the New Deming. It was later purchased by Augustine Wait and in 1892; he changed the name to the Arcade Hotel. Eight years later, he would remodel, expand, and call it the Decatur & Arcade Hotel. There was a horrible fire in 1904, which destroyed the building, but it was rebuilt on the same site a short time later. It was in 1915 however, when disaster struck.

On April 21, 1915, a spectacular fire broke out and destroyed the hotel, claiming two lives and damaging several of the surrounding structures. The blaze was believed to have started because of some oily rags that were left near the hotel's boiler. A night watchman discovered them smoldering and tried to put them out, but was driven back by thick smoke that began churning from the refuse. The blaze quickly spread and while all of the fire equipment in the city arrived on the scene within minutes, smoke was soon billowing from the lower windows. Water began to be pumped from the trucks but because the smoke was to thick to enter the basement, the firefighters had no idea of the exact location of the fire. It was said that a roar came up from the crowd assembled in Lincoln Square when the first flames appeared.

The fire came from the rear of the hotel and could be seen glowing through the front doors. The firemen began dragging hose into the building but within ten minutes, the blaze had entered the walls and was eating through the roof of the hotel. At that point, Fire Chief C.W. DeVore began directing his men to turn their attentions to the other buildings nearby, as there was no hope for the hotel. The nearby structures, including the Bachman Bros. & Martin Co. furniture store, the YMCA, the First Presbyterian Church and the Odd Fellows Building, were saved but as the north wall of the seven-story Arcade building collapsed, it struck the Bachman Bros. warehouse with a tremendous crash and a loud explosion. The furniture store was saved from heavier losses thanks to a heavy firewall that refused to give in and a new sprinkler system.

The two men killed in the fire were William E. Graham, an engineer for the Decatur Bridge Co. and C.S. Guild, a traveling salesman from Lockport, New York. The bodies were found in the ruins, although several other hotel guests were never found. Whether or not they escaped from the inferno is unknown. What is known is that the disaster could have been much worse. If it had not been raining before the fire broke out, it's possible that the entire west part of downtown, including many homes, could have been destroyed. The hotel was never rebuilt and the Lincoln Theater took the original building's place.

Many have pondered the question as to whether or not the spirits of the people killed in the hotel fire might walk in the dark corners of the Lincoln Theater. It now stands directly on the location of the former hotel and many have speculated that the ghosts could have passed into the new building and may have taken up residence there.

Fires in Decatur had been far too common in years past. A number of public buildings had been destroyed by blazes, including the Powers Opera House, which burned twice. Being built on the site of a hotel destroyed by fire must have made the designers of the Lincoln Theater especially aware of the possible dangers and they were determined to make this building "absolutely fireproof".

The new theater was constructed by Clarence Wait in 1916 on land that he had inherited from his father's estate. The Decatur architectural firm of Aschauer & Waggoner was hired to draw up plans for the theater and the buildings surrounding it. These buildings included the Odd Fellows Lodge and seven smaller stores that fronted Main Street with offices on the second floor. These smaller stores were given the name of Lincoln Square, which was also the name of the theater until it was shortened in 1930.

The theater was designed and built on a section of land that would be L-shaped, with an entrance in the middle of the block. To insure that the place was "fireproof", the original boilers were housed in the Odd Fellows Building and separated from the theater by a thick firewall. This wall, which was about two-feet thick, surrounded the entire building. The interior of the building was also carefully designed as the walls, floors, railings, ceilings, fixtures, and even the curtains, were all said to be impossible to burn. Architect Charles Aschauer claimed that the entire block could burn down, but this theater would be left standing and little did he know that there would be times when this boast would be tested!

The public got its first look at the interior of the new theater in October 1916 when John W. Dooley held a Christian Science lecture there. The formal and official grand opening took place at the end of the month, on October 27, 1916. The Lincoln opened to "standing room only" crowds of Decatur's finest citizens, dressed in black tie and formal wear and eager to see the new, glorious theater of which they had heard so much about. The first program to be presented was George M. Cohan's stage comedy, *Hit the Trail Holliday* starring Frank Otto. In addition to the show, speeches were given that night by Mayor Dan Dineen and by Clarence Wait, who once again bragged about the "fireproof" status of the theater and its solid and safe fire escapes.

The audience loved the show and raved about the spectacular design of the theater, from its private seating boxes, to the massive ivory-colored columns, to the 1,346 seats, all of which offered a splendid view and wonderful acoustics. Also new to Decatur was the mezzanine seating, which ran just below the balcony and offered seats that were only slightly above the level of the stage.

In those early years, the main emphasis at the Lincoln was on stage shows and vaudeville acts. The community also put the theater into use as well and it hosted many small, local productions and the Decatur High School commencement services each spring. Many famous stars appeared here, including, Ethel Barrymore, Al Jolson, Ed Wynn, Jeanette MacDonald, and many others. Audiences also thrilled to such attractions as a sparring exhibition by Jack Dempsey after his famous fight with Georges Carpentier.

In February 1926, the theater hired a 12-member orchestra to provide music for all stage productions and the silent films that were starting to gain popularity. Vaudeville still remained the most popular attraction the theater had to offer however and the orchestra's leader brought a young, unknown comedian named Bob Hope to the Lincoln in 1926 to show Decatur how to dance the "Charleston". Hope was just starting his career in those days and he would return often during the 1920's to appear in vaudeville shows and comedy productions.

One of the most enigmatic of the performers to allegedly appear at the Lincoln was the stage magician and master illusionist, Harry Houdini. Houdini was not yet a worldwide sensation by the time that he came to the Lincoln late 1910s, but he was well on his way to becoming one. According to Lincoln Theater legend, Houdini's visit has been permanently marked on the wooden stage of the theater by a narrow trap door that has been nicknamed the "Houdini Hole". Below the hole, metal hooks are imbedded into the ceiling of the basement as silent reminders of the magician's visit.

For a number of years, people believed that the hole in the stage had been cut for the magician to escape through during one of his illusions and that the hooks below had held some sort of safety net. However, this turned out to be incorrect. At the time Houdini would have played the Lincoln, he was perfecting an escape that used a very large water tank, into which he would be lowered upside-down and then have only a few moments to escape. The rectangular hole in the Lincoln stage was cut so that a hose could drop below the tank and empty into a drain in the basement. The metal hooks were actually used to hold the support ties for the drainage hose.

But was the "Houdini Hole" really used by Houdini? There are those who claim the famous magician never played at the Lincoln at all. They dismiss the recollections from those who remember his visit, believing that they are mistaking some other performer for the legendary illusionist. The name for the "hole" in the stage, they state, was a mistake and likely, those who remember a famous magician coming to the Lincoln have mistaken Harry Blackstone for Houdini.

There is no denying that Blackstone did perform at the Lincoln several times but those who have claimed to recall Houdini's visit remember Blackstone as well. A check of newspapers of the time offer few clues. There are advertisements for visits by Blackstone and even little known illusionists like "Alla Axiom", a "master mind reader and crystal gazer" but no mention of Houdini. How do we explain this if Houdini really played the Lincoln? According to one interview that I conducted with a staff member who worked at the theater for many years, there was no advertising for Houdini because he was not famous at the time. He was part of a vaudeville troupe that played the theater and received billing in the troupe's advertising but not with the theater. He was still a couple of years away from his great fame, this man explained, which is why no mention was made in Decatur newspapers of the day.

Still curious as to how so many people remembered Houdini --- even though others insisted that he never played the Lincoln -- I continued my research. I soon found other clues about Houdini and the Lincoln Theater. According to an interview with magician Harry Blackstone, Jr., the son of Blackstone, his father toured the vaudeville circuit, often following in the wake of Houdini. The two men had similar acts and while friendly, were fierce competitors. If one of them played a theater or circuit, the other soon followed. For this reason, the younger Blackstone stated, since his father played the Lincoln then this means that Houdini almost certainly did too.

But did he? Well, we will likely never know for sure. Someone, be it Houdini or Blackstone, left a permanent mark on the stage of the Lincoln Theater and an indelible mark on the history of this grand old place.

Moving pictures continued to increase in popularity in the city and Decatur was demanding more and more films to take the place of stage shows. Only major attractions were needed to fill in between the films, so the theater booked live emcees to host the films months in advance. This filled the need for live actors and celebrities and still managed to bring the moving picture crowd into the theater. Every movie became a major attraction with the orchestra playing overtures to accompany the action on the screen. A pianist, and later an organist, was hired to provide lighter music for the serials, newsreel footage and the comedy films.

In April 1928, the first "talkies" came to Decatur and played at the Empress Theater. The Lincoln began showing them 14 months later at the close of the vaudeville season. This would herald the end of the vaudeville days at the Lincoln, and perhaps in the entire city. The sound equipment was installed in the theater for films, making silent movies obsolete, and bandleader Billy Gail and his orchestra were promptly dismissed.

From that time on, two films were shown each week with one running from Sunday through Tuesday and the other from Wednesday to Saturday. The first talking films shown were *Nothing but the Truth* starring Richard Dix and a musical called *Desert Song*.

That same year, the Lincoln was purchased by the Great States chain of theaters, which also purchased the Empress and the Bijou. The building itself remained the property of Clarence Wait until his death in 1936. Ownership of the theater was then passed to his brothers, Arthur and Fao Wait.

Although movies had largely replaced live entertainment at the Lincoln, there were still special performances booked here on a regular basis. It was during one of these performances that the "fireproof" claims of the theater were first tested. In September 1942, Harry Blackstone returned to perform at the theater. The auditorium was filled with about 1,000 school children when fire broke out in the Rambo Drug store, located next door to the Lincoln Theater.

Alerted to the danger of smoke entering the theater and the building catching on fire, Blackstone remained calm and jokingly told the audience that for his next trick, he was going to make them all disappear from the theater in five minutes. He then directed them to leave, row by row, out of the alley doors and out of the fire escapes in the balcony. He promised the children that they were assisting him in a marvelous new illusion, which he would explain to them outside.

After he had successfully cleared the theater and learned that the danger was past, Blackstone is said to have sobbed with relief from the stress of his heroic evacuation of the theater. Years later, in 1960, while a guest on the television program "This is Your Life", he stated this had been the "greatest trick of his career".

The fire would last for four hours and would completely gut the drug store and Cook Jewelers, which shared the space. The fire was so intense that the floor of the building collapsed into the basement. It also heavily damaged an adjoining flower shop and beauty parlor, but no damage was reported to the Lincoln. Apparently, it really was "fireproof" after all!

These claims would be tested again in 1960 when another fire did major damage to buildings south of the theater. The section of the building that was located above the theater lobby would be virtually destroyed, which also explains why this section can be seen in older photographs but is not present today. The Lincoln itself, which was showing the film *The Bramble Bush* at the time, was only slightly damaged. The "fireproof" claims have not been tested since and the building has remained architecturally sound after more than 80 years.

The theater operated steadily for many years and was sold again in 1974 to Plitt Theaters Inc., which bought out the entire Great States chain. The Lincoln Theater only remained in the chain until December of that year, when management was passed to the Kerasotes chain that was based out of Springfield, Illinois. At this time, they already owned four of Decatur's other theaters. They leased the building on a month-to-month basis and in December 1980, were informed by William Wait that their lease would not be extended past the end of the year. Unfortunately, the Kerasotes chain had a reputation for stripping everything usable from a theater before they left it and they followed this same plan at the Lincoln. They removed much of the valuable equipment, from projectors to the interior mechanisms of the speakers. The projectors in the Lincoln in recent years have been borrowed from private individuals and salvaged from the Rogers Theater, while the speakers remained empty shells mounted on the walls in the balcony.

After that, the Lincoln closed down for many years, only opening occasionally for live music and barely attended events. By 1990, the building had deteriorated badly and was suffering from neglect. It had been abandoned by everyone except for the bats and pigeons that had taken up residence in the auditorium.

Thankfully, the Lincoln came to the attention of a restoration group and some life has been brought back to the old place. Thousands of dollars and countless hours of work have been put into the theater, but it still has a long way to go. The restoration effort has been a long and painfully slow project with possibly many years remaining before it will be completed. This has not stopped many local and national groups from performing here, however, and many times, during these performances, regular people have encountered things in the theater that can only be described as something well beyond the ordinary!

Stories have circulated about hauntings at the Lincoln Theater since at least the 1930s. Reports by witnesses from those early days of film in the theater have suggested that as least one ghost haunts the building. However, in more recent times, the numerous encounters here have led many to believe that a multitude of spirits may linger in the Lincoln.

The most famous ghost of the Lincoln is rooted in a legend from the vaudeville days. His name was "Red" and he was a stagehand at the Lincoln during the days of live performances. He was deeply attached to the theater and loved the place, working long shifts and coming to the theater on his day off just so that he could be among the actors and entertainers. It was said that Red always dreamed of becoming a performer himself, as he was a commanding presence with his bright, auburn hair, but he was simply too quiet and shy to ever take the stage. He contented himself to working behind the scenes and perhaps even standing on the stage at night, looking out on the empty theater. Perhaps he imagined an audience in those darkened seats, assembled to watch him perform in the latest show.

One night, during a performance, Red was working on the catwalks. This area is about 75 feet above the stage itself and was used in those days to lower props and scenery flats. Red was used to working up in those dizzying heights and it never really bothered him. Then, on that fateful night, the unthinkable happened.

Red slipped from the metal grid work and fell. He plunged downward and collided with the "pin rail" of the "sand trap", a concrete platform that is also located high above the stage. The "pin rail" is a metal bar with sharp hooks jutting from it. The ropes that controlled the flats and curtains were tied on these hooks. When Red collided with the rail, his arm was snagged by one of the hooks and torn from his body, thanks to the force and speed of his fall. He landed on the stage in a bloody heap with his arm still tangled on the rail overhead. Needless to say, he died moments later.

And he has been haunting the place ever since.....

At least that's what the stories say but unfortunately, the truth behind the tale isn't nearly as exciting.

There really was a stagehand nicknamed "Red" who worked at the Lincoln Theater during the vaudeville days. Red also had only one arm but he did not lose it (along with his life) in a horrific accident. He was a veteran of World War I and he had lost his arm during the fighting in Europe. When he returned to Decatur, he took a job as a stagehand at the Lincoln and soon became a "novelty" because he managed to do all of his work with one arm. In fact, he was faster than many of the other stagehands (most who were much younger than he was) at pulling the ropes and lowering the lights and they were using both of their arms. Red was a likable man and completely devoted to the theater. This was perhaps the reason he was so memorable to later generations of staff members as the "stagehand who never left the theater".

As mentioned, Red did not die in a terrible accident but he did die at the Lincoln Theater. According to my sources, he sat down to take a nap after his lunch one afternoon in 1927 and simply never woke up. He passed away in his sleep --- leaving an indelible impression behind. Soon, after people began to speak of a ghost at the Lincoln Theater, they immediately assumed that it was Red.

Over the years, dozens of witnesses have reported strange sounds and footsteps in the otherwise empty theater and these are sounds that cannot be explained away as simply the theater's acoustics. They have also reported whispers, strange voices and even a shadowy apparition in the theater's balcony. However, this strange figure is not described as looking like Red, but rather as a woman in a long, old-fashioned dress! This is only one of the many reports that cause some to believe there are a number of ghosts in the building. Several other witnesses have reported their own brushes with hazy forms and figures seen out of the corner of the eye ---- and none of these descriptions match! Could there be a legion of phantoms left behind in the theater?

In addition to visual sightings, there have been a number of other encounters as well, including the aforementioned footsteps and sounds. Many have experienced inexplicable cold chills in certain spots in the building and others claim to have been touched by unseen hands. Several others have mentioned seeing theater seats in the auditorium actually raise and lower by themselves, as if an unseen audience was watching the proceedings on the stage.

I had my own strange encounter a few years ago when I was working in the quiet theater one afternoon, making preparations for an upcoming Halloween show. I happened to be off to the side of the stage, behind some curtains, when I clearly heard someone walk up the steps and out onto the wooden stage. When I came out from behind the curtain, I was startled to find that there was no one there but me! I quickly searched the area, and even the rest of the theater, but the place was completely empty.

Other unexplained incidents have occurred around what may be the most haunted spot in the theater. It is a metal, spiral staircase that is located in the back corner of the stage. Many witnesses claim to have had unearthly encounters on and around the staircase. For example, in 1994, an entertainer who was performing in a traveling production reported that he saw a man lurking on this staircase. He was in the back corner changing his costume when he heard a voice whispering to him. When he looked up, he saw a shadowy figure on the steps. He was unable to describe the figure, but he was convinced that it was a man. He complained about the presence to a nearby theater staff member, but when they checked the staircase, they found it empty. The man was gone but there was nowhere that he could have vanished to! Strangely, the actor had no idea about the legends of the Lincoln, nor that the staircase was rumored to be haunted.

In addition, I can personally vouch for at least one encounter on this intimidating staircase, because it happened to me. I still have no other explanation for what occurred, other than to say that I was followed up the stairs by one of the theater's resident ghosts!

I was in the theater one evening in October 1995 with a reporter and a cameraman from a local television station. They had contacted me about haunted places in Central Illinois for a news special and one of the places that I took them to was the Lincoln Theater.

After an interview about the hauntings, I decided to join the cameraman, Robert Buchwald, for a trip up the spiral staircase. He took his camera along, hoping to film the theater's stage from this vantage point. It was a good thing that he brought it, because we would have had no other source of light to make the trip up there with. We rounded the staircase and then reached the top. We looked around the small and confined space for a few moments, exploring a small room that leads to the theater air ducts. Other than this dusty chamber, there is not much else to see up there. We stood talking for a few moments, and then what happened next was enough to convince even a skeptic like Robert Buchwald that there may be more to the Lincoln Theater than first meets the eye!

It seemed innocent enough at first. We had climbed the spiral staircase and left the reporter down on the stage by herself. We weren't surprised to soon hear the sound of her footsteps as she followed us up the stairs. Her hard-soled shoes made a distinctive sound as they echoed on the metal steps. Realizing that we had the only portable light, and the staircase was quite dark, Robert leaned over the railing with the camera so that the reporter would have some light to see by. Just as he did this, from out on the stage, we heard the sound of a voice calling out to us. We looked and saw the reporter standing in the middle of the stage ---- dozens of feet from the base of the steps and much too far away to have been climbing the staircase just moments before!

We suddenly realized that the footsteps on the staircase had not belonged to the reporter. So, who was climbing the staircase? We didn't know but when the sounds finally stopped, we didn't stay up there long enough to find out!

In addition to those encounters, I have been lucky enough to explore and investigate the Lincoln Theater on many other occasions. I believe that I have been just about everywhere there is to go in this old building and I have never gotten tired of wandering about in the darkness, wondering what might be around the next corner.

Starting in 1995, I have been able to organize a number of paranormal investigations in the theater, usually involving anywhere from 8-40 people. For most investigations, I would never dream of using that many researchers at one time, but the Lincoln is so vast, even a large investigating team will be swallowed up by all of the available space. Out of those investigations, there were several memorable happenings that are worthy of mention here.

During one of our investigations, in early 1997, ghost hunters who were staking out the basement of the theater (where the bathrooms were located) detected a moving "wave" of energy that managed to set off not only a motion detecting device, but also two different electro-magnetic field meters! The detectors are designed to pick up any strange fluctuations in the energy field of the location being measured and as far as could be determined, some sort of energy passed back and forth through this area and then inexplicably vanished. It should be noted that a small locker room area that is located off this basement has a tragic and horrific history. While there are no deaths recorded in this area, it's possible that sordid event of the past may have left some sort of impression here that is still being felt today.

Another investigation in 1997 found a small group of researchers in the dressing room below the stage. I had brought several people with me to check out some recent reports of footsteps and odd sounds that had been passed on about this area.

We had gathered in the darkened dressing rooms and were patiently waiting, hoping to pick up any unusual noises that might occur. I had been told by some performers in a stage show that had ended just a week or so before that they had been packing up for the night and heard the sound of hard-soled shoes crossing the floor and the sound of a man clearing his throat. They assumed that it was someone upstairs (the theater has excellent acoustics) but when they climbed the steps, they found no one else in the building. I couldn't help but think of my own encounters with phantom footsteps in the theater, so I decided that it might be a worthwhile report to check out.

We waited for about an hour without incident before we heard the sound of someone walking. The problem was that it was not coming from the concrete floor of the basement --- but rather from the wooden stage above our heads! I was convinced that someone must have entered the theater and was now ruining our investigation. Another researcher and myself decided to go upstairs and see who it was. We quickly climbed the steps to the upper level and found that the stage was completely dark. It was also very silent!

We had just heard someone walking around, literally seconds before, and I feared that our mad dash up the stairs may have startled them into silence. Although what someone could be doing walking around the stage in complete darkness was anybody's guess.

I called out: "Is anybody here?"

I couldn't help but wonder if perhaps they were afraid that we were the ghosts! There was no reply, so my friend handed me the flashlight that he had remembered to bring with him and I switched it on, checking out the stage area. It may, or may not, come as a surprise to the reader to learn that the stage was completely empty! There was no living person there who could have created the sounds of shoes walking back and forth over the boards.

Still pondering a possible explanation though, we then decided to check the auditorium and the lobby to see if the culprit may have fled when he heard us coming upstairs. We hurried to the front of the theater, but found the entire place to be deserted --- there was simply no one else there!

Unlike many other haunted locations, paranormal photographs from the Lincoln Theater are rare. I have experimented with a variety of film types and cameras and so far, have never been able to obtain any photographic evidence of my own to say that the theater is haunted. Many have tried to capture the ghosts here on film but perhaps the difficult and darkened conditions of the large building are simply outwitting the cameras that have been used. Of course, that's not to say that no anomalous photos exist from the Lincoln, they just seem to be few and far between.

In 1997, American Ghost Society researcher Nancy Napier had a strange encounter and snapped one of the best photos ever of spirit energy at the Lincoln Theater. During an investigation of the building, she went up into the balcony to take some photographs of the area. She was using a standard SLR 35mm camera (with flash) and was randomly taking a few photos. Her camera was working perfectly and she experienced no problems with it, before and after the incident that I am about to describe.

She was taking her fifth photograph when the camera suddenly malfunctioned. Simultaneously, a cold chill passed by her that caused (as she later described it) "the hair to stand up on my arms". The shutter of the camera opened and closed but strangely, the flash refused to work. Theoretically, with no lights on in the dark auditorium, the resulting photograph should have been ruined and dark. However, this would not be the case!

When the photo was developed and returned to her, Nancy was startled to discover that only the photo for which the flash had malfunctioned contained anything out of the ordinary. Apparently, the cold chill and the malfunctioning of the camera had been caused by the strange image that appeared on the developed print. The photograph showed a very white and intense ball of light that was only a few feet away from the camera. The image was clearly in motion and was obviously not some sort of camera reflection, or lens refraction, because her flash had not even been working properly. In addition, the ceiling of the balcony was too far away for even a working camera flash to have reflected off of it. It was truly a bizarre and unexplainable photograph!

While hard to explain photos are not often retrieved from the Lincoln, occasional snippets of strange video sometimes are. On Halloween night of 2001, during an overnight investigation, a number of investigators managed to record unusual lights in the theater using "night vision" cameras.

Perhaps the most astonishing images were caught by researcher Robert Johnson, who was armed with a Sony camera. Just moments after walking into the theater's auditorium with his camera, he turned to his right and began to film. Seconds later, two very bright white lights shot off at high speed and traveled along the back theater wall and then disappeared. The two lights traveled very quickly and with a definite path in mind. The lights were not merely free-floating dust or late season insects that ended up in the theater. What they actually were still remains a mystery --- but they certainly couldn't be explained away with ordinary means.

Our overnight investigations of the Lincoln Theater have continued and as recently as early 2007, strange incidents have taken place. One of the most recent "hot spots" in the theater has been the auditorium. It's possible that current happenings here have been caused by the remodeling that has been taking place since 2005. At that time, the Lincoln began undergoing its first stage of renovations, resulting in major repairs and changes to the entire building.

The auditorium has seen a lot of activity --- both of the normal and paranormal kind. One incident, which occurred in the late summer of 2006, I was hosting a Haunted Decatur Tour and we stopped at the theater, as we have been doing since 1994. At the time, work was being done on the large arch, just to the front of the stage, and the auditorium was almost completely filled with metal and wooden scaffolding. We walked down the side aisle of the theater and my assistants, Doug Hicks and David Pickett, assembled the tour group on the dark stage, facing out into the auditorium.

In order to keep things "atmospheric", we turn off all of the lights on the state and I tell the history of the theater while we stand there in the dark. I had only spoken for a few minutes when we all started to hear what sounded like someone walking around in the auditorium. We heard the sound of heavy boots, tromping back and forth and banging against the scaffolding that was assembled there. At first, I ignored the sounds and kept talking but soon, our tour guests on the stage began to notice the sounds, as well. People began shuffling their feet and whispering as the boots in the auditorium seemed to get closer and closer to where we were standing.

Finally, one of the tour guests spoke up: "Um, is there someone out in the auditorium?"

Once one guest spoke, others asked too and soon, Doug Hicks turned on his flashlight and began looking around in the auditorium. We all plainly saw that the auditorium was crammed with scaffolding and there would be no way for anyone to easily walk through it, especially in the dark.

We also saw that the auditorium was empty --- there was no one there!

Does the ghost of "One-Armed Red" really roam the dark corners and back hallways of the Lincoln Theater? Or is he just a legend created to explain the generations of strange phenomena that has been reported there? Could there be a large number of spirits still inside of the building, drawn to the energy of almost a century of sadness, heartbreak and tragedy?

Most importantly, is the Lincoln Theater really haunted at all?

If you are skeptical about the many tales of the theater, I challenge you to wait before answering these questions. Wait to ponder them until some night when you have the opportunity to come to the theater and sit in the dark auditorium --- by yourself. Is this place really haunted? Or is that just the sound of an old building settling in the shadows behind you?

Is it your imagination ---- or is it something else?

A Ghost Named Joe

In 1997, I had what I believe was my first real encounter with an intelligent, or "traditional", spirit. This type of haunting is actually quite rare and is best described as the personality of a person who once lived that has stayed behind in our world instead of passing on at the time of death. This may happen in the case of murder, a traumatic event, suicide or even because of some unfinished business in the person's life. At the time of death, the spirit refused to pass on because of these events. They may also linger because of emotions that tie them to the earth, from anger to love. It may not have been that the person did not pass on because they couldn't, but because they didn't want to.

In other cases, there is the chance that the spirit didn't even realize that he had died. This may occur when a death is sudden or unexpected, like with an accident or a murder. These spirits are now made up of the energy that once made up the personality of a living person. Now that the human body is gone, that energy is all that remains. These types of spirits will often be interactive with the residents of the location and can create some pretty dramatic hauntings.

I first encountered one of these elusive spirits in Springfield, Illinois at the Springfield Theatre Center. It was not a grand old movie house like the Lincoln Theater, it's really a plain, but pleasant, building that (until recently) was home to the Springfield Theatre Guild. Despite the unassuming facade and rather ordinary interior, it is also home to one of the city's best documented ghosts.

The Theatre Center is constructed from concrete block and is much larger than it appears on the outside, mostly due to the sprawling basement area of dressing rooms and storage areas. The auditorium of the theater is rather narrow and was built like a modern movie house with a sloping floor and flip-up seats.

For more than 50 years, strange and inexplicable events plagued this theater. Unexplained sounds and lights have been heard and seen; things have disappeared, seemingly at random; doors have opened and closed on their own; sets and prop pieces have moved and have fallen without human assistance; doors have opened and closed on their own; heavy objects have been hurled at unsuspecting victims; and of course, there is the pungent aroma of facial cream that seems to permeate the air on occasion. And strangely, that recognizably scented cream has been banned from the building for years!

Who is the spirit said to haunt this building? Those who work and perform here will tell you that he is the ghost of an actor named Joe.

The Springfield Theatre Guild was founded in 1947 and within a couple of years had managed to raise enough money to build a theater in which to hold their performances. The site was located at 101 East Lawrence Avenue and the construction began in 1950. The first theater season was in 1951 and they opened with the Broadway hit, *Born Yesterday.*

One of the actors involved during the early days of the Guild was Joe Neville, a rather strange and eccentric performer who was not well liked by many other cast members. Apparently, he was known for his arrogance and was unusually difficult to get along with. He also had a massive ego, but was a talented actor, so everyone made an effort to overlook his attitude. In addition to his acting ability, Joe was said to have had a questionable past, as well. Rumor had it that he had also done some acting and directing in England, under another name. After his death, his will was read and he apparently left a lot of land in England to various people in Springfield. The problem was that Joe didn't own any of the land! The will was his last practical joke on the people at the Theatre Guild.

As mentioned, Joe was regarded as a pretty strange and unpopular guy. His death was taken so lightly by other actors that the lead role he was slated to play in an upcoming production was simply given to another actor on the night before it was scheduled to open. I guess the show really must go on!

"If there was anyone who was going to come back as a ghost, it would be Joe," said Tom Shrewsbury, a long-time member of the Theatre Guild and a man who had more than one encounter with the theater's resident ghost. He was also one of the remaining actors who worked with Joe Neville in the old days of the Guild.

"I knew Joe from many, many years ago, back in the 1950's," Shrewsbury explained. "We were doing a show called *Mr. Barry's Etchings* and Joe played the lead. One night after dress rehearsal, Joe went home and committed suicide. There was apparently an audit of the books at that place where he worked and a lot of money had been misappropriated --- and it looked as though Joe would be caught the next day."

Many people feel that Joe's suicide is the reason that he haunts the theater. It may also be the unfinished business of the play that causes him to linger behind. He may have felt the audit cheated him out of his chance to play the lead role in the performance. As the theater was undoubtedly the only place where this bitter man was happy, his spirit probably has no desire to leave it. His need for attention, in life and in death, is evident.

As the years have passed, many staff members and performers have reported weird happenings here. They have also discovered that sometimes a disbelief in Joe's ghost can trigger the events to take place. One of the actors told me: "Whether you believe in him or not, you don't say out loud that you don't believe in him --- because then things happen."

He went on to describe an unusual occurrence that took place one evening when he and another man were building a set for an upcoming show. The friend who was working with him was skeptical about Joe's existence and made a point of stating this while onstage.

He told me: "The power saw he was using started up by itself and as soon as it did, some sheets of plywood fell over and a ladder that was standing nearby fell over on its own. The saw started to rev up again and right then my friend shouted 'I believe, I believe!'"

Other actors and staff members also tell tales of Joe's presence. These anecdotes involve props and objects falling from the rafters and striking people, staff members being pushed offstage and on one occasion, a filmy, white apparition that appeared on an overhead catwalk.

Colleen McLaughlin, one of the actors at the theater, had a number of experiences that qualified as being ghostly. She often noticed the tendency of things to appear and disappear around the theater. One night, during the run of a show, she had to make some very quick costume changes during a particular song. She ran offstage, changed and then went back on. A few moments later, she returned to change her clothing again. This time, she got a surprise.

She recalled: "Everything was missing. It turns out they [her costume] were behind a stairwell, all folded up neatly. No one used that stairwell during the production, and we have no idea how the clothes got there. They had been next to the piano when I came on and off stage. No one saw them disappear --- and no one could have taken them."

Other actors have experienced similar incidents on many occasions, including Rebecca Sykes, the former theater manager. One night during a show, the clothing she was supposed to change into also disappeared. It was found later strewn up and down a ladder in the back, a place where no one had gone during the show.

The actors are not the only ones troubled by the ghost, however. The people who build the sets and props sometimes have even stranger encounters.

One night, a stage crew volunteer was alone in the theater, painting a set for an upcoming show. He used a roll of tape to mark off areas where set pieces would be placed. He finished with one section and laid the tape aside. A few moments later, he reached for it, but it was gone! Thinking that he must have used the last of it, he decided to call it quits for the night. He closed up his paint cans and moved them up to the front of the stage. He went behind the curtain and was about the shut down the stage lights when he spotted his missing tape roll. It was propped up next to the last can of paint he had moved to the edge of the stage --- and there was no doubt that it had *not* been there seconds before! He left the theater in a hurry that night!

Another performance was using a ventriloquist's dummy as a prop. As usual, the dummy was locked in the prop cage, which was located just offstage, at the end of the evening. On the night before the show was scheduled to open, the dummy disappeared from the locked cage. Needless to say, everyone who had a key to the cage denied taking it out. One of the prop managers was forced to run out and replace the doll just before the curtain call. Later that night, after the show was over and the stage was cleared, one of the workers emptied the prop cage and took everything downstairs to a storage room. He came back upstairs, where a party was in progress, and he discovered the location of the original dummy, which had disappeared --- it was inexplicably sitting inside of the locked prop cage with its legs crossed.

That would have given anyone a good case of the creeps.

I had the chance to visit the Theatre Center in the early part of 1997 and spent several hours investigating the place and interviewing actors and staff members about their encounters with Joe's ghost. I heard a number of familiar stories, and some new ones, from theater regulars, who all expressed respect, and a sort of fondness, for the ghost that haunted the place.

Before interviewing the staff, I was able to wander about the building on my own. As mentioned, the lower regions of the theater are much larger that you might expect. Besides the spacious reception room, there are also many rooms for storage, bathrooms, a furnace room, and several small dressing rooms. I also wandered about the stage and the auditorium, not knowing what I would find, but hoping to find something.

I would not be disappointed.

My self-guided tour eventually led me down a back staircase from the stage to a dressing room at the bottom of the steps. This dressing room was apparently used mainly during the early days of the theater. A new addition to the building had been constructed years after the original work and the old room was replaced by newer dressing rooms upstairs. The room in the basement was seldom occupied, except apparently, by Joe. Of course, I didn't know that at the time!

As I walked into the room, I suddenly caught a strange smell near the center. I identified it immediately as the overpowering stench of Noxzema. To be honest, I really thought nothing of the smell. This was a theater after all, and the use of Noxzema was undoubtedly common. I shrugged the whole thing off and continued with my tour.

Later on, I got quite a surprise when Rebecca Sykes told me that one indication they had of Joe's ghost being present was the smell of Noxzema in the air. Because of this, superstitious actors had banned the use of the cream from the theater years before. So, whatever I had smelled in that room had not been the lingering odor of an actor who had recently removed his or her make-up.

I asked Rebecca how they had linked the smell to the ghost and she explained: "They say that Joe had this horrible rash on his legs that never seemed to heal. He used to slather layers of Noxzema on them. I guess that everywhere he went, you used to be able to smell it around him."

I would have loved to laugh the whole encounter in the dressing room off to nothing more than my overactive imagination, but that would be impossible to do since I had no idea of the tell-tale "smell" until *after* I actually caught a whiff of it!

While debunkers are bound to have a field day with such a subjective report, the encounter confirmed the presence of the ghost for me because the smell could not have been my imagination. I simply did not have the information to "create" such a distinctive odor in that particular location. I never even knew of the "ghostly smell" until hours after I first noticed it. I also could not have picked up a stray odor, as the balm had not been used in the theater for more than 30 years at the time of my investigation.

While this may not be concrete evidence for some, it was very convincing to me and I felt strongly that an interactive spirit was present at the site.

But let's go beyond this for a moment and investigate the mechanics of such an encounter. Without simply writing the whole thing off to "no one knows how the paranormal works", how could I have come into contact with a smell that was associated with a person when he was alive --- even though he is now a ghost?

Let's begin with the idea that I think we have compiled enough evidence to logically assume that Joe Neville is the resident ghost of the theater building. I think that it's safe to base this on the history of the place, the documentation that exists showing that Joe was a real person and that he died in the manner that is part of the theater's lore. It's also based on more than 25 independent accounts of the smell of Noxzema that accompanied paranormal activity. Needless to say, I became strongly convinced of the reality of the haunting after my own inexplicable encounter with the smell. Not knowing about the sign of the presence in advance ruled out (in my mind) any chance of it being just my imagination at work.

Now that we have established this, however, I still have to question how I could have actually come into contact with the smell. And this is why I wonder about it --- the smell that is associated with Joe's ghost should *not* be attached to his spirit! If we accept the idea that a spirit is the personality of someone who once lived and now remains behind as energy, then we can accept the idea that certain attributes of that person may remain behind as well. One such attribute might be the smell of that person. It's possible that someone could have a distinctive odor about them, perhaps a problem with body odor even, who knows?

In Joe's case, he also had a distinctive odor, however it was not a part of his actual makeup. It was an artificial odor of something that he applied to his body. How then could this odor exist as part of his energy after death? That's a good question and my only guess is that perhaps the spirit has more control over the energy attached to it than we ever imagined.

In the past, I have theorized about the various reasons why ghosts are reported wearing clothing. Outside of residual hauntings (where the ghosts are nothing more than imprints or memories), there are still many accounts of ghosts looking just as they did when alive, right down to the clothing they are wearing. I have come to feel that this occurs when the energy of the ghost interacts with the mind of the person seeing it. As the personality and attributes of the person remain within the energy that the spirit is now made up of, the affected mind now sees the spirit the way that it either once existed, or perhaps in the way that the spirit sees itself.

Could it work this same way with an artificial smell? Could the odor of Noxzema be such a part of the personality makeup of Joe Neville that his spirit exudes the smell just as he once did? It's certainly a possibility and I have no other way to explain just what I experienced that day at the Theatre Center. I believe that I literally came into close contact with Joe's ghost --- and experienced his distinctive smell to prove it!

Sounds from the Past?

Residual hauntings (believe it or not, a phrase that I coined back in 1997) have always been fascinating to me. I believe they are the most common type of haunting that ghost hunters run across and, over the years, I have encountered a number of them. The first one may have been at a house in Springfield, Illinois that is known as the Yates Mansion. The old mansion was the home of a former Illinois governor who used a turret in the house as a study and as a place to house his Civil War collection. Governor Yates liked to read and he would walk around the turret room as he did so. As the years passed, the sound of his footsteps would echo in the turret on nights of the full moon. After investigating this place, I did not come to the conclusion that his ghost was present but rather that the impression he left behind "replayed" itself on nights when the energy of the full moon was at its peak.

There seem to be many reasons why residual hauntings occur. The simplest way to explain this kind of activity is to compare it to an old film loop. By that I mean it can be a scene, or image, that plays over and over through the years. Many of the locations where these hauntings take place experience an event (or a series of events) that imprints itself on the atmosphere of the place. This event can suddenly discharge and play itself at various times, just as a recording would. The events are not always visual, as I mentioned, they are often replayed as smells, sounds and noises that have no apparent explanation. The famed "phantom footsteps" that are reported at many haunted locations (including the Yates Mansion) are a perfect example of this.

Often, the mysterious sounds or images that are recorded relate to traumatic events that have taken place and which have caused some sort of disturbance to occur there. This is the reason why so many battlefields, crime scenes and areas related to violence have become famous for their hauntings.

But this is not always the case. In other situations, the images have been created by a series of events that have been repeated over and over again. These frequent and repetitive releases of energy also seem to be capable of leaving a lasting impression. A good example of this can be realized from the large number of haunted staircases that have been reported over the years in homes and public buildings. It's possible that because of the number of times that people go up and down the stairs that the energy expended leaves a mark on the site. These locations act like giant storage batteries, saving up impressions of sights and sounds from the past. Then, as the years go by, these impressions appear again, as if a film projector has started to run.

Obviously, no one really knows for sure how these hauntings are created, but there are theories. Some believe that the building materials of the structure may absorb the energy to replay again later. Researchers have discovered that most buildings where residual hauntings take place are older structures. Could older building materials play a part in this? Possibly, but I think that it's more likely that the age of the building itself is the largest contributing factor. The number of people that pass through an old structure over time, and the tapestry of history played out in it, seems to be the main reason why these hauntings occur.

There may be other reasons as well. One idea that I suggested in the past connected underground water sources and residual hauntings. I have conducted a survey of such sites over the years and know of a number of locations where residual energy has been experienced, which also have a water source below the ground. One site, where I conducted a number of investigations and experiments, was the old gymnasium at Millikin University in Illinois.

The college's old gymnasium was added to the campus in 1911, about eight years after the school was opened to students. When construction was started on the building, the designers still had to contend with some of the problems of the past. One major issue was the small stream that still ran across the back part of the campus. It had been dubbed the "River Sticks" by the students and it was all that remained of the lake that was once the centerpiece of a nearby park. It was learned that the stream was fed by a natural spring and that a water table existed beneath the entire campus. In spite of this, the builders managed to force the water underground, where it still remains today.

The gymnasium was used constantly for quite some time but as the years passed, the old Gym was replaced by the Griswold Physical Education Center. Today, only a weight room and a dance studio are left to remind us that the building was once the sports center for the college. Since the departure of most sports activities, the upstairs portion of the gym, with its high ceilings and elevated running track, has been abandoned by the athletes. It has been used by the theater department for many years as an area for both prop storage and as space to build sets for upcoming performances. It is in this part of the building where ghostly sounds from the past echo into the present.

Countless students claim to have had strange encounters in the building and most of these encounters seem to tell of events from the past repeating in the present day. These events, strangely enough, repeat in the form of sounds. Visitors, staff members and students, who have come to the upstairs portion of the building, told of hearing voices, laughter, cheers, applause, whistles blowing and even the sound of a basketball bouncing across the floor when no one else is present.

One student told me of coming to the old gym one night and having an encounter of his own. He said: "It was my freshman year and we were loading a show downtown at the Lincoln Theater. It was about midnight and we had forgotten a prop and they sent me back to get it."

He walked into the dark, upstairs gymnasium and was surprised to hear the sound of someone loudly bouncing a basketball across the floor. Curious, he quickly reached for a light switch but when the lights came up, he found the room was deserted. A quick search of the building revealed not only that no one else was there, but that there were no basketballs there either!

A Millikin theater alumnus named Allison Smith had an eerie story to tell me that occurred during her tenure at the university in the middle 1970's. At that time, she had been a costume designer for the theater department and was working late one evening in the gym. Although she was sure that she was alone in the building, she began to hear the sounds of a young woman crying from somewhere downstairs.

The office she was using was up on the highest floor (the level with the elevated running track) and she stepped out into the foyer at the top of the stairs. She could hear the cries drifting up from the shadows below. The staircase and the lower floors were dimly lit and she was chilled by the mournful and eerie sound.

Allison decided to go downstairs and check on the crying girl. She felt badly for her and stated that she felt something was terribly wrong. With each descending step, the crying grew louder until it became almost a warbling scream. Determined, Allison quickened her pace and reached the bottom of the steps. The cries were coming from the gymnasium itself and she tried to see where the other girl might be, but it was too dark. Just around the corner, Allison found the electrical box and she switched on a light. Just as she did so, the crying immediately stopped!

A thorough search of the building revealed that there was no one else inside and that all of the doors had been locked. Allison never solved the mystery of the "crying girl" but she never forgot it either.

A former Millikin security guard told me of an event he experienced during the holiday season of 1994. At that time of the year, the campus was mostly deserted and because most of the buildings are empty, the security staff had to make sure that everything is locked up tight. The watchman entered the old gym and from upstairs, he could hear the sound of someone running around the elevated track that circled the gym and overlooked the basketball court from the third floor.

He explained: "I honestly thought that someone had gotten into the building and was running around upstairs. I hadn't been on the job very long and I really didn't know anything about the building. I just knew there was a weight room downstairs, so I figured that the gym was still actually a gym and that students might work out here. I certainly didn't know the place was supposed to be haunted!"

He cautiously climbed the stairs to the highest floor and stepped through a doorway and onto the track. He looked around with his flashlight, peering first from the dizzying heights to the floor below and then around the track itself. The echo of the pounding footsteps circled quickly away from him, rounding the track to the far side of the gymnasium. He turned his flashlight in that direction, sure that he would be able to see someone in the glare. However, he quickly discovered that no one was there --- and not only that, he realized the track was completely blocked with stored props and set pieces! There was no way that anyone could be running around the track, and yet, he could distinctly hear the sound of the running feet! Unnerved, he scrambled for the lights and flipped them on and the sound abruptly stopped. A search of the building revealed that no living person was present.

He told me later: "I just got out of there... fast! And I didn't go back to the gym over that entire holiday season. All that I did was check the door outside because I never went in!"

I had my own encounter with the "phantom sounds" of the old gym in 1997 (and this would not be the only strange thing I experienced here). After hearing all of the stories from both students and staff members about the strange sounds that "haunted" the place, I was able to get permission to spend an evening in the building. I brought two other investigators along with me and we were determined to record anything odd that occurred, or at least to experience it for ourselves.

For me to say that serious boredom set in would be an understatement. We sat in the dark gymnasium for more than two hours, listening for anything out of the ordinary --- then we heard it! It seemed to be someone walking across the wooden floor and the sound was so real that I could literally hear the floorboards creaking under the weight of each step this person took. The footsteps crossed from one side of the room and were heading quickly toward the other.

The first thing that I did was to make sure of where my friends were. The gym was dark, but not so dark that I couldn't see them sitting just a few feet away. I saw that they were also peering in my direction, making sure that I was not a prankster, taking on the role of the "walking ghost". Once we insured that no one from our small group was the culprit, we decided to try and find out if the "extra" person in the room was solid or spectral. The only way to do this (short of running across the room and attempting to tackle the phantom) was to try and illuminate the person using one of our flashlights. I followed the sound of the footsteps and then shined the bright light over in that direction.

As soon as I did, the footsteps immediately halted! It was as if it had been merely a recording and the device used to generate the sound had been abruptly switched off. And not only was the gym now silent, but it was empty, as well. I had half expected to find some befuddled student standing there in the glare of my light, having wandered into the middle of our "ghost hunt", but there was no one there.

As others who had experienced strange events in the gym had done, we searched the building. I confess that I still expected to find a student or staff member who had been playing a trick on us, but the place was totally empty.

This type of experience has been repeated many times in the building with inexplicable sounds being heard and then ceasing when the lights are turned on. Could this be the connection to the haunting? There are many places on the Millikin University campus where electrical disturbances are common. In many locations, these anomalies cause cameras and stereos to stop working, televisions to shut off and lights to turn on and off. I had a couple of weird experiences myself while on campus that concerned bizarre behavior by electrical objects. One of my experiences took place in the old Gym and the other while walking about the campus.

In 1996, I was on campus recording strange events experienced by Millikin students and I found that my tape recorder refused to work correctly in some places. Strangely, it would work fine in others! While I was walking around campus, I was also taking photos with a camera that I had been using for some time and which had a fresh battery in it. Throughout the day, I had frequent problems with the camera, leading me to believe that the battery might be faulty. There was nothing remarkable about this until I played back the tapes of the interviews.

The tapes had been recording ordinary conversations and also discussions that had nothing to do with ghostly encounters. At every point on the tape that I mentioned I was having trouble with my camera, the tape made a weird, whirring noise as though something was interfering with the recording. Was it just a coincidence? Was something just wrong with the tape recorder? Maybe so, but I should add that both the camera and the recorder worked perfectly later on.

To make matters worse, the recorder was working perfectly when I walked into the old Gym that afternoon but a few moments later, it inexplicably stopped working and everything on the tape was blank! Because of this, I returned to the Gym a few days later with a video camera and planned to record the rest of my interviews. I had just installed a freshly charged battery in the camera, but it went dead after just 12 minutes of filming! The battery had been completely drained.

Oddly enough, though, that's not the strangest thing that occurred to me in the building. I was in the old Gym again in 1997, working with a documentary film crew that was doing a segment on the ghosts of Decatur and on this day, Millikin University, in particular. The crew was setting up an array of lights for an interview and as everyone was busy, they asked if I would mind switching on one of the bright flood lights. I reached over and casually flipped the switch on the light and it flashed brightly on for probably 10 seconds or less, and then it blinked back out again.

Puzzled, one of the crew members looked over and asked why I had turned the light back off again. I told him that I hadn't. The light had turned off by itself.

He came over to investigate (thinking that something might be wrong with the light) and I turned around and looked behind the light on the floor to see if someone may have accidentally unplugged it or something. I didn't think there had been anyone behind me, but I thought that I had better look. Instead of finding the cord loosely strung out on the floor and pulled away from the plug, I found it neatly fastened into an extension cord that was tightly coiled up on the floor. There was one problem though --- the extension cord had never been plugged in at all and because of this, neither had the light! It had somehow flashed on by itself and then turned back off again!

What surge of power could have caused this light to turn on and could it be the same type of energy that manages to drain batteries and flashlights and to cause recorders and video cameras to behave strangely? If so, could it also be the reason for the haunting in the building?

It's possible that the source of the strange activity reported all over the Millikin campus is the lake that was once located where the university stands today. When the water was forced underground, the water table remained beneath the campus. This could be why Millikin seems to act like a giant battery, storing up energy to replay over and over again. On the other hand, this water source may also be responsible for the resident ghosts as well. Spirits and supernatural energy are often attracted to water and their energy may be generated in much the same way that an electrical current is.

As for the gymnasium itself, it is located directly over the site of the old lake and the underground water table is certainly present at this location. Thanks to years of sporting events, parties and dances, there has certainly been a lot of people through the building over the years and perhaps a residual haunting would explain the reports of phantom clapping, cheering, whistles, basketballs and footsteps that have come from the place. Further credence is given to the water / electrical theory because in most of the cases where the witnesses have reported anomalous sounds and have turned on a light (or another electrical appliance), the noises have suddenly stopped. Could the change in one electrical current somehow affect the other one?

Obviously, there are no clear answers as to why strange things continue to happen at the old Gym. Is it paranormal electrical interference or ghostly Millikin alumni from years gone by? It's impossible to say but regardless of why the weird happenings take place, the old gym remains a strange and haunted place. It is an odd sort of "mystery spot" where the past is still present in a way that we don't yet understand.

The McPike Mansion

Shortly after moving to Alton, Illinois in 1998, I began hearing stories about the place that many referred to as "Alton's most haunted house". I soon discovered that if you lived anywhere in the region, from Alton to St. Louis, you couldn't help but hear about the infamous McPike Mansion, located on Alby Street.

I took an immediate interest in the place and the owner, Sharyn Luedke, would credit me with helping those who lived far outside of the area to think of the mansion as a very haunted place, as well. I wrote about the house and even helped to get it featured on television networks like Fox, ABC and the Travel Channel. Many asked me if the stories that they heard about the old house were really true. I can answer those queries quite simply with just one word --- "yes".

The McPike Mansion was built in 1869 for a man named Henry Guest McPike, a prominent Alton citizen.

McPike's family could be traced back to Scotland. His ancestry included a number of patriots who fought during the Revolutionary War, including Captain Mose Guest McPike, of New Jersey, and Captain James McPike, both of whom were at Valley Forge with George Washington. James McPike came west to Kentucky in 1795, bringing with him his sons, John and Richard. Henry McPike was a son of John McPike and came to Alton as a very young man in 1847.

McPike soon became active in the business and political community of Alton and, over a period of years, was involved in a number of different companies, working as a real estate agent, box manufacturer, and insurance executive, along with other things. He also became the president of the oldest horticultural society in Illinois.

His political aspirations did not get off to a quick start, although he did have an interest in the abolitionist movement. His father had been the editor of a Whig newspaper (the Whig party later became the Republicans in the time of Abraham Lincoln) and was an early advocate of the abolition of slavery. He was also one of the organizers of the debates between Abraham Lincoln and Stephen Douglas in Alton and had a place on the platform during the event. In spite of this, McPike never sought political office, although it was offered to him many times. During the Civil War, he was called upon to act as Deputy Provost Marshall of the District and this placed him in a management position in the War Department. After this, he acted as a representative in many conventions and with the city council and interest in politics eventually led to him service as the mayor of Alton in 1887 and 1891.

The McPike Mansion was constructed in an Italianate-Victorian style and became known as one of the most elaborate homes in Alton. It contained 16 rooms and a vaulted wine cellar and was originally built on a country estate of 15 acres that McPike called "Mount Lookout". Thanks to McPike's interest in all things horticultural, the estate was planted with rare trees and shrubs, orchards, flowers and extensive vineyards. The owner became the propagator of the McPike grape, which was known across the country. The grape was praised for its wine-making properties and it won gold medals in almost every competition in which it was entered.

There is no question that this was one of the most beautiful homes in the area. The McPike family lived on at the estate for some time after the death of Henry McPike, but records are unclear about some of the dates. It has been stated that they stayed in the house until around 1936, while others records say that the home was owned by Paul A. Laichinger at this time and that he purchased the house in 1925 and lived there until his death around 1945. Laichinger either lived in the house or rented it out to tenants, but it's likely that it became a rooming house after his death. There have been a number of people who have come forward and have spoken to the current owners about living in an apartment in the house in years past. One woman even mentioned the strange experiences she and her family had with ghosts in the house --- long before the place earned its reputation for being haunted.

For years, the house remained silent and empty but then it was sold to an individual who planned to develop the four acres of property by demolishing the house and turning the site into a shopping center. When the new owner encountered problems with the city in regards to the zoning of the property, the plans for the store were scrapped and the house was abandoned once again. It was not long after this that the condition of the McPike Mansion started to go rapidly downhill.

The word was out that anyone who was looking for anything from the house could easily come in and take it. Soon, thieves and vandals descended on the place. They stole everything from the house that was not nailed down and many things that were, from the marble fireplace mantels to the toilets. The staircase banisters soon disappeared, as well as the massive interior doors that had been custom-made for the home's twelve-foot ceilings. Chandeliers and light fixtures were torn out, radiators were removed and even plumbing fixtures and copper pipes were taken. Perhaps even worse than the scavengers were the vandals that followed in their wake. Soon, spray-painted graffiti covered the walls, windows were broken and plaster walls were broken apart. It was destruction for the sheer thrill of it, which is the worst kind of crime to commit on an old house.

Time has not been kind to the old house either. In the 1980s, the box gutters failed and water began to seep into the house. The roof started to deteriorate and leak, causing the floors to fall into such ruin that many of them became unsafe to walk on. With all of the window glass broken out of the house, the damaged interior was left to the elements and the days of Mount Lookout seemed to be numbered.

In 1990, the house was purchased by a contractor from St. Louis named Gary Hendrix. He had come to Alton in search of a modest Victorian home but became entranced with the McPike Mansion instead. Even after viewing all of the destruction that the elements and the vandals had wreaked on the house, he still had hope for the place and almost immediately began working to renovate it. As a stickler for detail, his plans for the house were extensive and he estimated that it would take him at least two years to restore the mansion to its former glory. He began re-making the eaves brackets of the house with old lumber (since modern lumber was not the same) and planned to floor the solarium with white marble, along with many other improvements and enhancements. When he finished the work on the interior, he planned to also build a new carriage house for the property and a Victorian gazebo for the lawn.

He said in a 1991 interview: "My mother always laughs when I start one of my restoration projects and tells me that I will never get it done."

In this case, it appears that Hendrix's mother was correct because in 1994 the house was on the market again and very little had been accomplished from the list of grand plans that the contractor had for the property.

But hope does remain that the McPike Mansion will not become just a memory. In 1994, Sharyn and George Luedke purchased the house at auction. Sharyn, a teacher in the Edwardsville School District, stopped by the house on the day that it was to be auctioned off. She and her husband, an associate professor at Southern Illinois University Edwardsville, had always dreamed of buying an old house and fixing it up and almost on a lark, Sharyn put in a bid on the house. She was more than a little surprised to later learn that she had won it. A few months later, when the brick ranch house next door to the mansion came up for sale, the Luedkes sold their home in Godfrey and moved to Alby Street so that they could be closer to the mansion.

The struggle to restore the house has continued to be an uphill battle for them. They hope to eventually renovate it and open it as a bed and breakfast but they were disappointed to learn that, contrary to the assurances they had received on the day of the auction, no grant money was available for the house from any federal, state or local agencies. The house had been added to the National Register of Historic Places back in 1980 but that was the extent of the attention that it had received from such agencies. The Luedkes soon discovered that they were on their own but they were not ready to give up on the old place just yet.

Their first break came when Bob St. Peters, the president of the Alton Area Landmarks Association, nominated the house for inclusion on the list of Illinois' Top 10 Endangered Places. The list focuses on historic properties that are architecturally significant but are at risk because of deterioration, demolition, improper development or bad public policy. As a result of the publicity generated by the list, the Luedkes did receive a couple of small grants to help generate architectural reports about what could be done with the house, but not much else. They have continued the fight, though, facing a myriad of problems with the city, and by time and weather, as well. Their valiant effort continues to make sure that the McPike Mansion remains a part of the city's present and future --- and not just its past.

And if even a fraction of the stories about the haunting here are true, then the importance of saving the house becomes even clearer!

But how did the house become so haunted in the first place? That is perhaps one of the questions that I am most frequently asked when I start talking about hauntings in Alton. There have been all manner of rumors and false stories started about the house, including that it has been the site of various murders and suicides over the years. Fortunately, such tales have no truth to them. Yes, there have been deaths in the house, as is the case with many old homes, but none have been sufficiently traumatic enough to seemingly cause the mysterious activity that has been reported here. In spite of this, ghost stories abound in this mansion, including many first-hand accounts from reliable people with absolutely no reason to lie. The mansion just seems to be "haunted by yesterday", as the events of the past have truly left an impression here that is re-lived in the present as more than one ghostly presence.

Sharyn Luedke came to believe the house was haunted almost from the beginning of her involvement with it. Her own unusual encounters in the house carry much more weight than the claims of trespassers and curiosity-seekers who come to the house simply because it looks haunted. There have been hundreds of stories that have circulated about the mansion, from the chilling to the downright silly, but Sharyn's claims that the ghost of Paul Laichinger haunts the place seem to be the most credible. He is one of the few spirits who is alleged to haunt the mansion for which a real historical connection exists.

As mentioned earlier, Laichinger owned the house during the early part of the last century and died here in 1945. He was also preceded in death by his young son, who also may linger here. In an earlier part of this account, I briefly mentioned that a woman had contacted Sharyn who had lived in the mansion during the time that it was a boarding house. As a punishment for misbehaving, she and her sister often had to sit by themselves on a staircase outside of their apartment. On many occasions, the girls both heard the sound of a child running and playing upstairs --- even though there were no other children living in the building.

As for Laichinger himself, he passed away from an illness that had been caused by years of heavy smoking. It is not uncommon for visitors to the house to smell strong whiffs of cigarette smoke in the place --- even though no smoking has been permitted in the structure in decades. Sharyn also told me that on one occasion, a group of people gathered at the house not only smelled the smoke but actually saw a cloud of it appear in the area above their heads.

Sharyn says that she had her first encounter with Laichinger's ghost about six weeks after she bought the house. She was on the property watering some plants and saw a man standing in the window, looking out toward where she was standing in the front yard. A chill came over her but she noted that the man (who vanished moments later) was wearing a striped shirt and a tie. Sharyn later obtained a photograph of Paul Laichinger wearing an identical outfit. She has since come to believe that it was his presence that she witnessed. Many people have since told her that Laichinger had loved the house. In some cases, those who pass on have returned to locations because they simply did not want to leave them. Could this be the case with Paul Laichinger?

Another spirit in the house is thought to be a domestic servant that Sharyn has dubbed "Sarah". She was little more than a presence with an assumed name until a man came by the house one day and presented the Luedkes with some books that he had removed from the house nearly two decades before. One of the books had the name "Sarah Wells" written inside of it. Since that time, Sharyn has been touched (actually hugged) by this spirit and she and her husband have occasionally caught the scent of lilac on the third floor. They believe the odor is directly connected to this ghost and have been unable to come up with no other explanation as to why the smell so mysteriously comes and goes.

In the summer of 1999, one of the strangest, and hardest to explain, events occurred at the house. A video that was made at the time of the incident has since appeared on television and has yet to be debunked, even by skeptics and experts in special effects. One weekend that summer, a mutual friend of mine and Sharyn's was in town from out of state. Her name is Rene Kruse and she is a professor at California University in California, Pennsylvania. Sharyn was taking her on a tour of the house and they descended down into the basement. As it happened, Rene was making a video of the tour and managed to capture what happened next on the tape.

As she turned a corner in the basement, an eerie white "mist" appeared and moved toward the small group that was with her. The mist, which was unlike anything that she had ever seen before, literally enveloped the group. Rene later described it to me as having what seemed like an "electrical charge" about it. It swirled all around them, which was seen on camera, and then inexplicably dissipated and moved off. Rene was able to follow the mist to several different locations in the basement and as she would get near it, it would move and start to swirl around her. The mist was not being moved by air currents, as there was no outside air coming into the underground area, and instead seemed to move about as though it had an intelligence behind it. This occurred several times before it vanished for good and did not return.

The entire incident was witnessed by those present and was also recorded on the videotape. The mist remains an absolute mystery but the tape has been examined by everyone from videographers to debunkers and ghost researchers and so far, no one has been able to provide information to adequately explain what it is or how it was able to behave in the manner that it did. A clip from the video was even shown on a program on ABC-Television and turned out to be one of the only segments on the show that the experts were unable to duplicate and explain away.

I was present for another weird incident that occurred in the house in 2001. That summer, I had the chance to spend the night in the house with some friends who had come down from Chicago. Among them was Dale Kaczmarek, the president of the Ghost Research Society, and an investigator with nearly three decades of experience with the paranormal, Rene Kruse and authors Jim Graczyk and David Goodwin. Our extended investigation of the house revealed little in the way of activity but there was an event that occurred that weekend that did convince me once and for all that there is something haunting the place.

At one point over the weekend, a small group of us were gathered in the old McPike wine cellar. This vaulted and brick room is located just below the level of the basement and has been the site of a number of eerie happenings over the years. This night turned out to be no exception.

Not long after everyone had gathered in the chamber, Dale's wife, Ruth, began to complain of being claustrophobic. Not sure of how to get out of the house from the basement, Rene Kruse offered to take her upstairs and outside, so she could get some fresh air. The two ladies departed and the group waited for Rene to return. A few minutes later, sounds were clearly heard as it seemed she was coming back. Footsteps crossed the upstairs hall and traveled through the house, then descended the stairs to the basement. The steps were clearly heard as all of the basement stairs were crossed and then could also be heard as they walked across the basement floor. A few moments later, the metal door to the wine cellar scraped open. The bottom of the door barely cleared the stone floor of the basement and as the door is opened up, it made a squealing sound, which could be heard on several recording devices that were running at the time. Everyone who was present turned to look as the door swung open --- but no one came in. Thinking that Rene was perhaps trying to play a joke on the group, Dale Kaczmarek walked over and peered out into the gloomy basement. He looked both ways but there was no one to see. He spoke aloud: "There's no one here."

A few minutes later, Rene actually did come down the stairs and when she was told about what happened, insisted that she had been outside the entire time. Ruth Kaczmarek was able to confirm this and stated that no one had entered the house while they were out front. This added just one more mystery to the long line of strange events at the McPike Mansion and to this day, also remains unexplained.

I remain convinced that there are more mysteries and questions about the McPike Mansion than there are real solutions. There have been dozens of paranormal investigations carried out here, as well as hundreds of stories that have been told by ordinary people who never expected to find anything out of the ordinary about this crumbling old house. It is an eerie and mysterious place and yet a wonderful one at the same time. It is a part of Alton's haunted history that we dare not lose and one that we can hopefully enjoy for many, many years to come.

Prospect Place: Haunted by History

If there is one thing that I have learned over the years, it's that you never know where you might find a haunted place. I have often given out the criteria about where to look for hauntings, from private homes to graveyards, cemeteries, battlefield and hospitals. Sometimes, though, you just stumble upon them by accident. That's what happened to me when I "discovered" Prospect Place, near the small town of Dresden, Ohio, in April 2003.

I was traveling across country at the time, on my way to Pennsylvania to speak at a ghost conference, and was rather lazily searching for some places of interest to see along the way. By chance, I ran across an article in the *Coshocton Tribune* about an old mansion near Dresden that was undergoing renovations. Not only had it once been a location "station" on the Underground Railroad but it was reportedly haunted, as well!

Even though the house was not open to the public, I took a chance and contacted the owner about possibly visiting the place. He readily agreed and so, I headed off in search of Prospect Place -- and ended up taking a haunting journey back in time.

George W. Adams & Prospect Place

George Adams came to Ohio from Virginia in 1808. His father had been a prosperous plantation owner with more than 500 acres of land in Faquier and Loudon Counties, a large number of slaves and a tremendous fortune. With the death of his father, when George was a young man, he inherited the entire estate and proceeded to do something that few Virginia gentlemen of the time would have done -- he sold the plantation and freed his slaves. Adams was a devout Christian and abolitionist and believed that for one man to own another was a sin against God. He took the money from the sale of the plantation and purchased a large tract of land in Ohio, as well as wagons and provisions to move west to this new land. Ohio had been entered into the Union as a "free state" in 1803 and offered great promise in the eyes of the young man.

The family, which consisted of his wife and daughter (whose names have been lost to history) and his three sons, Samuel, Edward and George Willison, arrived in Ohio almost nine months after departing Virginia. This region was still a frontier at that time and aside from the famed Cumberland Road, there were few good trails. Harsh weather conditions forced them to find shelter for the winter and continue their journey in the spring. They eventually settled on the eastern side of the Muskingum River, near the tiny village of Dresden in central Ohio.

At that time, Dresden was little more than a collection of homes and a few businesses but as the century progressed, it became a wealthy community of merchants along what was then one of the most important trade routes of the time, the Ohio & Erie Canal. The canal was constructed just north of Dresden in the 1830s and opened the town to business from all over the world. It would play an important part in the life and business interest of the Adams' family.

Not long after the canal was completed, George Adams died and the 150 acres that he had purchased in Ohio were passed on to his sons, Edward and George Willison (I have found no record of what became of Samuel). Unfortunately, the land was nearly all there was left to give though. The money from the Virginia plantation had been exhausted by the purchase of the Ohio property and the expense of the trip west. The two younger Adams' did not let this deter them however and they saw an opportunity to capitalize on the new canal. For many years, local farmers had been taking their grain to Zanesville (about 20 miles away) to be milled into flour. George W. and Edward decided that by selling the land their father had left them, they could raise the money to build a mill on the Muskingum and Coshocton County lines.

The mill would be directly on the canal, which would provide power for the water wheel and would also allow the flour from the mill to be directly transported directly to faraway ports like New Orleans. The location of the mill turned out to be even more beneficial when a side cut canal was dug that allowed the Muskingum River to be linked to the canal. Not surprisingly, it became a great success.

Both men married and began to raise families. They also built identical homes that cost over $40,000 each, a tremendous sum in those days. Edward built his mansion just behind the mill in a little community that became known as "Adams Mills". This house still stands today and is known as the Prescott Gray House, in honor of a later owner. George's house was identical in every way to the home of his brother but it as constructed in a field near the canal and just north of the small town of Trinway. During the time that he resided in this house, he and his wife raised five children and he became a member of the Ohio General Assembly at age 32.

He formed a stock company in order to build a suspension bridge across the Muskingum River in the early 1850s and later sold it to the county commissioners. The bridge was designed by the famous John Augustus Roebling, who later, along with his son, designed the Brooklyn Bridge in New York. The bridge was later destroyed in 1913 during a horrific flood. A barn was pulled from its foundations by the flood waters and was washed downstream, where it collided with the bridge. The current metal link suspension bridge in Dresden replaced it in 1914.

George and his family were happy in the house and prospered until tragedy struck in the winter of 1850. His wife, Clarissa, suddenly fell ill and died. Adams was heartbroken and mourned for several years, struggling to recover from his loss. Not long after his depression finally lifted, he became engaged to a young woman named Mary. The two of them were deeply in love, despite the fact that Mary was some 20 years younger than her prospective husband. After the wedding, she came to live with George and his children in the mansion near the canal. But happiness was not to be found for them in this house...

There are several stories about what may have occurred in the house during the early days of Mary's residency there. Whatever the cause for the strange events, the end result is that the family moved out and George began construction on a new, much grander home. Stories and rumors persist as to why Adams would have moved out of the house that he once loved so much. Some say that it was merely a "house of bad memories" for him since his first wife was not long passed on but others insist that it was Mary who prompted the move.

These stories have it that the ghost of Clarissa Adams began making appearances in the house not long after her husband's marriage to the pretty, much younger woman. Unable to deal with the literal "specter" of George's late wife, Mary insisted that a new house be built --- and one that had never belonged to another woman. Adams, eager to please his new wife, quickly agreed. He would build a "fairy tale castle" for her, he said, and the ground was soon broken for the house that would come be called Prospect Place.

Prospect Place

As the laborers were being hired and ground was being cleared for the mansion, Adams built a small, two-story frame house near the Adams Warehouse in Dresden where he and his family could live until the new house was completed. From here, he and his family often journeyed out toward Trinway to watch as the great brick structure rose a towering three stories with a cupola as a crown. Another wing was added, which rose two stories, and another wing was added to the north (almost an entirely separate house) for the servants. The roof was covered in copper panels and ornate woodwork was added to the roofline and then painted with bright colors. By the summer of 1856, the house was nearly completed.

Then, on the night before the family was due to move in, the amazing house caught fire and burned to the ground. A bucket brigade of neighbors and volunteers from the surrounding community hurried to the house but they arrived too late and were unable to get close to the inferno. There was no immediate explanation for what had happened but local rumor had it that the house had been set on fire by an elderly Native American woman who lived nearby. She had a fearsome reputation in the community and most referred to her simply as "Satan". She had been angry with George Adams when he purchased the land to build the house because it contained a number of burial grounds. She had reportedly threatened that terrible things would happen if the land was disturbed and many saw the fire as the result of her warnings.

However, there is a more likely explanation for the fire. According to most stories, the fire was actually set by a brick layer who had been hired for the project named George Blackburn. He was a drunkard and thief who also worked as a brick layer around Dresden. Allegedly, while drunk one night, he bragged to someone that he had set the Adams' house on fire so that he could generate more work for himself. Since Adams was so well-liked in the community, word of this quickly reached him and he had Blackburn arrested. The brick layer was tried and found guilty and sent to the penitentiary in Columbus as punishment. Ironically though, Blackburn had been hired to help build the prison and knew his way around the place. He promptly escaped. His days were numbered when he returned to Muskingum County, though. One night, while attempting to rob the house of a local farmer, his head was split open by the homeowner's ax.

Meanwhile, Prospect Place, which had been named by George Adams because he wanted to the house to be a prospect for a better future, was immediately rebuilt. The second version stood on the same foundation as the first and was almost identical. Likely, Adams even made a number of small changes that made the new version of the house even more to his liking. The house was massive and offered sitting rooms for the ladies and parlors for the men, a number of bedrooms, a wing for the servants, elaborate plaster work, marble fireplace mantels, a grand staircase and even a unique feature that was simply not found in homes of the day --- indoor plumbing. George was so enamored of his young wife that he had built for her a bathroom with a tub and flushing toilets. A hand-operated piston pump in the basement was used to pump water upstairs to a copper holding tank that worked by way of gravity. One of the strangest features of the place though -- and one that would not be rediscovered until recent times -- was a cistern that was located below the house in the basement. It had a secret purpose and one that would remain the greatest mystery of the house for many years to come.

The Railroad comes to Prospect Place

The Adams family lived in the house for many years and were, by all reports, very happy. George and Mary had two children of their own, John Jay and Elizabeth "Lizzie" Adams, while living at Prospect Place and on the surface, they appeared to be simply a pleasant, respected family with a thriving business and bright outlook for the future. And while they were all of these things, George Adams was also secretly involved in a highly and dangerous illegal activity that threatened not only his family but his wonderful home, as well.

Like his father before him, Adams was an ardent abolitionist and he became involved with the Underground Railroad movement in Ohio. The Underground Railroad was as secret system of homes, barns, businesses and other buildings that were used to assist slaves as they escaped from bondage in the southern states and came north to freedom. Those who helped the slaves were referred to as "conductors" and buildings where the refugees hid during the daylight hours and waited for darkness before moving on were called "stations". George Adams first became a part of the Underground Railroad in the 1840s, often going himself, or funding men who retrieved escaped slaves, and helped them to make it to the north. Originally, his mill was used as a "station" but by the middle 1850s, when it seemed that a Civil War was eminent, Adams moved the operation to his home. In this way, his business would not be endangered and the operation would be even more secure.

No matter well hidden it was, though, the operation was still a dangerous one. It was illegal in the northern states to harbor or assist escaped slaves and Adams risked arrest and imprisonment by continuing to do so. He did take many precautions, however, and some believe that a few of the more unique and elaborate additions to Prospect Place were created in order to further the abolitionist cause. There are stories that say that the cupola that was built high atop the house was often used as a signal post for other conductors. Whenever a lighted lantern was placed in the window, they knew that it was safe for the fugitives to be brought to the house. It is also generally believed that the cistern that was located in the home's basement was dug to provide an inside water supply so that residents could fetch water without being seen. In those days, slave catchers and bounty hunters would stake out the wells of homes that were suspected of being Underground Railroad stations. They could monitor how much water was being used and see if there were extra people in the house.

One popular story that has been perpetuated over the years is that of a tunnel that allegedly once ran from the basement of Prospect Place to the nearby river. Restoration of the house has revealed no such tunnel, though. When I visited the house, I was shown what may be the source of the story --- an eight-foot long tunnel that leads to a window in the outside wall. It is believed that this was once a root cellar and that it did offer access to and from the subterranean sub-basements of the house, which may have been used by the escaped slaves. Unfortunately though, as with many other similar houses from the time period, there is no way that we can know for sure. Because of the clandestine nature of the operation, and because it was illegal, no real records were kept to deny or confirm much of anything. It is generally accepted that Adams and Prospect Place were involved in the Underground Railroad, thanks to the clues that do remain behind. It has never questioned that Adams was a staunch supporter of the Union during the Civil War.

In the early 1860s, Adams donated large sums of money for the war effort and he maintained an "open door" policy for any Federal soldier or officer who passed through the area and needed a place to stay. At various times, when Ohio seemed threatened by Confederate forces, Prospect Place was designated to become the Union headquarters in the region. Luckily though, Ohio was never seriously in danger, although many men from the area did serve in the military during this period.

When the war ended, Adams financed a huge celebration in Dresden that reportedly lasted for two weeks and only came to an end when word reached the community of the assassination of President Abraham Lincoln.

The years following the Civil War continued to be prosperous and happy ones for the Adams family. Anna, George's oldest daughter, married William Cox Jr., a young man who lived in the nearly home, River Dale. The house had been built by Jonathan Cass, a Revolutionary War veteran from New Hampshire, who sold the house to the Cox family in the early 1800s. The elder William Cox had been an Irish-born officer in the British Army, who had given up his commission to come to America. The families were close friends and reportedly approved of the match between their children.

In the last years of his life, Adams involved himself in the railroad industry and became the director of the Steubenville & Indiana Railroad. He was also the owner and director of the Cincinnati & Muskingum Valley Railroad until his death on August 31, 1879.

At the time of his passing, George W. Adams had an estate worth an estimated $14 million. It was divided among his family members in his will, with his wife Mary receiving $7 million of it. She and her youngest son, John, moved back to Zanesville, where she was originally from. The remaining estate was split equally among all of the children, giving them $1 million each. Prospect Place was inherited by Anna and her husband, William Cox. It was shortly after this that one of the great mysteries of the family came about.

The Vanishing of William Cox

In the years that followed his inheriting of Prospect Place, William Cox spent huge amounts of money renovating the mansion and throwing large parties and galas on the grounds and in the grand ballroom on the top floor. The parties hosted at Prospect Place became known far and wide and at one reception, held for a new Episcopal bishop and with over 200 people in attendance, ice cream was served for the very first time in Muskingum County. Cox had commissioned a special refrigerated train car to deliver it to the party. There were whispers and rumors about the amounts of money that Cox was spending but none of them were taken seriously until one day shortly after the turn of the last century. On a Friday afternoon in November, he informed his family that he was going to Zanesville on business --- and vanished without a trace.

For days afterward, Cox's family, and the local authorities, attempted to unravel the mystery of his disappearance. By all indications, he disappeared under his own power and left several strange and contradictory clues behind. Anna hired a detective to try and track him down but he found nothing. Cox had left home on Friday, November 15, explaining that he was going to Zanesville and would not be home for dinner. When he arrived in Trinway, though, he spoke to a man named Henry Park and told him that he needed someone to do an errand for him in Zanesville because Cox had business in Columbus that he urgently needed to attend to. Park replied this his wife was leaving on the train for Zanesville and would gladly take care of Cox's errand. Cox then gave him $255 and asked that his wife pay it on Cox's account at the A.E. Starr & Co. office. Cox then boarded a train for Columbus and this was the last time that he was seen near Dresden.

The detective that Anna hired was able to trace Cox to Schrader's Hotel in Columbus. According to witnesses that he interviewed, Cox had checked into the hotel in the company of a man that he refused to register. He and the clerk argued over the matter, which is why the man remembered the incident at all. He gave a good description of the stranger but the clue led nowhere --- until a letter arrived for Anna one day a few months later.

The letter that arrived came from a young woman named Jennie Adams, who had grown up in Dresden but who had moved to San Francisco several years before. She wrote that she had been walking a few days before and that William Cox had passed her on the street. Not knowing anything about his disappearance and happy to see an old acquaintance from home, she hurried up to him, calling his name and asking for news from home. The man glared at her and, according to her letter, seemed annoyed and quickly pushed past her. He refused to speak and refused to acknowledge her at all. She started after him and when he looked back over his shoulder and saw her following him, he ducked into a cigar store. Jennie, thinking still that Cox did not recognize her, followed him inside, only to have the man hide from her and then hurry out another entrance. Obviously, she thought his actions were very strange and so she wrote to her friend, Anna, and inquired as to his behavior. She was sure that the man she had seen had been William and she asked Anna the reason why he acted in such a bizarre way. Anna, who had no idea of her husband's whereabouts, was surprised by the letter.

In the letter, she also referred to another man who was with Cox that day on the street. Her description of the man exactly matched that of the strange man described by the clerk at Schrader's Hotel. Who this man could have been is unknown --- as is the reason for Cox's disappearance in the first place.

There have been those who have suggested that he managed to spend most of Anna's fortune and then vanished in shame but this seems unlikely for Anna lived comfortably in Prospect Place for years afterward. Could he have been involved in some illegal activity, forcing him to leave Ohio? Or could the reason have been a sordid one, at least by the standards of the time? Some have suggested that perhaps William was a homosexual, in a time less open than our own, and that perhaps the mysterious man was his lover. The two of them may have left Ohio, thinking they would never be seen again. Jennie Adams' chance sighting of them on the streets of San Francisco was a piece of ill luck for them but Anna never chose to pursue it.

Officially, William Cox was never seen again.

The Story Continues

The story of the Cox family and Prospect Place continued. George Cox, Anna's son and the grandson of George W. Adams, grew up in the house and later was educated as an engineer. He worked on President Franklin D. Roosevelt's Tennessee Valley Authority dam projects all over the south and lived most of his life in Georgia and Florida. He maintained two consuming passions in his life and spent a great deal of money on both. The first was the unsuccessful search for any trace of his missing father and the second was Prospect Place. He owned the house through the 1960s but never lived there. He attempted to keep up with the march of time at the house but eventually, he gave up on it --- just as he gave up on ever finding out what happened to William.

In the late 1960's, George sold the house to the Cox Gravel Company, which was owned by Gene Cox (no relation to George and his family). The gravel company opened the house for tours in 1976, during the American Bicentennial celebration, but paid little attention to it other than that. By the 1970s, time had started to take its toll on the house.

Nearly a century and a half after its construction, the once beautiful home was now empty and abandoned in a field of weeds. The leaking roof had caused the floors to become unsafe and to collapse. Wind blew in through the broken windows and during the 1980s, frequent forays into the house by vandals resulted in graffiti being spray-painted on the walls, the marble fireplace mantels to be broken into pieces and even the curving three-story staircase had been stolen. By 1988, the house was in ruins and Prospect Place was scheduled to be demolished.

But then in stepped Dave Longaberger, the founder of the Ohio basket-making empire, history buff and preservationist. Dave had been raised near the mansion and he couldn't stand to see the old place torn down. He had already purchased and renovated a number of other local, historic buildings and did the same for Prospect Place. He bought the house and the Longaberger company soon started repairs. A new roof was installed, windows repaired and some demolition was completed to make way for new construction. Unfortunately though, Dave became ill and died before he could see the restoration completed. It seemed that the mansion was doomed once more.

Once again, though, Prospect Place was rescued --- this time by George Adams. And the name was no coincidence as this new Adams was the great, great grandson of the original owner. He was able to purchase the house from Longaberger, who was still providing security for the place, thanks to the company's assistance. Adams explained that no one else would finance the place for him but Longaberger just wanted to see Dave's vision of restoration fulfilled. Adams moved into the house soon after, becoming the first occupant since 1969, and began a slow restoration process that was sometimes more archaeological dig than home renovation. Relics recovered inside of the house have included old shoes, melted glass from the fire that burned the original house and of course, the secret cistern in the basement.

The first year of renovations included repairing the unsafe floors, fixing much of the damaged masonry, restoring water and electrical service to the house, installing new furnaces and an alarm system, repairing the windows and a number of new locks and safety equipment.

It was around this time that he discovered something very interesting about the house. Prospect Place, along with a rich history, also boasted a variety of resident spirits.

The Haunting of Prospect Place

My visit to Prospect Place occurred in April 2003 after I contacted George Adams and asked about seeing the place. He graciously agreed but unable to be there himself, he left me in the capable hands of one of his friends, Jerry Taylor, who met me at the house and took me on an extensive tour of the property. He was a wealth of information on the old place and never hesitated to answer any of my questions -- including those about the alleged haunts.

Like the stories of the Underground Railroad and Prospect Place, there have been many stories told locally about the ghosts here over the years. Like many of the tales of escaped slaves have shown to be true, the stories of the ghosts who haunt the place may eventually move beyond legends and lore and enter the world of reality. This can be an eerie place and not surprisingly, the reported encounters with ghosts here reflect this. Many visitors who have come to the house claim to have had paranormal encounters within the walls and these experiences run the gamut of sights and sounds that include voices in empty rooms, the laughter of a child, hair-raising whispers, shadowy apparitions and even the ghost of a man in formal attire who has been seen standing near the main staircase on an upper floor. Could this be the echo of a servant from time's past -- or perhaps, as some have suggested, the ghost of George W. Adams himself? Some stories say that he loved the place so much that his spirit simply refuses to leave it.

It has been a long held tradition in Dresden and Trinway that the halls of Prospect Place still play host to the spirits of the former owners --- and to those who connection with the place is fleeting at best. It will likely come as no surprise to most readers to learn that the basement here is believed to be especially haunted. Most feel that the ghosts who linger here are those of slaves who sought refuge here during the period when it was a station on the Underground Railroad. There have been reported sightings here of a black woman who seems to have some sort of injury to her head. She is often seen in the basement rooms, usually only for a moment, before she disappears.

There is also another story that might explain the hauntings in the basement, especially those reports of cold chills being felt and the anguished cries that have sometimes been heard. According to this story, there was apparently a train wreck that occurred near Dresden one hot summer day in the late 1800s. A passenger train had been stopped on the tracks because of a problem with the locomotive and another train came along and collided with it from behind. The engine of the second trail barreled into the passenger cars and its boiler exploded. Many of the passengers died instantly, while others were badly burned. There were many injuries, but no hospital nearby. As it happened, Prospect Place was the closest house to the accident site and so the cool basement of the house was turned into a temporary hospital for the injured passengers. A number of them succumbed to their wounds while waiting for assistance, however, and it is said that many of their ghosts still haunt the dark subterranean rooms.

The most widely-known story about the house in the area involving ghosts tells of a young girl (possibly a servant girl) who died after falling from a portico on the house during one harsh winter the 1860s. The stories vary as to what happened next but in the most common version of the tale, her body could not be buried because the ground was too frozen to dig her grave. Because of this, her body was kept on ice in the basement of the house until spring. She was the daughter of a local family and so her mother came each day to visit her until her corpse was finally laid to rest.

Since that time, visitors have often reported seeing her ghost in the hallways and especially around one of the fireplaces in the former servant's quarters. Childish laughter has also been heard in the house, as well as the sobs of the grieving mother. There have been many instances of people encountering the ghost, or hearing her voice and identifying it as that of a little girl, who have no idea that the spirit of a little girl allegedly haunts the place --- or even that the house is regarded as haunted at all!

Another ghost that has been seen is that of a man in period clothing who has been reported near a staircase on an upper floor. The man has often been described as having a large mustache and he has been identified as either a servant who once worked in the house or even a party-goer from the days when Anna and William Cox hosted numerous lavish events and receptions in the ballroom. Some believe that he might even be George W. Adams himself. As Adams was never known for having a mustache (but rather a large beard instead) it seems unlikely that it might be him. If it is a former owner though, could this phantom be that of William Cox -- inexorably drawn back to the house and the family that he abandoned? Could he be doomed to wander the corridors of this place after the betrayal of it so many years ago?

As you can see, there are many mysteries that still remain at Prospect Place and during my visit, I was able to leave with one of my own. As Jerry Taylor was leading me out of the basement, after regaling me with tales of the many ghosts rumored to linger there, I got the distinct impression that someone was behind me. As stated already, I make no claims of being psychic (or even remotely sensitive) but sometimes feelings like this are hard to ignore. Just before I reached the staircase, I turned around and looked back over my shoulder. I saw nothing --- but I heard the definite sound of footsteps walking on the crumbling floor in one of the back rooms.

I asked Jerry to wait for one moment and then hurried around the corner of the room where I had heard the sounds. The room was empty --- there was no one there. Did I really hear footsteps? Or was my imagination hard at work after hearing about the myriad of basement spirits?

Who knows?

The Hauntings of Gettysburg

In the course of looking for ghosts, I have had the opportunity to travel literally all over the country. On these trips, I am always on the lookout for interesting places and, of course, haunted ones. This has given me the chance to experience hundreds of spirited spots all over America, although I have to say that it has been a very small percentage of these places where anything "paranormal" occurred during my visit.

However, there is a single historic site that I have visited and on several occasions, have experienced things that I cannot explain. I have come to consider this place, Gettysburg, Pennsylvania, to be the most haunted small town in the country. According to local lore and to reliable first-hand accounts, this small city is teeming with ghosts. And given it's past, is it any wonder that it would be?

Most Civil War enthusiasts would say the battle that was fought near the small Pennsylvania town of Gettysburg in 1863 was the greatest battle of the war. At the very least, it is considered the turning point that led to the fall of the Confederacy. For ghost hunters, the mere mention of Gettysburg conjures up images of haunted buildings, strange battlefield encounters and restless ghosts.

The Battle of Gettysburg

By the early summer of 1863, the war in the east was going well for the Confederacy, which convinced General Robert E. Lee that an invasion of the north would be of benefit to the southern army. So, moving in secret, Lee began his northern thrust on June 3, 1863. He marched his troops into the Shenandoah Valley and pushed them on, using the mountains as a shield.

Although unaware of Lee's plans, the Army of the Potomac, under the command of Joseph Hooker, realized that a major enemy troop movement was underway, following a cavalry engagement at Brandy Station on June 9. Hooker then cautiously followed Lee's march to the north, keeping his army east of the mountains and between Washington and the Confederates. On June 15, Lee overwhelmed a Union force at Winchester and then continued northward. By June 28, all of the Confederate troops had crossed over into Union territory. They were still widely scattered out, but all were converging on the Pennsylvania capital of Harrisburg.

Meanwhile, tension between Washington and General Hooker was increasing. Once again, Lincoln was disappointed by the inaction of one of his generals and on June 28, he appointed George Meade to replace Hooker as the head of the Army of the Potomac.

Coincidentally, on this same day, General Lee received a message that the Union Army was on the move, heading toward his new location. This came as a shock to Lee, as he had been depending on General Jeb Stuart to keep him aware of all enemy activity. Although no one knew it at the time, Stuart had seemingly vanished. He was involved in a daring raid east of the Federal army and all communications with the main Confederate force had been cut off.

With the news that the Federal Army was aware of his plans, Lee sent out an order to concentrate the Confederate forces at Cashtown, a small village between Chambersburg and Gettysburg. The Confederate Army was now in place to the north and west of Gettysburg, while Meade pushed the Federal Army from the south, moving northward from the area around Frederick and Emmitsburg, Maryland.

Both armies were in the dark as to the whereabouts of the other on June 30, the day that cavalry units under command of General John Buford rode into Gettysburg.

Before this time, there was nothing to set Gettysburg apart from hundreds of other small communities in America. The population of the small town numbered about 2,400 souls and aside from a thriving carriage industry, its only claims to fame were its two colleges, the Lutheran Theological Seminary and Pennsylvania College (Gettysburg College). It was nothing more than a sleepy little Pennsylvania town in 1863 --- but all that was about to change.

Buford's cavalry rode into town on June 30 and established a picket line on the other side of the Lutheran Seminary to guard approaches to the town from the west. By coincidence, a brigade of Confederate Infantry under General John Pettigrew, of A.P. Hill's Corps, had been sent to Gettysburg from Cashtown to scout out the area that same day. Legend has it that the Confederates were there looking for shoes, but they were actually on a reconnaissance mission. For whatever reason the two groups bumped into each other, it seems likely, with two large armies in such close proximity of each other, they were bound to run into each other at some point. However, once the Confederates spotted the Union pickets, they rode to the west to report the enemy's presence.

Early in the morning of July 1, two Confederate brigades were sent to investigate the Federal presence in Gettysburg. Within a short time of the Confederate arrival, a skirmish had broken out between the rebels and Buford's men. Although Buford knew that he was greatly outnumbered, and in a bad position, he chose to stand his ground and send for help from two Union corps that were a short distance to the south. The Confederates also sent for reinforcements and soon, both armies were headed toward Gettysburg.

For the next two hours, Buford's men, fighting dismounted, managed to hold off a number of Confederate attacks from the area known as McPherson's farm. Buford was later relieved by the arrival of General John Reynold's corps. One division crossed an unfinished railroad cut to the north of the Chambersburg Pike and formed a battle line. Another Confederate brigade was at the same time attacking McPherson's Woods, which lay to the south of the Pike. General Reynolds himself led the Federal "Iron Brigade" into the woods, where he was killed instantly by enemy fire. Reynolds was the second in command of the Army of the Potomac and would be the highest-ranking officer to perish during the three days of fighting at Gettysburg.

Around the middle of the day, the fighting broke off and the field was fairly quiet until the middle of the afternoon. The Confederate corps commanded by Hill and Ewell advanced against the Federals along a two-mile stretch that ran between the western and northern approaches to Gettysburg. Confederate reinforcements continued to arrive throughout the afternoon and around 4:00 p.m., General Jubal Early's division struck the right flank of the Union's XI Corps, which was under command of General Francis Barlow. The attack caused Howard's entire line to begin to crumble.

The corps began retreating into Gettysburg, where they almost collided with retreating Federal troops, who at the same moment had collapsed to Confederate pressure near the McPherson farm. Falling back from two different directions, the Union troops became confused and disoriented in the small town and stumbled along to the shelter of Cemetery Hill, a reserve position located on the southern outskirts of Gettysburg. Here, Union General Winfield Scott Hancock rallied the men into defensive positions on this hill, and along nearby Culp's Hill, as well. The elated Confederates followed and captured the entire town, along with over 2,500 Union soldiers.

And here they halted.... Strangely, Lee's forces made no attempt to storm Cemetery Hill that night. One has to wonder what may have been the outcome of the battle if they had. Instead, Lee had given orders to Ewell to renew the attack before nightfall "if practicable". Unfortunately, Ewell took Lee's courteous order as having a choice of whether to fight, or to retire from the field. He chose incorrectly. Ewell decided his men needed rest and the first day's fighting came to an end.

Lee arrived in Gettysburg that afternoon and established his headquarters in a house along the Chambersburg Pike. Here, he began to make plans for the following day. Even though he was in poor health and suffering from diarrhea,

Lee remained confident about the Confederate chances in the battle ahead. He felt the Union Army was weakened by its recent defeats at Fredericksburg and Chancellorsville and by yet another change in command. If he pressed hard enough, the Federals would break.

Throughout the night, the two armies continued to gather and by morning about 65,000 Confederate troops faced a Union force of around 85,000. The northern lines had assumed what has become known as the "Fishhook" formation. Cemetery Hill, became the curve of the fishhook, while Culp's Hill, located just to the east, became the hook, and right flank, of the Union line. Hancock's corps occupied the shank of the formation and they stretched south through the open fields to Cemetery Ridge. The Union left was defended by troops under General Daniel Sickles, a former politician who was best known for killing his wife's lover before the war. Secretary of War Edwin Stanton had been his attorney and had gotten him acquitted by using the first plea of "temporary insanity".

Sickles spent the entire morning of July 2 disobeying orders. He had shifted his corps position on lower Cemetery Ridge out into the Peach Orchard, which stood on a flat-topped ridge about a half-mile in front of the Union line. This managed to leave the hills known as Little Round Top and Big Round Top, and the Union's left flank, completely undefended. When Meade got wind of this, he angrily ordered him back into position, but before the corps could be moved, Longstreet had begun his attack.

As Lee studied the Union formation on the field that morning, he noted that the Federal fishhook was overlooked by hills on both ends. Culp's Hill and Cemetery Hill stood above the right and the Big and Little Round Tops loomed over the left. Lee's plan called for the Confederates to take the hills, sending Ewell to attack Culp's Hill and Longstreet the Round Tops.

Little fighting took place during the morning and afternoon, aside from scattered fire from skirmishes. Lee's plan called for attack on both Union flanks at the same time, but the assault was delayed for several hours as Longstreet shifted his two corps into position on the southern edge of Seminary Ridge.

At the same time, Sickles was shifting his own line to the more forward position. By the time Longstreet was ready to attack, Sickle's new line extended northwestward from the tangle of boulders at Devil's Den, through Rose Woods and the Wheat Field, and then sharply to the northeast where it crossed the Peach Orchard and continued along the Emmitsburg Road. The new position was nearly impossible to defend and not only did it not connect its right flank to the left flank of II Corps, but it also left Little Round Top completely unoccupied.

The Confederate attack against the left Union flank began just after 4:00 p.m. One of the first points to be struck was the Devil's Den, which fell to Hood's men after a bitter struggle that lasted for several hours. In waves, Longstreet's brigades swept over the Rose Woods and the Wheat Field and then advanced on the Federal positions at the Peach Orchard and along the Emmitsburg Road.

The fighting continued on through the afternoon and while Sickle's beaten line was reinforced by troops under George Sykes, Sickles himself was severely wounded near his headquarters at the Trostle Farm. The Confederates were relentless and after four hours of battle, all of the Union positions along Sickle's line were overrun.

Meanwhile, during the initial attack, the 15th Alabama managed to make it to the summit of Big Round Top. From here, Confederate Colonel William C. Oates realized that the summit of Little Round Top was virtually undefended. If he could haul guns to the top of the hill, he would be directly above the Federal lines and could destroy them.

As luck would have it, Little Round Top had also come under the scrutiny of the Union command. Meade had dispatched the army's chief engineer, General Gouverner Warren, and a lieutenant of engineers named Washington Roebling, to the summit of Little Round Top to bring back a report of the state of the battle. They found only a handful of Union signalmen on the hill and one look around sent them into shock. Warren quickly realized what was going to happen as he saw Sickles corps pinned down below and Confederate troops coming up the ravine that separated the Little and Big Round Tops.

He sent for reinforcements at once and the last of the four regiments ordered to the hill was the 20th Maine, under the command of Colonel Joshua Lawrence Chamberlain, a professor of rhetoric and languages at Maine's Bowdoin College. The Chamberlain's orders were to hold Little Round Top "at all hazards" and with less than 400 men, he started up the south slope and took shelter behind rocks and trees. Fortunately, at the last moment, Chamberlain sent a company of men across the hollow between the hills to bolster the left flank of the defense. Less than 10 minutes later, Oates and his Confederates arrived, attacking before the company could take shelter on the left. The rebels opened fire and Chamberlain later stated that he assumed his men had been wiped out with the first volley of fire.

The Maine men attacked but the Confederates re-grouped and charged again and again, slowly gaining ground and swinging around to Chamberlain's left. He ordered that portion of his line to drop back, forming again at right angles to the rest of the regiment. The men dropped back, continuing to fire as they regrouped.

In less than an hour, over 40,000 rounds had been fired on Little Round Top and still the Federals held firm. The rebels had driven them from their position five times and yet each time, Chamberlain's men fought their way back again. He would lose 130 of his 386 men, a loss of nearly one-third of his force. He would describe the conflict: "At times I saw around me more of the enemy than my own men; gaps opening, swallowing; closing again.. and all around, a strange, mingled roar."

The sounds of battle behind Chamberlain grew louder and he assumed they had been surrounded. His men had finally run out of ammunition and the only choices that remained to them were to surrender --- or to die. Chamberlain refused to give up. He ordered his men to fix bayonets. Then, while the right corner of the regiment stood firm, the men were told to wheel around like a great hinge toward the right.

The attacking Confederates were so stunned by the maniacal charge of the

Federals that many of them actually dropped their weapons and surrendered. Others began to run, only to get another, more gruesome surprise --- the company of men that Chamberlain had sent over to guard the left flank had *not* been killed by the initial Confederate attack. They suddenly appeared from behind a stone wall and opened fire on the retreating rebels.

The remaining Confederates broke and ran. Colonel Oates would later admit "we ran like a herd of wild cattle". The Confederate dead literally covered the ground and while fighting continued on other parts of the slope, the summit of Little Round Top was secure.

Joshua Lawrence Chamberlain would go on to receive the Congressional Medal of Honor for his actions that day.

While the heroics of the men from Maine had saved Little Round Top, things were not going as well on other parts of the Union front. Sickle's corps was in desperate straits as the Confederates continued to attack. A Confederate artillery blast removed the lower portion of General Sickle's leg and he was carried from the field, still calmly smoking a cigar.

Union reinforcements continued to arrive and fighting raged through the Devil's Den and the Valley of Death. The Federal troops, as they crossed the Wheat Field, opened a gap on Cemetery Ridge and a Confederate brigade began a drive toward it. Hancock spotted the opening and ordered a single, small regiment, the 1st Minnesota, to countercharge and hold the gap. The Minnesota regiment, made up of only 262 men, raced toward the opening with fixed bayonets --- and came face-to-face with 1,600 Confederates. The stunned rebels fell back and the gap in the lines was closed, although only 47 members of the 1st Minnesota came through the skirmish unhurt.

By the end of the day, the lack of coordination in Lee's attacks cost them the fight. Despite Longstreet's success against Sickles, the Confederate offensive had only worked in some locations and the plan of attacking both flanks at the same time had not worked at all. In fact, it was almost sundown before two divisions of Ewell's corps even began their assault on the hook and curve of the Union's right flank.

The Confederates had clashed with Union troops on the eastern slopes of Culp's Hill, which had previously been fortified with earthworks, strengthened by felled trees and rocks. The Federals, although badly outnumbered, used the works to their advantage and the rebels failed to dislodge them from the hill.

Meanwhile, two brigades under Jubal Early met with even less luck in their attempt to capture Cemetery Hill. The Confederates initially managed to break through the Federal lines at the northern base of the hill in the early evening but soon suffered a devastating blow from Union artillery on Steven's Knoll. The fighting on the hill became hand-to-hand combat but with no reinforcements from the Confederate infantry units on the south edge of Gettysburg, the rebels soon retreated.

At the end of the second day of battle, Meade's fishhook remained intact.

The third day of battle began badly for the Confederates, further adding to the belief that Lee had concocted during the night --- that he must attack the

Federal forces at the center. The failure of his attempts to crush the Union flanks suggested that Meade had fortified these areas at the expense of the center. By midday of July 3, Lee decided that the Confederates would make one last attack. It would be a direct frontal assault against Cemetery Ridge. Lee's plan called for an artillery bombardment to weaken the Union line on the ridge, followed by an infantry attack.

During the morning hours, even Jeb Stuart had suffered at the hands of the Yankees. The cavalry commander had arrived in Gettysburg the afternoon before to be greeted by Lee's anger. One officer recalled later that Lee had even raised a hand as if to strike Stuart, as one would discipline an errant child, which perhaps was how Lee saw his relationship with the younger man. He chastised the cavalryman: "I have not heard from you in days, and you the eyes and ears of my army."

But Lee's anger quickly passed and on the morning of the third day, he put Stuart's men to work, launching an attack on the Federal rear. But the once weak Union cavalry stopped him, thanks to a series of reckless charges led by a 23-year-old general named George Armstrong Custer.

Now, everything depended on the success of Longstreet's assault on the Union center. Longstreet opposed attacking in this manner, knowing what his own rebel gunners had accomplished at Fredericksburg when Union troops had advanced across an open expanse in much the same manner. But Lee disagreed and ordered Longstreet to prepare the advance. He reportedly told his general: "The enemy is there and I am going to strike him."

The man that Lee chose to lead the advance was a friend and compatriot of Longstreet, General George Pickett, a rather peculiar, but well-liked officer with a beard and long, curly hair. Pickett's men waited in the woods on the opposite side of a long field from the Union center. They passed the time by throwing green apples at each other. They laughed and joked, knowing that what faced them was a nearly impossible task.

At just after 1:00 p.m., the Confederate artillery assault on Cemetery Ridge began. The earth shook as the cannons pounded the ridge, trying to weaken the Union line. General Meade had just left his commanders at the lunch table when the barrage started. As an orderly was serving butter, a shell literally tore him in two.

The top of the hill seemed to be tearing apart. Great mounds of earth were catapulted into the air and shells furrowed into the hillside, destroying grave markers and upending stones. Soon, the Union guns began to return fire and the casualty rate began to climb for the Confederate infantry, who were waiting in the woods for the signal to advance. But after about an hour, Meade ordered the Federal guns to silence, hoping to conserve ammunition for the fight that he was sure was coming. And also to lure the Confederates out into the open field.

Pickett came to Longstreet and asked if his men should go forward. The Federal guns had been destroyed and nothing lay between the Confederates and the destruction of the Federal center but Union infantry. The time was now ripe for an attack, he believed.

Longstreet was unable to speak and he merely nodded his head, convinced that he was sending his friend to his death. Pickett hurriedly scribbled a note to his teen-aged fiancée and handed it to Longstreet to mail. Then, with his usual flair for dramatics, he gave the order to attack.

Three divisions, numbering about 13,000 men, started out of the woods and towards the stone wall at the edge of Cemetery Ridge. Although history remembers this advance as "Pickett's Charge", it was hardly a quick attack. The men walked at a brisk pace, covering only about 100 yards of the open field by the minute.

One northern officer later recalled: "It was the most beautiful thing I ever saw."

Union cannons on Cemetery Ridge and Little Round Top began to sound, opening fire on the right side of the advancing line. Men were killed with every shot, but the Confederates still kept coming. Behind the stone wall, Union troops waited, holding their fire until the Rebels came closer. Finally, the order was given by General Alexander Hays and 11 cannon and 1,700 muskets went off at once.

Hundreds died in the first volley but the rest continued to come. The Confederates reached the Union line at just one place, a crook in the wall that has become known as the "Angle". They were led by General Lewis A. Armistead, who jumped the wall and managed to capture a Union battery before he was shot down. All of the other Confederates who breached the wall were captured, killed or wounded. Soon, those Confederates remaining on the field broke and ran or gave themselves up as prisoners.

The assault was over --- a complete and utter failure.

As the Confederates staggered back to Seminary Ridge, Lee rode out among them, urging them to regroup. He was said to have told them: "It was all my fault. Get together and let us do the best we can towards saving what is left of us."

Pickett had watched the advance with disbelief. Half of his men, over 6,500, had been killed or captured; 16 of his 17 field officers were gone, along with three brigadier generals and eight colonels. When Lee ordered him to rally his division for possible counterattack by the Federals, Pickett replied: "General Lee, I have no division now."

In the years to come, Pickett would never forgive Lee for what happened that day, always believing that his commander had sent his men into the field to be needlessly slaughtered.

By the end of the third day, the Battle of Gettysburg was over. The fighting had spilled across the hills and through the forests and even into the streets of Gettysburg itself.

The next day, July 4, both armies remained on the battlefield, with Meade and Lee each waiting for the other to move. When nothing of significance occurred that day, Lee realized that his invasion of the north had come to an end. He was now far from his supply line and was running low on ammunition, not to mention the fact that the Confederacy could not afford the over 28,000 casualties they had sustained. It was time to return home. That afternoon, Lee began his long retreat back to Virginia while Meade, despite urgings from

Washington, declined to attack the retreating force.

Behind them, the streets and fields of Gettysburg were littered with the bodies of the dead, slowly decaying in the heat of the Pennsylvania summer. The people of the town were also left with thousands of the wounded to attend to and homes and businesses were quickly turned into field hospitals. One local woman remembered: "Wounded men were brought into our houses and laid side-by-side in our halls and rooms. Carpets were so saturated with blood as to be unfit for further use. Walls were bloodstained, as well as books that were used as pillows."

The dead also lined the streets and walkways, rotting in the summer sun. A Federal soldier wrote: "Corpses, swollen to twice their original size, actually burst asunder.... several human, or inhuman, corpses sat upright against a fence, with arms extended in the air and faces hideous with something very like a fixed leer..."

In terms of significance, Gettysburg will always be remembered as one of the greatest battles in American history. It was the turning point in the war and it was probably not a coincidence (in the greater scheme of things, at least) that the day after the battle ended, also marked the fall of Vicksburg to General Grant. The war had just taken a darker turn for the Confederacy.

The battle would have a lingering effect on the country, not only for the armies of the Civil War, but for the America itself --- an effect that still lingers today.

Gettysburg Ghosts

It goes without saying that the Battle of Gettysburg left a tremendous mark on the small town and on the fields where the fighting actually took place. Few are surprised to learn that many of the buildings in Gettysburg and many locations on the battlefield are now believed to be haunted. In places where so much death and destruction took place, the stories of ghosts and spirits often follow.

And the ghostly tales of Gettysburg are not confined to what has been deemed "the battlefield" that is located outside of the city limits. During the fighting here in 1863, there were many who bled and died within the city itself. During the battle, fighting raged up and down the streets of Gettysburg and thousands died here. There are dozens of homes and businesses in town that are believed to be haunted . One of them, the Farnsworth House, is now a bed and breakfast. I have spent the night in this house on two occasions and while nothing out of the ordinary occurred when I was there, I have spoken to a number of people who have had strange experiences here.

The Farnsworth House was built in 1810 and expanded in 1833 by John McFarland. During the battle, the house was occupied by the Sweney family and was eventually opened as an inn by the George Black family in the early 1900s. Today, the house is a showcase of history and it retains the original walls, flooring and rafters --- and some believe it also retains a few of the occupants who passed through the house years ago.

During the battle, the house was occupied by Confederate sharpshooters, who used the garret (attic) of the house as a vantage point to fire at the Union troops on Cemetery Hill, just a few hundred yards away. According to the legends, a sharpshooter was taking aim at a door on a house a short distance away, between the Sweney House and the Federal lines. He was using the doorknob as a target to see just how hard the wind was blowing. He fired and when he did, the bullet pierced the wooden door and struck and killed a woman named Jennie Wade, who was in the kitchen kneading dough. She became the only civilian who was killed during the battle.

It has been said that the deeds and the presence of these sharpshooters have left an indelible mark on the Farnsworth House. According to the ghostly traditions of the place, the sound of a jew's-harp has been heard drifting down from the attic when no one is present there --- a musical instrument commonly played by soldiers during the Civil War.

After the battle, the house was used as a Federal headquarters, further adding to the history. The battle itself also left a mark on the place in the form of more than 100 bullet holes, which can be seen on the south side of the house. Most of these marks still remain, even after all of these years, and many of the bullets removed from the wall are on display inside.

In 1972, the house was turned into a restaurant and an inn. The staff members are a veritable treasure chest of stories relating to hauntings at the Farnsworth House, from the spectral sharpshooters to tales of guests who have heard phantom footsteps on the stairs, have detected unexplained noises, have felt invisible intruders sitting on the ends of their bed, and more.

Staff members have reported seeing movement out of the corner of the eye, only to turn and find nothing there. Some have also reported seeing shadows moving through the dining room at night, after everyone else has gone home. A quick search finds that the place is deserted. There are also a number of reports of footsteps pacing through the main floor at night, and of employees hearing these footsteps following behind them, only to turn and see no one is there. On other occasions, employees and customers have been tapped on the shoulder, or touched, by unseen hands.

On one visit to the house, I had the chance to spend the night in the garret area with a television crew from the BBC in England. We arrived at the house in late July, with temperatures that ranged from 90 to 95 degrees. The rooms where we stayed were quite cool but the attic area was at least 20 degrees warmer than it was outside! Needless to say, this put a damper on our investigations and we braved a few hours in the confined space before giving up. During this time, we attempted to monitor the area with infrared video cameras and TriField Natural EM Meters. Unfortunately though, we were so soaked with sweat and exhausted from the heat that we had a hard time concentrating on what we were supposed to be doing. It was certainly a lesson about *when* not to do an investigation!

Another strange experience in Gettysburg, this time with a residual haunting, occurred while on the city streets. The incident occurred while I was taking on one of the "ghost tours" of the city. It was a rainy evening and we were walking along Baltimore Street in a small group and we stopped along the street for the guide to recount another of his ghostly tales. I didn't think much about it at the time, but as I stood there, I caught the overpowering smell of peppermint. As I said, I thought nothing of it, believing that perhaps someone close by was eating a piece of candy. Another tour guest looked over at me and wrinkled her nose up. The smell was quite strong and I guessed from her facial expression that she smelled the peppermint too.

Our guide began his talk, telling of how people have experienced the images of soldiers running past them on this street in the wee hours of the morning and then he mentioned the other strange phenomena that was connected to Baltimore Street.

He told of how people walking along the street would often be struck by the scent of vanilla or peppermint, for no apparent reason. According to the legend, in the days following the Gettysburg battle, the bodies of the men who lay in the town started to decay and to smell quite bad. Ladies who would leave their homes would soak handkerchiefs in vanilla or peppermint and press them to their faces to combat the odor of decomposing flesh.

It is said that people still encounter these "phantom smells" today --- and I would have to agree with that because I certainly smelled the scent of peppermint. Was it my imagination? And was it the imagination of other guests on the tour who also picked up the smell? I don't believe that it was. We smelled something that not only should not have been there, but was a smell that I did not realize I was supposed to be smelling until I was told about it afterward.

The Haunted Battlefield

There are scores of ghostly stories and supernatural incidents that have been recorded and experienced by everyday people across the official confines of the Gettysburg Battlefield. Factor into this number the encounters of those ghost seekers who have purposely traveled to the battlefield in search of spirits, and the number of strange tales becomes an amazing one.

There are a number of once private residences scattered across the battlefield that have reportedly played host to the spirits over the years that have passed since the battle. Most of these homes are now the property of the National Park Service and often they serve as residences to park rangers and personnel who stay in the houses to keep them occupied and in good repair. Nearly all of the nearby homes were used during the battle as makeshift field hospitals during the fighting. Many believe that such incidents may be what has caused them to gain reputations for being haunted over the years.

Not surprisingly, as employees of the United States Government, the rangers are usually very reluctant to discuss their supernatural encounters on the battlefield. Those who do speak, usually do so off the record, which nevertheless, creates a fairly impressive documentation of events beyond our understanding.

Nearly all of the historians and battlefield guides from the area who will speak to someone about ghosts usually preface their comments with something like: "I don't believe in ghosts, but...."

And then they might proceed to tell you about times when they (or one of their co-workers) have heard things they cannot explain on the battlefield like guns or shouting or have seen phantom regiments of men, or horses when no riders should be present. Such encounters are not uncommon and if you are lucky enough to find someone who will share them with you, you can count on some fascinating tales.

One night, I was taken out on the battlefield at night by a historian who lived in the Gettysburg area. I had asked him about strange happenings and rather than tell me about it, he wanted to show me instead. We went out that night, parked our vehicle and then climbed out to stand in the darkness. We stood there for about 10 minutes in absolute silence before I finally whispered to him and asked what we were doing. He motioned for me to be quiet and to listen.

I waited about five more minutes and then I heard it. It came from the distance and was eerily clear. The rumble and thunder that came from the forests and rocks of the battlefield could not have been anything other than the renowned "Guns of Gettysburg". These booming sounds of cannons and gunfire have been reported for many years and are believed to be the "ghostly" echo of the artillery from the battle in 1863. Can I explain this phenomenon? Not really, other than to think that these sounds are impressions from the horrendous events that took place here.

And they would not be the last phantom happenings that I would experience on this battlefield.

The Devil's Den

If there is a single place on the Gettysburg battlefield more haunted than any other, it would be the area that is known as the Devil's Den. The lore and legend of the Devil's Den was undoubtedly created by the fighting that took place here on July 2, 1863. However, other strange tales surrounded this place long before the battle was ever fought.

According to early accounts from the area, the tangled, outcropping of rocks was a Native American hunting ground for centuries and some say that a huge battle was once fought here. It was called the "Battle of the Crows" and during many perished during the bloody fighting. A Gettysburg writer named Emmanuel Bushman wrote in an 1880 article of the "many unnatural and supernatural sights and sounds" that were reported in the area of the Round Tops and what he called the Indian Fields. He wrote that the early settlers had told stories of ghosts that had been seen there and that Indian "war-whoops" could still be heard on certain nights.

Also, according to local legend, the name "Devil's Den" was actually in use before the battle took place. How the area got its name, though, remains a mystery. Many believe that the strange atmosphere of the area itself may have contributed to the designation. Another legend persists that the Devil's Den was always known for being infested with snakes. The legends say that one gigantic snake in particular eluded the local hunters for many years and they were never able to capture or kill him. He was allegedly nicknamed "the Devil" and thus, the area of rocks was called his "den".

No matter how the area got its name, it was apparently already considered a strange and "haunted" spot before the battle, at least according to Emmanuel

Bushman. In the years that would follow, the Devil's Den would gain an even more fearsome reputation. The fighting here, which took place on the second day of the battle, was especially brutal and bloody. Control of the rocky area went back and forth between the Confederate and the Federal troops and hundreds were mowed down in the narrow rocky field that has been dubbed the "Slaughter Pen".

After hours of bloody fighting the Confederates finally controlled the area. The fight for the Devil's Den may have been the most confusing and intense skirmish on the battlefield that day. The heat of the afternoon and the collapse of the battle lines, thanks to the difficult terrain, caused the entire chain of events to happen so fast that many of the men were almost stunned to find the battle was over.

Stranger yet were the reports from the men who were ordered to stand guard in the tangle of boulders that night. Many of them later spoke of the macabre and unnerving surroundings and of sharing the space in the looming boulders with the bodies of the dead.

Days later, the Federals would return to the Devil's Den, this time triumphant as the battle had come to an end with a Confederate defeat. As men approached, they were stunned by the scene that greeted them. The hills and boulders were covered in blood and carnage and the dead lay scattered about in every direction. One of the first soldiers to enter the area recalled that some of the dead men "had torn and twisted leaves and grass in their agonies and their mouths filled with soil... they had literally bitten the dust."

Another Federal soldier, A.P. Chase of the 146th New York described a scene of horror that July 4 afternoon. As he climbed the stones, he found "those rocky crevices full of dead Rebel sharpshooters, most of them still grasping their rifles."

That afternoon, the rain began to fall in a heavy downpour that lasted for several hours. The dead men, who were already bloated beyond recognition, were now drenched and beginning to decay. No one knows just how long the dead remained unburied around the Devil's Den but it could have been days or even a few weeks. And many of the bodies were said to not have been buried at all, but merely tossed into the deep crevices between the rocks.

The stories about the Devil's Den being haunted began not long after the battle itself. Local legend had it that two hunters had wandered onto the battlefield one day and had gotten lost in the woods near the rocky ridge. They had completely lost their way when one of them looked up and saw the dim figure of a man standing atop the boulders. He gestured with one hand as if pointing the way and the hunter realized it was in that direction they needed to travel. He looked back to thank the man --- but the apparition had vanished.

Even those who are skeptical about the hauntings at Gettysburg, and who claim that the stories of ghosts here are a recent addition to the battlefield, admit that there have always been tales recalled about supernatural doings at the Devil's Den. While admittedly, most of these stories are of a rather recent vintage, Emmanuel Bushman wrote of "many unnatural and supernatural sights and sounds" back in 1880 and local lore has always included odd happenings in the area.

One afternoon in the early 1970s, a woman was said to have gone into the National Park Service information center to inquire about the possibility of ghosts on the battlefield. One can imagine just how many times this question must come up. Although the official position of the park is to neither confirm nor deny the ghostly tales, the ranger on duty was reported to have asked why the woman wanted to know.

The visitor quickly explained that she had been out on the battlefield that morning, photographing the scenery. She had stopped her car at the Devil's Den and had gotten out to take some photos in the early morning light. The woman stated that she had walked into the field of smaller boulders, which are scattered in front of the Den itself and had paused to take a photo. Just as she raised the camera to her eye, she sensed the uncomfortable feeling of someone standing beside her. When she turned to look, she saw that a man had approached her.

She described this man as looking like a "hippie", with long, dirty hair, ragged clothing, a big floppy hat and noticeably, no shoes. The man looked at her and then simply said: "What you are looking for is over there." He pointed over behind her.

The woman turned her head to see just what the unkempt fellow was pointing at and when she turned around again, he had vanished. There was no trace of him anywhere.

A month or so later, the same ranger was on duty at the information desk when another photographer came in and asked almost the same question. He too had been taking photos at the Devil's Den. This time, however, he had taken a photo about a month before in which the image of a man had appeared on the exposed frame --- a man who had not been there when the photo was taken!

When asked what the man looked like, he also described the man as looking like a "hippie" (remember, this was the early 1970s) and also mentioned his long hair, old clothing and the fact that he was barefoot. Could this have been the same man? And if so, who was he?

During the war, many of the Confederate soldiers, and especially those connected with the fighting at the Devil's Den, were from Texas. At that time, this was America's most remote frontier and most of these men did not receive packages from home containing shoes and clothing, as many of the men from states in the immediate vicinity did. Because of this, the "wild" Texas boys were often unkempt and dirty, lacking shoes and new clothing.

Could this reported specter be one of the soldiers from Texas, still haunting the rocks of the Devil's Den? Since those reports from the 1970s, this same soldier (or at least one fitting his description) has been reported several times in and around the rocks of the Devil's Den. According to some of the stories, a number of visitors have mistaken the man for a Civil War re-enactor and have even had their photographs taken with him. The accounts go on to say that when they return home and have their film rolls developed, the man is always missing from the photo.

In spring 1998, I had the chance to conduct a number of investigations on the battlefield with my friend Chris Waterston and several other investigators.

Chris and I obtained permission to do some research at the home that had been used as General Lee's Headquarters during the battle and then went on to several locations on the battlefield itself. The night was largely uneventful until we reached the Devil's Den.

After climbing in and around the rocks for awhile, plus setting up some cameras and recording equipment, Chris and I were walking along the edge of the road at the base the rocks. We were silent as we walked and then suddenly, both of us were startled by a bizarre sound that came from just behind us. The noise we heard was the loud snorting of a horse and it was followed by the distinct sound of jingling reins and the strong smell of a sweaty animal. Both Chris and I spun around at the same time and looked behind us. There was nothing there!

I asked him: "What was that?" I must have jumped about three feet when the sound occurred. It had come so suddenly, and was so close behind us, that I was totally unnerved. I knew that Chris was too --- although he still won't admit how startled he was! However, he never ceases to give me grief about my own reaction.

"What did you hear?" Chris asked wisely.

I answered quickly: "It sounded just like a horse to me and it definitely smelled like one."

He nodded quickly. He had experienced the same thing, and at the exact same time. How could we explain away so a unique, shared experience, except to say that we had a brush with the paranormal!

A Real-Life Haunted House?

As I continued my research into the psychical field, I soon found that each investigation was a learning experience of one type of another. The reader should keep in mind that even though the middle 1990s were not so long ago chronologically, it was quite some time back when it came to the use of electronic equipment for paranormal research. These devices had only recently started to be adapted for investigations and many of us were still learning how to effectively use them.

The investigation where I learned that electronic equipment could actually pick up paranormal activity, and where I learned how important corresponding activity can be, took place in a suburban area of Indianapolis. I had been contacted by a man who was then a police officer in the city and he told me that he knew of a house that was allegedly haunted and wanted to see what I would make of it. The house, which had been known as the Rand family home for many years, was once located along Southport Road on the edge of Indianapolis. What I would not learn until after the investigation was the history of the house --- and also what strange events had prompted this level-headed police officer to contact me about it.

The house was originally known as the Nicholson Mansion. It had been constructed in 1870 by David Nicholson, a contractor for the new Marion County Courthouse in Indianapolis. During the six years that he worked on the courthouse, he also worked on his own home near the small town of Valley Mills. From 1903 to the 1960s, the house was owned by the Rand family.

In 1997, the house was scheduled to be demolished but at the last minute, was saved by a restoration group, which had the house removed from its foundations and transported on two trailers to an empty field a short distance away.

The mansion was not moved without incident, however. During the trip, a photographer from an Indianapolis newspaper took a public interest photograph of the house and it was printed in the following day's edition of the paper. Soon after, telephone calls began flooding into the newspaper office from readers who were sure that they saw the image of a little girl staring out one of the windows of the house as it was being moved. Obviously, no one had been inside at the time. An examination of the photograph did appear to show a little girl staring out the window and attempts to recreate the photo from the same angles revealed nothing out of the ordinary.

The police officer contacted me a short time later and asked me to come and take a look at the place. He did not reveal the story of what had occurred to me, or show me the photograph, until after the investigation was completed. This made what occurred inside of the house that evening all the more exciting!

I traveled to Indianapolis in the company of a number of American Ghost Society investigators and we met the police officer, who took us to the empty field where the Nicholson Mansion had been transported. Interestingly, the house was still divided into two parts (the open ends were sealed off with plywood sheets) and the pieces were still resting on the huge trailers that they had been transported on. This is very important information so that the reader can understand what is to follow --- the house had no electricity, no gas, no running water and in fact, had no connection to anything that might cause artificial energy sources to appear inside of the building. It was not even resting on the ground at the time we entered it!

We decided to go into the main section of the house for the investigation. The second trailer actually contained only a small, additional wing that had been added to the house in later years, so we felt comfortable focusing on the largest section. I entered the house with several other investigators, including Michael and John Barrett, through what would have been the basement entrance. We gained access up some stairs and squeezed through a hole in the door that would have led cellar if the house been sitting on the ground. Our police officer guide, as well as Nancy Napier and several other investigators, remained outside, photographing and videotaping the exterior of the house.

Once we got inside, we discovered that the house was largely empty. Except for a piano that had, for some reason, been left in the living room, we found little besides architectural pieces and extra wood stacked in various places on the first floor. The rooms were in poor condition, having weathered both time and intruders, but the house was apparently not beyond repair. A quick search revealed it to be completely empty though --- or was it?

We used the time that we had to our best advantage, measuring, recording and documenting the house as quickly as we could. We did have permission to be inside of the structure but we had arrived in the early evening and the available light was fading fast. The house was too dangerous to remain inside of after dark.

Our search of the first floor revealed nothing strange. None of the equipment that we had brought inside with us had picked up anything out of the ordinary. There was not a single reading that could be picked up inside of the structure. As far as the equipment was concerned, it was a bare, empty and abandoned shell of wood.

However, that would not remain the case when we climbed up to the second floor. The first area that we examined was the bathroom at the back of the house, where our police officer escort hinted that strange things had been seen. What he did not tell us then was that it was from the bathroom window that the alleged apparition of the little girl had been photographed, peering out as the house was being moved.

We didn't manage to record or document anything out of the ordinary, though, so we moved on to the other rooms. It was at the front of the house, in one of the bedrooms, when the TriField Meter that I carried with me began to suddenly go out of control! It was totally quiet and without activity when I walked into the room. However, as I neared a window in the far corner of the room, the meter immediately jumped. In fact, the readings were so intense that the needle on the scale buried itself at the highest end of the screen. And strangely, it did not remain in that one place either. As I moved back and forth, whatever was causing the readings to occur moved as well, although the energy (or whatever it was) stayed close to the area around the window. Remember that the house had no electricity, gas or running water attached to it. There was simply nothing artificial that could have been causing these readings to occur, which incidentally, had been picked up nowhere else in the house.

At the same time that this was occurring in the bedroom, Michael Barrett called to me from the doorway. He was standing just inside of the room from the upstairs hallway and could see the anomalous readings that I was picking up on the meter. He could also see what was occurring out in the hallway as well. As the bizarre readings were being recorded, the other investigators were experiencing something else in the hall. Just a short distance away from the bedroom was a back staircase that led downstairs. This was not the same set of stairs by which we had accessed the second floor, but a secondary one in the back part of the house. Hanging above the staircase, and above a landing where the stairs shifted in an alternate direction, was an electrical light on a chain.

At the exact moment when I called out that I was picking up the strong readings in the bedroom, the light above the staircase began to move under its own power. It swung backwards and forward and even rotated in circles, moving at such a high rate of speed that it could not have been caused by the mere motion of the house or by any wind that might have somehow begun to blow through the place.

When they called out about the erratic behavior of the light, I hurried away from the window and out into the hall. We stood there watching (John Barrett videotaped the motion) for several minutes as the light twisted, turned and jerked back and forth. Several times, the light actually stopped in mid-swing, balanced in the air at an angle, before plunging back down again and continuing its inexplicable dance. Finally, after about four minutes, it abruptly came to a halt. It did not swing slowly until it finally ran out of motion - it stopped immediately --- as if a hand had reached out and had taken hold of it. We waited for a few moments but the light did not move again.

After this, I turned and went back into the bedroom again, heading straight for the area around the window where I had earlier recorded the readings. Whatever had caused it was gone, as if there had never been any readings there at all. The needle on the meter did not budge at all. Whatever had been there had departed.

Interestingly, these were not the only incidents to occur during the same period of time. Outside of the house, Nancy Napier was snapping photos of the exterior. When her film was later developed, she discovered that one of the photographs of the house contained a series of white streaks and smears that appeared to be in motion. We were later able to determine that the photo had been taken roughly at the same time the readings were being picked up in the bedroom and the light was moving by itself in the bedroom.

We left the house a little while later and our guide began to tell us about the history of the house, the strange photograph taken by the newspaper and some information that he was able to find out by talking to neighbors who once lived near the mansion. According to their stories, the house had long been haunted by the benign spirit of an old woman and by the ghost of a little girl who had been killed in an accident near the house. The police officer believed that the ghost of the girl may have been the spirit who was photographed looking out of the window. However, he could find nothing to back up the story of the old woman --- at least not at first.

At the time of the investigation, the officer had been assigned to one of the school districts in the Indianapolis area, which put him into contact with many of the school employees. He happened to mention the newspaper photograph to one of the bus drivers one day and the woman spoke up that she was not surprised to hear about it --- she already knew that house was haunted! For years, she had driven a route that had her picking up some children at a corner near the house. On a number of occasions, she had seen an old woman standing near an upstairs window, looking down on the street outside. She mentioned this in passing to one of the children and they explained to her that the woman was a ghost. She didn't know it at that time but the driver later learned that there was no one living in the house.

Before I told the officer where the strange readings had been picked up with the equipment, I asked him which window the old woman had been seen looking out of. Not surprisingly, it turned out that it was around the same window where the meter had started to behave so strangely!

Did we encounter the ghost of that old lady on the night of our investigation? Perhaps, or perhaps it was the little girl instead. Who knows for sure? However, I do believe that we encountered something --- there was simply no reasonable explanation for the things that occurred. I remain convinced today that the house was haunted!

The First Time that I Saw a Ghost

Over the years, I have been to literally hundreds of locations that were alleged to be haunted. I wish that I could state with some amount of conviction that all of them were "genuinely haunted", but I can't. Many stories of ghosts and things that go bump in the night are merely that, simply stories, legends and lore. It's often hard to know where truth ends and imagination begins. This is one of the main reasons that I decided to delve into ghost research in the first place --- to separate the fact from the fantasy. However, there is one location that I have visited that I can truly say is haunted, for my experiences here go far beyond just ghostly tales. You see, this location was the place where I first saw a ghost!

Located along a secluded road in the woods of northwest Indiana is a private residence and farm that has been the scene of reported paranormal phenomena for years. The owner of the farm has often stated that the strange events here began not long after she moved in. It started innocently enough when she decided to build a barn on the foundations of a small cabin that had once stood on the property. The original structure had burned down many years before and all that remained of it was the building's stone outline. It was here that, legend has it, a previous resident of the farm died when the cabin burned to the ground. And it was here where the new owner had a horse barn erected.

However, the death of this luckless farmer may not have been the true beginning of the haunting. It is believed the spot was haunted for many years before that, and even perhaps before the region itself was ever settled. Legends say that the land may have been along a trail by which Native Americans who once lived here traveled each winter to Indiana's Grand Marshes. The lore has it that some of the Indians died on the journey south, and that the Native Americans searched for places to bury their dead near water sources and underground springs. Not surprisingly, the land that makes up this "haunted farm" has both --- a small pond that is located not far from the barn and an underground spring that is the source of its water. Many who have come to the farm believe that the source of the haunting may lie near the mouth of this spring.

After years of research, I have come to believe that underground springs and natural water sources attract and enhance ghosts and supernatural activity but they also seem to be a source of unusual energy, as well. This energy can not only attract spirits to the area, but can also have a "ghost-like" effect on people, animals and lights, radios and television sets. In fact, I was more than willing to believe that the area was nothing more than a magnetic "mystery spot" until my own experience convinced me that there was more here than meets the eye.

After moving to the farm, the owner began reporting some very strange happenings. Even guests and visitors to the farm have had their own strange encounters. Incidents included eerie voices; lights turning on and off by themselves; things vanishing and then turning up again in other places; strange moving cold spots in the house and the barn; water faucets turning on without assistance; odd knocking sounds; a rocking chair that moves by itself and much more. The owner also told me that the farm seemed to have a strange effect on her horses and dogs too and they often seemed to see, or sense, something that wasn't visible to her. Strangely, she had also noticed the tendency for kitchen knives and scissors to disappear and then re-appear at various times. One knife literally vanished for 10 years before being discovered again in plain sight on the floor of the barn.

Even though the owner was content to co-exist with whatever was causing the weird events on her farm, she repeatedly invited ghost hunters and researchers to conduct investigations of the place. After being in contact with some of these groups, I was told of cameras and video cameras that mysterious turned on and off; new batteries that drained in moments; equipment that sometimes refused to work and then started working again somewhere else on the farm; strange noises and cold chills that could not be explained; and inexplicable surges of energy that were detected with electronic devices.

Needless to say, as both a writer in search of ghost stories and as an investigator in search of authentic haunts, I was intrigued by the reports from this location. And while I love a good story, the chance of experiencing something truly unexplainable has always been one of the greatest benefits of my work. With that in mind, I decided to accompany three members of the American Ghost Society on an investigation of the "haunted farm" in July 2001.

I met up with them in Chicago and they took me out to the wilds of Northwest Indiana to find the barn. The group was made up of Michelle and Tom Bonadurer, Rob Johnson and myself. We arrived at the farm as darkness was just beginning to fall and we found it to be a very warm and humid night. And if the ghosts turned out to be as plentiful as the mosquitoes, we were bound to have an eventful evening!

After a tour of the farm and the barn, we settled in to our investigation. Thanks to maps of the property that had been made by Rob Johnson, marking the previous active sites on the farm, we had areas around which to center the investigation. We separated into two groups with Tom and Rob filming and photographing outside and with Michelle and I staking out the barn. I was soon reminded about what most people don't know about ghost hunting. This, of course, is the fact that you spend many hours of your hunt simply sitting around waiting for something to happen. It can be a tedious experience and, aside from slapping mosquitoes, there was little for us to do.

In spite of this, though, the initial part of the evening was not without incident. During the first two hours or so, between all of us, we lost three brand new sets of batteries. They had literally been loaded (and had been working!) prior to leaving the house and walking around the farm. In just moments, they had been drained. While this was odd, it would not compare with what happened in the barn later on that night!

Before I get to that though, let me explain the layout of the building. The barn is entered through a doorway that faces the house (about 40 yards away). To the left of the doorway is a lean-to / overhang that is used for storage and to the right is the corner of the barn and a gate that enters a grassy lot. Behind the door into the barn is a short hallway, or foyer, that leads straight ahead to the main body of the barn. On the left side of the foyer is a narrow, wooden staircase that leads up to the loft. Straight ahead down the foyer is a horse stall. If you turn to the left, you enter the wide corridor that runs down the center of the barn. There are horse stalls on either side and on the night of the investigation, there were four horses in the barn. At the opposite ends of the main aisle were large, sliding doors that allowed the horses access from the building. Both doors were locked and secured on this evening.

I had been in the barn several times that night, sitting in pitch darkness and helping to maintain the video cameras, recorders and ghost hunting equipment that we had brought along. Aside from the sounds of some very large barn rats scurrying around in the shadows, nothing out of the ordinary occurred until much later. Before that, we took several breaks for cold drinks and to re-apply much-needed insect repellant.

As we neared the fourth hour of the investigation, Rob and I decided to return to the barn while Tom and Michelle stayed outside. By this time, the batteries had died on the video camera and the extra batteries had also been drained. We were now without video but Rob and I decided to stake out the barn and see if anything strange occurred. We had been in the building approximately 40 minutes, talking and ignoring the sounds of the rats lurking nearby, when we heard a loud noise that came from inside of the building with us. Even afterward, I have been unable to describe what it sounded like. I can only say that it was some sort of "groan" and that it was loud enough that it startled both of us. To make matters worse, the sound also spooked the horses and they began to snort, stomp and move about in their stalls. This is especially important in that one of the horses was a former military mount and is never frightened by anything! Whatever made the noise we heard, though, had the ability to scare this horse and the others as well.

Both Rob and I were especially unnerved by this latest development and in fact, Rob even mentioned to me that he was surprised the horses were acting so skittish --- and then we both stopped talking!

The foyer to the barn suddenly began to illuminate with a brilliant white light! It was extremely noticeable in that the barn was pitch dark at that time. As we stood there, the light filled the foyer, as if someone had just walked inside with a lantern. As it happened, that's exactly what we thought --- that Tom and Michelle had entered the barn. Or at least that's what we thought until what happened next!

The light seemed to draw itself through the wall of the foyer and into the first horse stall. As it did so, the foyer drew dark and the light caused the back wall of the first stall to be illuminated. The white was bright enough that it cast a glow toward us and through the wooden slats of the stall. It was about the height of a person off the ground and almost flat and one-dimensional looking. It entered the first stall and then with the speed of a fast walk, it passed through the wall of each stall, all the way down the length of the barn and then vanished out the back wall!

Now, I should state that these impressions are based on my recollection of the events because at the time they occurred, neither Rob nor I comprehended what was happening. Even moments later, we assumed that Tom and Michelle were outside of the barn and had carried a flashlight past the outside wall of the building. I assumed (as did Rob) that a light outside of the barn could be seen through cracks and chinks in the wall. We soon found that this was not the case!

Almost as soon as the light disappeared, I called Michelle and Tom on the radio and asked where they were, still thinking they were just outside. To my surprise, they were still at the house and not been near the barn. In addition, there was no one else outside and no vehicles had passed on the road. I ran outside and called to Rob to tell me when he could see my light. I began to shine it along the outside wall of the building, parallel with where we had seen the light inside --- but Rob could see nothing! No light could penetrate the building! This meant that the light we had both seen had to have been inside with us!

Had we just come face-to-face with one of the farm's resident ghosts? In all honesty, I believe that we did! You see, we spent the next hour going over and over the incident and trying to re-create the sighting in every possible way that we could. However, we could not duplicate the odd sighting --- it was absolutely impossible! As Sir Arthur Conan Doyle once wrote, "Eliminate the impossible and whatever remains, no matter how improbable, must be the truth".

In all of my years of writing about ghosts, I have had many strange experiences, but up until this time, I had never actually seen a ghost. The importance (at least to me) of what had actually happened in that barn would not sink in until later, when my always skeptical mind began to realize that no explanation existed for what I had seen. Even now, as I write this, I am only just beginning to understand that Rob Johnson and I saw a ghost that night on a farm in Indiana.

So, do you ask me if I believe this farm is haunted? I have to say that I do. Are they really ghosts here? And to that I can say --- if seeing is believing, then yes, there are ghosts on this farm. I saw one!

3. FROM THE OTHER SIDE

Ghost Hunting in Graveyards

It is a common belief among most ghost hunters that cemeteries are not usually the best places to find ghosts. While most would fancy a misty, abandoned graveyard to be the perfect setting for a ghost story, true stories in such a setting are not as common as you might believe. Almost all of us would agree that a place becomes haunted after a traumatic event or unexpected death occurs at that location. History is filled with stories of houses that have become haunted after a murder has taken place there, or after some horrible event occurs that echoes over the decades as a haunting.

But what of a haunted cemetery? Do such places really exist? Most assuredly they do, but ghosts who haunt cemeteries seem to be a different sort than those you might find lingering in a haunted house. Most of these ghosts seem to be connected to the cemetery in some way that excludes events that occurred during their lifetime. As most spirits reportedly remain in this world because of some sort of unfinished business in life, this seems to leave out a cemetery as a place where such business might remain undone.

Graveyard ghosts seem to have a few things in common. These spirits seems to be connected to the burial ground because of events that occurred after their deaths, rather than before. In other cases, the ghosts seem to be seeking eternal rest that eludes them at the spot where their physical bodies are currently found. Cemeteries gain a reputation for being haunted for reasons that include the desecration of the dead and grave robbery, unmarked or forgotten burials, natural disasters that disturb resting places, or sometimes even because the deceased was not properly buried at all.

I have long been intrigued with cemeteries and with the ghosts who are said to haunt them. However, looking for ghosts in a cemetery can often cause a dilemma and it is here where we find ourselves straddling the fine line between "ghost hunting" and "ghost research".

The reason that we run into problems investigating locations like cemeteries (or perhaps I should say *especially* cemeteries) is the way that such investigations are often conducted. Conducting paranormal research in cemeteries really shouldn't be that much different than conducting an investigation in someone's home or in a building. Every investigation has to be organized and there has to be a point to it, otherwise we can't legitimately call it "research" or even an "investigation". To be able to conduct an actual investigation, we have to have rules and criteria to go by. The ghost hunter should have his own checklist of items to be studied at the site because while wandering around in a cemetery taking pictures is fun, it does *not* constitute an actual investigation.

The first thing to do when preparing for a cemetery vigil is to choose the site. This should not be done by simply picking a cemetery at random. Despite what some people apparently believe, not every cemetery is haunted. However, there are hundreds of sites where strange stories have been told, dark history has taken place and where people have encountered things that cannot be explained.

Once you do find a place that seems promising, start looking into the history of it so that you can decide if it is a location for legitimate research. You can make your decision based on the information learned by answering the following questions:

1. What is the history of this location?
2. What events have taken place here to lead you to believe that it might have become haunted?
3. What paranormal events have been reported in the past?

If the answers to these questions lead you to suspect that something ghostly may be taking place at the location, then you should consider organizing an investigation. In the *Ghost Hunter's Guidebook*, I go into great detail about how such investigations can be conducted so that authentic evidence can be collected.

One of the biggest problems that you will run into when investigating a cemetery, though, is the "ghost lore" of the place. This is the one thing that will have almost any investigator chasing false leads and looking for history that does not exist. "Ghost lore" is the practice that society has of trying to explain strange events by attaching a legend to them. In many cases, stories of a "lady in white" or a "headless railroad brakeman" (and think about how many of those are out there!) have been invented to try and add understanding to sightings of ghostly white mists and mysterious glowing lights. Without these chilling stories, the weird locations might never be explained. To put it simply, people just have a need to try and explain things --- they crave a reason for everything, supernatural or not.

In many cases, these locations truly are what we would consider haunted. Unfortunately, though, the true facts behind the haunting may not have anything to do with the legend that is associated with it. There may be another reason entirely for the strange phenomena reported but what often occurred was that, many years ago, local residents felt the need to attach an explanation to events they could not understand. A witness may have glimpsed some sort of pale apparition that looked like a flowing dress, and thus, the legend of a "lady in white" was born.

Cemeteries seem to be especially prone to this, as the mystery of death gives birth to legends of its own. By following the trail of the "ghost lore" to the local graveyard, we have to be careful about believing everything that we hear about the place. Many of the stories that make up the so-called "history" of the place are liable to be filled more with legend than anything else. Still, though, even the folklore can be a place to start with many locations. Those tales had to get started for some reason, right?

My own investigations into cemetery ghosts have been many, but like most ghost hunters, most of them have been uneventful. I have chased stories and hauntings from vanishing hitchhikers to glowing tombstones and usually have come up with nothing. Thankfully though, I love a good story and as a writer, graveyards have given me years of tales, legends and eerie haunts. How many have been authentic cases of the paranormal? Not as many as I would have liked, but of course, not all of them have been fruitless...

Graveyards & Ghost Lights

My first introduction to graveyard ghosts was through the lore of the cemetery --- the ghostly stories that involved those spirits who returned from the grave for one reason or another. In the first chapter of the book, I recounted an adventure that I had in a desecrated graveyard called Peck Cemetery in Illinois and while that may have been my first experience, it was not my last.

The first graveyard investigations that I got involved with were at Greenwood Cemetery in Decatur, Illinois. If there is a single location in downstate Illinois that is more haunted than any other, it would undoubtedly be Greenwood.

The beginnings of the cemetery are a mystery. There is no record to say when the first burials took place here, or even just how many were laid to rest in these grounds. It was not the city's first official burial ground, but the Native Americans who lived here first did use it as a burial site, as did the early settlers. The only trace they left behind were the large numbers of unmarked graves, scattered about the present-day grounds. During the decade of the 1830s, it is believed that local settlers began to use this area also and legend has it that even a few runaway slaves who did not survive their journey on the Underground Railroad were buried on the grounds under the cover of night.

In March 1857, the Greenwood Cemetery Association was organized and the cemetery was incorporated into the city of Decatur. By 1900, Greenwood had become the most fashionable place in Decatur in which to be buried. It had also become quite popular as a recreational park and it was not uncommon to see noontime visitors enjoying their lunch on the grassy hills. Unfortunately though, by the 1920s, the cemetery was broke and could no longer be maintained. It was allowed to revert back to nature and it wasn't long before the once beautiful cemetery began to resemble a forgotten graveyard with overgrown brush, fallen branches and tipped and broken gravestones. Hundreds of graves were left unattended and allowed to fall into disrepair. The stories and legends that would "haunt" Greenwood for years to come had taken root in the desolate conditions that existed in the oldest section of the graveyard. Tales of wandering spirits and glowing apparitions began to be told about the cemetery and decay and decline came close to bringing about the destruction of the place. The cemetery became a forgotten spot in Decatur, remembered only as a spooky novelty.

The next decades, however, would bring a great change. At this point, the cemetery was nearly in ruins. The roads were now only partially covered mud and cinder tracks that were so deeply rutted that they were no longer passable. The oaks, which had added beauty to the cemetery, had now become its greatest curse. The falls of leaves, which had not been raked away in years, were knee-deep in some places. Fallen branches from the trees littered the grounds, which were overgrown and tangled with weeds and brush. Water, time and vandals had wreaked havoc on Greenwood's grave markers. Years of rain, harsh weather and a lack of care had caused many stones to fall at angles and many more were simply lost altogether. Others lay broken and damaged beyond repair, having given up the fight with the elements.

In 1957, though, ownership and operation of the cemetery was taken over by the city of Decatur and the township crews planned to maintain it. The city could not handle the cost of the cemetery's restoration, so a number of organizations and private individuals volunteered to donate time and labor to save it. The restoration was largely a success and despite a few setbacks, Greenwood Cemetery has managed to prosper over the years. Despite this, the place has not lost its eerie reputation and the stories of ghosts and the unexplained still mingle with fact and fiction, blending a strangeness that is unparalleled by any other location in the haunted heart of Illinois.

There are many stories that plague the history of Greenwood Cemetery, including that of a bride who committed suicide when her fiancée was murdered and now haunts a lonely hill within the cemetery; Confederate prisoners who perished aboard a train that was passing through the city and who were buried on a hillside, only to restlessly haunt the area; a phantom woman who appears on a staircase; and more.

However, the most enduring mystery of the cemetery is likely the oldest. And it's the one piece of local lore that first drew me to the graveyard in the first place. The story involves the "ghost lights" that appear on the south side of the burial grounds. These small globes of light have been reported here for many decades and are still reported today. I saw these lights myself a few years back and while I have no logical explanation for what they are, or why they appear here, the lore of the cemetery tells a strange and tragic story.

The legend tells of a flood that occurred many years ago, around 1905, which wiped out a portion of the cemetery. The Sangamon River, located just south of the cemetery, had been dammed in the late 1800s and was often prone to floods. During one particularly wet spring, the river overflowed its banks and washed into the lower sections of the cemetery. Tombstones were knocked over and the surging water even managed to wash away graves and to force buried caskets to the surface. Many of them, as these were the days before Lake Decatur had been formed, went careening downstream on the swollen river.

Once the water receded, it took many days to find the battered remains of the coffins and many were never found at all. For some time after, farmers and fishermen were startled to find caskets, and even corpses, washing up on river banks some miles away. There were many questions as to the identities of the bodies and because of this, many of them were buried again in unmarked and common graves. These new graves were placed on higher ground, up on the southern hills of Greenwood.

Since that time, it has been said that the mysterious lights have appeared on these hills. The stories say that the lights are the spirits of those whose bodies washed away in the flood. Their wandering ghosts are now doomed to search forever for the place where their remains are now buried.

Dozens of trustworthy witnesses have claimed to see the "spook lights" on the hill, moving in and out among the old, weathered stones. The mystery of the lights has managed to elude all those who have attempted to solve it. Many have tried to pass them off as reflections from cars passing over the lake --- but what of sightings that date back to before Lake Decatur ever existed? In those days, a covered bridge over the Sangamon River took travelers along the old county highway and for many years, not a single automobile crossed it, as motorcars had not yet come to Decatur.

Whether the cause is natural or supernatural, the lights can still be seen along the edge of the graveyard today. Want to see them for yourself? Seek out the south hills of Greenwood some night by finding the parking lot that is located across the road from the cemetery fence. Here, you can sit and observe the hills. You have to have a lot of patience, and may even have to make more than one trip, but eventually, you might be lucky enough to see the "ghost lights".

My own patience paid off for the first time back in 1991. I had been told about the "ghost lights" for several years from people who came to me with their strange stories. In fact, I first heard about the lights from family members who, when they were teenagers (and this would have been in the early 1930s), used to park their cars along the road south of the cemetery in hopes that the lights would appear. I first starting seeking out the lights for myself in the late 1980s but it would take several years before my persistence paid off.

One night, a friend that I worked with and I drove down to the road behind the cemetery to try and look for the lights. At that time, this area was much more overgrown than it is now and the old road that used to run through an area called "Hell Hollow" was still in use and had not yet been torn out by the city. I remember it being very dark that night and strangely quiet. Aside from the stray sounds of animals in the nearby woods, only the ripple of the Sangamon River could be heard as it passed behind us.

We waited there, sitting on the hood of the car, for about two hours, quietly talking and watching the hills that stretched out in front of us. It was a cloudy night, but just enough of the moon seeped through the clouds to softly illuminate the stones of the cemetery in the distance. My friend, Larry, spotted the first light as it moved at a fairly quick rate of speed from the lower part of the hill to the top. It vanished in a second, almost as if it had been switched off. More lights followed and I began to see them too as they darted and zipped among the trees and the stones, some shooting upward and others speeding off into the darkness and fading away. The "light show" lasted for about 15 minutes and then no more of them were seen.

After all of these years though, I still have no idea how to explain what I saw on those hills. The lights appeared to be about the size of softballs and were white in color and tinged with a faint blue. They had an electric sort of glare to them, as though they were light bulbs that were surging with energy. What could have created them?

Obviously, it's very possible that these lights might have a natural explanation. I do believe that they are paranormal in origin, but are possibly only paranormal in the sense that we don't have an explanation for what causes them yet. Many researchers have cited the causes for "spook lights" as being railroad tracks, power lines or sources of water. Almost every "spook light" location has one (or more) of these things in common. In the case of the Greenwood lights, we have all three. The lights are seen on a hillside that is only a few yards away from the Illinois Central rail line. In addition, there are power lines running next to the tracks and both the railroad tracks and the power lines cross over the Sangamon River. Given all of that, I would say that it's possible, and perhaps even likely, that the Greenwood lights have an explanation that is of this world, rather than the next one. In other words, they are not likely the restless souls of the dead.

I will tell you though, as you are sitting out on the south side of the cemetery in the dark and happen to catch a glimpse of the famous Greenwood "ghost lights", it's easier to believe they are ghosts than anything that we can explain away as a glitch of nature!

The Ongoing Mystery of Portals

As time passed and I became more interested (and spending much more time) in cemeteries, my research began to lead me into areas that were not specifically tied to the spirits of the dead. In 1997, following a series of experiences in graveyards, I proposed the idea that some cemeteries might actually be "doorways" or "portals" between this world and the next. The idea was dismissed by many investigators who were more experienced that I was but my ongoing research continues to lead me to believe there might be something to this idea. But what are these "portals" and why have I come to believe the theory of them is worthy of continued investigation?

Earlier on in this chapter, I mentioned that cemeteries are rarely haunted in the traditional way. In spite of this, though, weird activity, hauntings, bizarre photographs and reports continue to come from graveyards all over the country. How and why can this be?

The theory behind some cemetery phenomena has been linked to what a few researchers call "portals" or "doorways". Dismissed by some and embraced by others, the idea of a portal is still mostly theory and conjecture but in my opinion, the idea explains a lot of things about cemetery hauntings and even some short-lived paranormal flaps or outbreaks.

The idea of a "portal", or a "doorway", to another dimension is not a new one. It has been suggested that there exist places all over the world that serve as "doorways" from our world to another. These doorways may provide access for entities to come into our world. They may be the spirits of people who have lived before, or they may be something else altogether. Some researchers even believe that they could be used otherworldly beings from some dimension that we cannot even comprehend. In famous cases like the "Mothman" or the "Mad Gasser" of Mattoon, Illinois, it may even be possible that such a portal opened for a short time in a specific area, allowing these figures to wreak havoc for a brief period, only to later vanish without a trace.

I know this all sounds far-fetched, but it may not be as strange as it seems. The entities that have been sighted, reported and even photographed around what many believe to be portals could be the spirits of the dead --- or perhaps something stranger. If locations like this do exist, and they are some sort of doorway, it's possible that these spots may have been labeled as being "haunted" over the years by people who saw something near them that they couldn't explain, isn't it? I think it's possible that this has happened many times. In fact, I would even suggest that these places did not "become" haunted as traditional locations do (through death or tragic events), but had been "haunted" for many, many years already.

Some have suggested that portals might be linked to what are referred to as "ley lines". The idea that a number of unusual, or sacred, spots are often located in a particular area, or along a straight line, was suggested by Alfred Watkins in 1925. The idea came to him when he was examining a map of Herefordshire, England and noticed an alignment of ancient sites. He gave such alignments the name of "ley", a Saxon word that meant "a clearing in the woodland".

Since that time, the idea has been expanded beyond ancient sites and has enveloped strange and haunted sites, as well. Many believe that the ley lines cross the entire world and feel that locations where the lines cross are especially energy-filled. Such sites might even be described as "portals".

Some of the most common sites alleged to be portals have been cemeteries. For years, ghost hunters and researchers have collected not only strange stories of haunted cemeteries, but dozens of anomalous photographs too. In many cases, there seems to be no reason why the cemetery might be haunted unless it might somehow provide access for spirits, or entities, to pass from one world to the next.

Of course, some of the cemeteries are haunted in the traditional manner, but it's the ones that aren't that cause such a puzzle. Going back to what was mentioned earlier, it's possible that these sites were "haunted" long before the cemetery was ever located there. Might it be possible that some sort of "psychic draw" to the area was what caused our ancestors to locate a cemetery at that spot in the first place? Perhaps they felt there was something "sacred" or "spiritual" about the place and without realizing why, placed a burial ground on the location and made it a protected spot. According to American Indian lore (and my own discussions with several Native Americans), the early inhabitants of this country chose their burial grounds in a conscious manner, looking for a place to bury the dead that they felt was more closely connected to the next world. Many of these locations, including many disturbed sites, are now considered "haunted" or at least inhabited by spirits.

So why not our own cemeteries? Could our own burial grounds have been chosen in the same way, although perhaps unknowingly? These sites could now mark doorways between this world and the next. The strange entities that have been photographed around such sites could be the traveling spirits of the dead --- or perhaps something worse?

Cemeteries are not the only places to find these portals. I believe they may exist in other locations too, including in places where we would least expect them. These "glitch" areas might be found anywhere, even under a home or building. In fact, these doorways, and the unknown entities that pass through them, might be the explanation for some of the strange sightings that have plagued paranormal research for years. For some time, investigators have attempted to dispel the myths that "ghosts are evil" and that they "hurt people", but what if we are wrong? Or perhaps even partially wrong?

Normally, I don't believe that ghosts hurt people. By that, I mean that people involved in a haunting are not normally injured by the discarnate spirits of the dead. There are certainly instances of people being hurt, though, but usually because they are struck by an object in a poltergeist outbreak or trip over a shifted piece of furniture. In fact, you are more likely to be hurt running away in terror from ghostly activity than you are by the activity itself!

But what about people who get hurt in other ways? These are the cases that worry everyone and the cases that give rise to the stories of "evil spirits" and dangerous ghosts. In some of these cases, we hear accounts of violent acts, terrifying visions and even strange beings that may have never been human at all. Can we always take such stories seriously? Perhaps not, but they are out there and what if these cases involve entities who are not ghosts at all? Could they be strange spirits who have passed into this world by way of the "portals" that we have been discussing?

This is interesting to think about. If this might be true, such a theory would certainly provide answers for puzzling cases when traditional methods of ghost investigations have not worked. It might also provide a solution as to how stories of "evil spirits", "demons" and even "negative ghosts" have gotten started. Obviously, this is all just conjecture at this point, but consider this:

I am acquainted with a "sensitive" who lives in the Midwest and who works with people who have haunted homes and businesses. His goal is to assist both the witnesses with their ghost problems and the lingering spirits to pass over to the next world. Let me say that while I have no first-hand knowledge of how this works, or how it is possible, he has been very successful at what he does and has helped a lot of people.

Anyway, some time back, he got involved in a case where the witnesses complained of very strange, almost non-human creatures, which appeared in their home and caused damage to the property. On one occasion, a relative who was visiting them was even injured by one of these entities. My friend was called and he went to the house to try and assist the spirits in passing over. Instead, he encountered something that he had never experienced before.

He told me: "I have never seen anything like it. Whatever was there, these things were not ghosts. In past cases, I have been involved with as many as three or four spirits at a time. There were dozens of them here and they seemed to be moving back and forth through some sort of doorway."

It is interesting to note that the house had been constructed near an area that is purported to be an Indian burial ground.

In this chapter, I want to discuss a couple of the cemeteries that I have done research in that I believe were "portal areas". Strangely, the entire cemetery could not be considered a portal in either case. This is something else that I have noted about such locations. Both of these cemeteries had certain areas in them where activity was the strongest. In fact, I would even go as far as to say that all of the activity in the graveyard was centered around this spot. Going back to what I mentioned earlier, it is almost as if the creators of the cemetery unconsciously highlighted the area in some way, placing distinctive gravestones or architecture in these areas to set them apart from the rest of the cemetery.

Old Union Cemetery

My first investigation into a cemetery that I came to believe contained a portal area was in early 1996. The graveyard is known as Old Union Cemetery and it's located in a remote section of Central Illinois. The cemetery saw its first burials in 1831 and it closed down less than 100 years later in 1931 after a fire destroyed the Union Christian Church that was located at the edge of the grounds. As time passed, the road past the cemetery, which had once been a busy stage line between Bloomington and Springfield was abandoned and the graveyard was largely forgotten. Although it is well-kept by workers from the local township, the cemetery is no longer visible from any road. The forest now surrounds it, hiding it away from history. Old records say that over 500 of the early residents of this area were buried in the grounds but less than 100 of their grave markers remain.

Old Union Cemetery first came to my attention thanks to reports from a sheriff's deputy and two independent witnesses who had worked for the local township. The police officer and the caretakers told me stories of glowing balls of light that were often seen among the tombstones of the cemetery grounds. In addition, the caretakers also told me of one part of the graveyard that they avoided working in if possible. Both of them told me, without knowing that anyone else had mentioned it, that one particular section made them feel very strange and uncomfortable. They had no reason to explain what bothered them about it --- it simply made their flesh crawl.

This section of the cemetery was an area in the far corner of the grounds, that almost touched the woods that loomed over the burial ground. The section was apparently some sort of private plot that contained a now unreadable tombstone. It was surrounded by an iron fence that was cast with the images of willow trees as a decorative motif. Each corner of the plot had a metal post to which the sides of the fence connected. The design of the posts was rather intricate as well, twisted and turned to stand about four feet tall.

I wanted to describe this fence in more detail because it was unlike anything else in the cemetery. Keep in mind that this is a simple, country cemetery with standard granite stones and very little in the way of decoration or design. This fenced-in plot was not only very much out of place (in regards to the architecture of the cemetery) but it was located in a very odd position within the grounds. The plot was located right at the edge of the woods, at least 20 yards away from not only the main portion of the cemetery, but from the closest other graves as well.

This fits in with the theory that I mentioned earlier about how the designers of some cemeteries seem to highlight certain areas in ways that are unlike anything else that can be found in the graveyard. I don't think that it's any coincidence that the fenced area is the center of the strange activity at Old Union Cemetery.

My first visit to burial grounds took place on a warm afternoon in the spring of 1996. There was nothing odd or spooky about the day and frankly, not much spooky about the cemetery itself either. I was accompanied to the graveyard by another investigator, who lived in the area, and who was able to track down the secluded location. We drove back to the woods by way of an old farm road beside a field. We crossed a grassy area and then found ourselves rounding a curve and entering the cemetery itself. As mentioned, it was completely surrounded by the forest but aside from this, it looked a lot like just about every other small cemetery that you can find along country roads all over the Midwest. There were no signs of vandalism, damage or anything else that might explain why ghostly stories were being told about the place. In spite of this, it was hard to ignore the tales of strange lights that were so often being seen.

Our plan that afternoon was to map out the cemetery and to look things over so that we could return one night for a full-fledged investigation. Neither of us wanted to show up here some night after dark and stumble into an open grave, so we thought it best to get a lay of the land. We spent about an hour walking around the area and poking into the woods to see what was on the other side of them. We found nothing but more woods and farm fields that lay some distance off. There are no houses in the immediate area, so when we did conduct our investigation, we knew that we could count on not picking up lights or sounds in the distance that might be coming from hidden structures.

One of the last areas that we looked over was the fenced-in section at the back of the cemetery. Perhaps it was my imagination at work, but this was the only area of the burial ground where I felt the least bit odd. As mentioned previously, I make no claims to any sort of psychic ability but it was hard not to wonder if I was feeling the same thing those caretakers had felt while mowing the grass around this small plot. Out of curiosity, my friend and I decided that we would set up a few pieces of equipment around the area and see if we detected anything with our tools that might explain the unusual reports.

The sun was just beginning to dip slightly below the tops of the trees as we unpacked the gear. The temperature that afternoon was in the lower 70's and it was quite comfortable in shirt sleeves. How then could I explain away what we discovered with the equipment?

The first inkling that something was out of the ordinary around the burial plot came when I unpacked my TriField Natural EM Meter and placed it on the stone inside of the fence. The meter began to fluctuate back and forth, peaking suddenly and without explanation.

This particular TriField Meter is one of the best electromagnetic field meters on the market. Electromagnetic Field Meters (EMF Meters) are the most commonly used devices for ghost hunters today. Largely, they are also the most reliable. Electronic devices have been adapted to use in the paranormal research field as a way of giving confirmation of our instincts. They are also used to detect energy that we cannot see with the naked eye. Researchers believe that ghosts, or paranormal energy, are electromagnetic in origin. The energy that a ghost gives off (or uses) causes a disruption in the magnetic field of the location and thus, becomes detectable using measuring devices. For electronic devices to be useful in an investigation, though, the researcher must search for corresponding activity to go along with the anomalies the EMF meter picks up. No single piece of evidence can stand alone, but coming up with several different things that are corresponding, like witness accounts, photographs, temperature changes and more, an investigation reveals some things that cannot easily be explained.

There don't seem to be any "ideal" readings when it comes to using these meters but it is worthwhile to search for sudden surges and drops that cannot be explained away.

Investigations like the one at the Nicholson Mansion in Indiana have convinced me that EMF detectors do work when hunting ghosts, or at least when tracking paranormal energy. Because of this, the odd readings in Old Union Cemetery seemed to verify to me the reports from those who claimed this section of the cemetery was "haunted" in some way. However, I should add that I will often discard readings that I pick up with the equipment if they are not backed up by anything else. I am always searching for corresponding activity, even at a place such as this one, with no power lines or artificial sources from which the equipment fluctuations could come. I was soon to find my "corresponding activity", however.

Moments after the TriField meter began to behave erratically, my friend began working with a portable, infrared temperature device and after placing it nearby, soon discovered that the temperature inside of the fenced-in area was almost 40 degrees colder than the air in the rest of the cemetery! But how could this be? And how does something like this work to pick up temperature readings when there was nothing to see with the human eye?

Infrared thermometers are believed to be able track down a paranormal presence by taking instant temperature readings from a location and by detecting any changes that might be sudden or extreme. To state it simply, it checks for "cold spots" (unexplained temperature variances) that are believed to signal that a ghost is present. It is thought that a ghost uses the energy in a particular spot to manifest itself and by doing so, creates a cold mass. The energy may be invisible to the eye but still detectable using one of these devices.

Researchers have detected these cold spots, which can be very extreme, in both indoor and outdoor locations, from haunted houses to cemeteries. They have also collected a number of photographs that have been taken while the devices were picking up intensely cold spots. These "spots" were invisible and yet registered for the thermal device. The developed photos show the researcher holding one of these devices and, often, just beyond their reach, is an anomalous mist or image. My own experiences with photos like this has convinced me that there are useful applications for these devices in paranormal investigation.

Not everyone was convinced though. In spite of interesting evidence, many researchers have argued that these thermometers can only work when they come into contact with something solid. These questions came up regarding the old non-contact thermometers that were pointed and used like a gun. These devices could be used reliably, under the right conditions, but often were not. During the late 1990s, we were still using them for investigations (along with infrared, stationary devices that took temperature readings directly at the location) but in recent years, have turned strictly to temperature probes that pick up changes in the immediate area.

As mentioned, though, even the non-contact thermometers could be used reliably under controlled conditions (i.e. not pointing them into the sky) and I do not believe that they had to contact something solid in order to record a temperature. I have documented evidence to say that firefighters sometimes use these devices to record the temperature of a fire. As fire is not a solid object, and yet the probes still works, what can it be recording?

I do not argue the fact that the infrared beam of the device does need to come into contact with *something* to register a reading. However, in the research that I did after the first investigation at Old Union Cemetery, I spoke to a technician who worked for the makers of one of the best IR probes on the market (the Omega OS-521) in the middle 1990s. During our discussions, she explained to me how the device worked and that it had to make contact with something to register a reading. After showing her the photos that I had of strange mists that were giving off cold readings at the time the photos were taken, she agreed that such a "mass" could give off the temperature changes necessary to register on the device.

She explained that the thermometer reads the infrared energy of an object and converts that into a temperature. A basic hand-held thermal scanner is set at a level of about 98% of the energy given off. The good news is that rock, bricks, trees and cemetery headstones are also at about this same level and that's why these devices worked for paranormal investigations when used correctly. Based on the evidence we had at the time, it seemed that "spirit energy" was on a different level than that and that's why it could be picked up using one of these devices. Of course, these days, a question of whether or not non-contact thermometers work for paranormal investigations is no longer as valid as it once was since most investigators have now switched to more reliable devices. I did feel that this discussion was warranted, however, in showing how our Old Union Cemetery investigations in the 1990s were as controlled as possible at the time.

The temperatures recorded inside of the fenced area that afternoon were achieved using a stationary, digital thermometer but my friend did have a non-contact device, as well. He used this to check the temperature of the surrounding area since readings from inside of the fence ranged from 30 to 36 degrees. As best as we could tell, the surrounding area of the cemetery was 68 degrees, which was an extreme difference.

We took a number of photographs to document the area that day but nothing out of the ordinary turned up in them. However, this would not be the case as we continued our investigations at this location.

We returned to the cemetery a short time later for the first of several investigations. As with the first trip, all of the activity that we documented with our equipment centered around this same part of the cemetery.

In addition to bizarre temperature drops, the fenced area also seemed to be the source for small, glowing balls of light that turned up in the developed photographs from the place. During our second investigation, which lasted about two hours, we managed to come back with 14 unusual photos, all of which were later sent to an independent lab for analysis. They had no explanation for the balls of lights and stated that they were not developing flaws or anything wrong with the film itself. The balls of light were seen hovering, or captured in motion, in several areas of the cemetery. Most were photographed near the fenced section.

Perhaps the strangest photograph --- and weirdest incident ---- was an image that was taken of one of the investigators who came with us to the cemetery. In the photo, one of the odd, gold-colored lights was very close to her face, even though nothing was seen by the naked eye at the time. Oddest about this, though, was the seeming "allergic reaction" that occurred at the same time the light was photographed around her. Her eyes became very red and began to water and she broke out with blotchy, red hives. It is unknown whether or not the reaction was caused by the proximity of the gold light, but it would certainly be a strange coincidence if it was not. In the end, this incident remains a mystery.

The temperature drops that occurred that night were experienced by both stationary and hand-held sensors. We saw nothing that could have caused the fluctuations, but they happened several times, always around the fenced area at the back of the cemetery. It was clear that this was the focal point of the activity.

I returned to the cemetery about three months later in the company of two other investigators. We arrived in the late afternoon to once again test the area where the fenced section is located for additional daytime activity. I have always maintained that if a location is really haunted, then it's going to be active both in the daylight and after dark. I think it's a common misconception that hauntings only take place at night --- and I think Old Union Cemetery certainly dispels that myth!

Shortly after we unpacked our equipment, one of the other investigators announced that he had seen movement around the center of the graveyard. Thinking that it might have been a bird, he asked us to keep watch with him for a few minutes. As we stood watching, I suddenly saw a yellowish-colored blur streak past us and vanish near the woods. The other two saw the shape too and this single light was followed by others. Amazingly, we were watching the cemetery's "spook lights" with not only our naked eyes --- but in broad daylight! Even when we had been in the cemetery at night, we had not seen the lights but we saw them in the daylight instead. What made this day different than the others when we had been present?

I have no idea but I can tell you that it never happened to me again. At no time after this, in subsequent investigations, did I ever see the strange lights, or anything else that I would consider to be paranormal. However, I did bring back more weird photos of the place. Recently though, a friend of mine, who visited the cemetery, also reported seeing the lights in the daytime. When he told me about them, he had no idea that the lights had been reported during the daylight hours before. Thinking quickly, he managed to snap a couple of quick photos as the lights buzzed past him. The photos were blurry but if you looked at them closely, the eerie globes were visible.

Anderson Cemetery a.k.a. "Graveyard X"

Over the last decade or so, I have probably received more requests for information about (and directions to) the elusive burial ground known as "Graveyard X" than I have any other site that I have investigated. And while I am still not going to reveal its location within these pages, I will pass on to the curious that while some readers may think they know the location of this mysterious cemetery, it's likely that they do not. It has been pointed out to me on numerous occasions that there is more than one Anderson Cemetery in Illinois (where this one is located) but all that I can tell you is that I made an agreement not to reveal the whereabouts of this cemetery when I first starting doing research here.

In addition to keeping silent as the location, I have also worked to try and prevent the cemetery from being overrun by would-be "ghost hunters" and vandals by doing all that I can to cover my tracks in regards to this place. I have even gone as far as to weave several locations into one and offered photographs of the place that are misleading, at best. It has been pointed out as well that both in the photos and in the documentary that was filmed in "Graveyard X", the cemetery is very recognizable. And I will agree that it is ---

but one of the basic rules of filming any sort of television program is that separate sections of the show can be filmed in many areas and then edited to appear as one. Artistic license can be taken with the historical aspects of the place, as well.

Of course, I can't say one way or another just what has occurred here in regards to keeping the location of the cemetery secret but I will urge the reader not to take anything that they think they know for granted.

With all of that said though, let me assure you that Anderson Cemetery (as we'll call Graveyard X here) is a very haunted place. In fact, it was because of my investigations at this place that I first began to research more deeply the idea of "portals" and doorways between this world and another. I could find no other explanation for the strange events that had been reported here, the eerie happenings, the bizarre photographs and first-hand accounts. There was no reason for this cemetery to be haunted --- and yet it was.

Anderson Cemetery is not a place that you are going to find on any maps. It is a typical rural cemetery that is well hidden by curving back roads, thick woods and wind-swept fields of grain. It's not a place that most people would go to, or would care to find, unless they had relatives buried there and had a reason to visit. Unlike many other cemeteries that are regarded as haunted, it is not vandalized and is in fact in good condition, well-maintained by the local township crew and still in use today.

Over the years, I have visited literally hundreds of places that are alleged to be haunted, but by all indications, Anderson Cemetery may be one of the most actively haunted spots that I have ever been to. Strangely though, its history suggests nothing that would have made it become that way.

It is located on land that once belonged to a local farmer named Tavner Anderson. Prior to 1867, the graveyard was nothing more than a wooded section of his property. It did not become a burial ground until the internment of a small child took place there. A family that was passing through the area on their way west came to the Anderson house with a child that had fallen ill and died. They asked if the child might be buried somewhere on the farm. Anderson selected a clearing in the woods where a high knoll was located and on this site the cemetery was started. The small hill can still be seen in the cemetery today, although any grave marker made for the young girl has long since deteriorated.

I first heard about this cemetery in the middle 1990s from a man who had grown up in the area where it is located. For some time, there had been stories about people reporting strange lights and unusual sounds in the cemetery at night. It is very isolated and surrounded on three sides by heavy woods, so it was unlikely these lights and noises were coming from a nearby farmhouse or road. It was also supposed to be haunted, a claim that was met with much skepticism by the man who told me about it.

It was not until his made his own trip the cemetery that he began to believe there might be something behind the tales that he had been told. One night, he drove out to the graveyard and stayed for several hours. A short time after he arrived, he got his first glimpse of one of the eerie lights that others were allegedly seeing. It floated up from behind one of the graves, flashed for a moment, and then vanished seemingly into nowhere. Soon, he saw several more of them but could find no explanation as to what they might be. Stunned, he attempted several times to photograph them, but he was sure that his camera and reflexes were too slow to catch them. When his film was developed though, he got the surprise of his life!

The finished photos showed what can only be called a number of "misty shapes and apparitions". I confess that when I saw these photographs and heard the man's stories about Anderson Cemetery, I was intrigued. In fact, I was intrigued enough to almost immediately schedule an investigation to the site with members of the American Ghost Society. The location was so hard to find though that we had to meet with the original witness in a nearby town and literally follow him to the cemetery.

We arrived at Anderson Cemetery just about the time the sun was going down, which is not an optimal time to arrive since no one should be stumbling around in the dark. In spite of this of the late hour, we were able to map out the cemetery and to coordinate enough so that we were not on top of one another and were able to use equipment and to photograph the area without interfering with the other researchers.

The first investigation paid off with little in the way of documented evidence except for several strange photographs. Several of them were ones that I managed to take myself. One of them clearly appeared to show a white, human-like face that looked directly into the camera! It was pretty unnerving to say the least and some time later, it was sent to the Kodak Laboratories for an explanation. However, they had no idea what the weird image might be. They merely stated that it was not a problem with the film, the developing or the camera. They refused to comment on what the images might be, though, especially the one that looked so much like a human face.

My research into Anderson Cemetery continued and I began looking for any history about the place that might provide a clue as to why the cemetery was haunted. I began speaking to people in the area, including residents and police officers who patrolled the area, about their own experiences with the graveyard. I continued to hear the accounts of the strange lights and of the sound of voices that could be heard in the cemetery at night. According to my sources, the voices of children at play were sometimes heard, literally coming from nowhere. This eerie sensation was experienced by six independent witnesses that I spoke with and has since been verified by others, as well. I should add that I have searched diligently for a logical explanation as to where this sound could be coming from but there are no houses near the cemetery --- and why would children be playing and laughing near the cemetery during the early morning hours, when several of the witnesses have reported the sounds?

I returned to Anderson Cemetery the following summer to conduct another investigation during the daylight hours. I unpacked my equipment and began trying to monitor the cemetery, searching for anything out of the ordinary. I found it after about an hour. There was one particular part of the cemetery where the temperature was noticeably colder than anywhere else, in fact about 40 degrees colder! Remember that this was a summer afternoon and the temperature that day (according to a gauge that I brought with me) was 89 degrees. The temperature in this area of the cemetery was only 53. How could I explain this away naturally?

Using the maps and charts that we had put together during our various investigations, I marked the area from which the cold temperatures were found. I discovered that not only were the unusual temperature readings confined to one section of the cemetery, but so were the readings that we had picked up with our equipment and the strange photographs that had been taken. All of the activity at the cemetery came from one small area that was roughly the shape of a triangle. The angles of the line were marked with a stone bench at one corner, a large, arched stone at another and strangely, the third corner was marked with the largest stone in the cemetery. Like the fenced area at Old Union Cemetery, all of these stones were unlike anything else that could be found in the graveyard. Stranger yet, the tallest stone that marked the third corner of the triangle was it was located on top of the mound where the original grave in the cemetery was located! It was this small hill, located in the woods, where Tavner Anderson had buried the little girl around who the cemetery was started. If we take the theory of a possible portal seriously, then this can be no coincidence!

More than a year after I first began delving into the strangeness of Anderson Cemetery, I returned there in the company of ghost researcher Bob Schott, who was filming an installment of the now defunct series "Adventures Beyond". We were accompanied to the graveyard by Tim Harte and Mike Hollinshead, creators of a sophisticated computer tracking system. The device was designed to take readings in allegedly haunted locations and then analyze the gathered data and determine the nature of the haunting. The system read changes in electro-magnetic fields, temperature changes, visible light, seismic vibrations and other areas. The experiments with this system were closely controlled and monitored with motion detectors and video cameras. To try and cover all of the possibilities with this experiment, we decided to do it using the computer system to monitor an old-fashioned séance.

A table was set up and a small group of average (non-psychic) people gathered around it with a Ouija board. These people were completely unaware of the past history of the place and were asked to simply try and communicate with anything that might be present. Whether you believe in the validity of Ouija boards or not, it was a fascinating --- and often chilling --- experiment. In a relatively short time, the sitters claimed to be in contact with something supernatural. Later, they would say that at times, the pointer on the board was moving so fast that their fingers were not even touching it! It should be noted that later viewings of the film that was shot that night would confirm that this occurred.

Stranger still, the spirited communicator claimed to be that of a small child who had been buried there before it was a cemetery. What was so strange about this is that, as you might remember, the first burial that took place here was that of a little girl who had died while passing through the area. Not a single one of the people involved in the séance knew this at the time! I was the only person who possessed this information and I was not involved in the séance except as a monitor. I didn't pass on any of the information to the sitters in the séance, so there was, realistically, no way that they could have known about this. Was it a coincidence? Perhaps, but it seems unlikely.

It seems especially unlikely when considered in connection with the results achieved by Tim and Mike's computer system. According to the read-outs and graphs, there were things occurring in the cemetery during the séance that could not be explained! These anomalous spikes and dips were totally out of the ordinary and showed severe fluctuations in electro-magnetic radiation that could not be explained by natural means. Even stranger still was the fact that these fluctuations were occurring in response to the questions asked by the sitters! It seemed as though some sort of intelligent energy was present in the graveyard.

Tim Harte later told me: "I couldn't explain why this was happening. The readings were completely unexplainable. Whatever was going on, it seemed to occur at the same time the people at the table would ask a question. The computer would show a massive change then, pause for a moment, and then spike again. It was almost like something was answering."

I can tell you that the events that occurred during this séance were truly a part of the most intense paranormal investigation that I have ever been involved in. Bob Schott would later state (correctly, I believe) that it was "the most intense activity ever captured on film".

As the séance was taking place, other pieces of equipment were also being used to monitor the area. TriField Natural EM Meters had been placed around the séance table and the electromagnetic field around the table actually dipped and spiked in response to the questions being asked with the Ouija board, just as the computer system monitors did. We also photographed the area heavily, all during the séance, and managed to capture a number of photos that showed white, anomalous images that were hovering in the vicinity of the table.

The séance was also monitored using a television camera that had been fitted with a Generation III Night Vision lens, which was reportedly 5 times more sensitive than the equipment used by the U.S. Military during the first Gulf War. The lens was so advanced (at that time) that it had not been available on the civilian market until a short time before the investigation. It had been loaned to Schott by the manufacturer, a company that deals specifically with sensitive government and military contracts. The company that made the equipment later took a look at a copy of the film that we shot that night in the cemetery and were puzzled by what they saw. They, along with other film experts, ran the clip over and over and put it through all sorts of tests to determine if it had been hoaxed or if it was merely an accidental image that had been caused by camera flashes or some sort of reflection. In their final report on the footage, they stated that they had no explanation for the strange anomaly and that it could only be paranormal in origin.

The image that was filmed was documented using not only the television camera, but also by several handheld infrared temperature detectors. The séance was monitored using these detectors, in the hands of Bob Schott and myself. We circled the table and took readings directly from the center of the séance. Impossibly, on this warm summer night, we picked up temperatures that dipped down as low as 10 degrees above zero! How was this possible? I have no idea but it was all documented on film and the readings were recorded using not only different temperature scanners but scanners made by totally different companies.

The startling image that appeared on the film came at a high point in the séance. After more than 30 minutes of strange readings, inexplicable replies from the Ouija board and strong temperature drops, one of the participants in the séance, Charles, announced that he felt something cold creeping across his back. During a playback of this video shot that night, I discovered that Charles actually said this several times before I heard him and went to check it out.

I hurried around behind where Charles was sitting and aimed the infrared beam of the temperature scanner at his back. If you have ever worked with one of these devices and have aimed it at a person's body, you usually get a reading that is only a few degrees below the person's body temperature, thanks to the clothing they are wearing. That was not the case this time, however! Even though it should be absolutely impossible, I pulled the trigger on the scanner and it registered a reading of only 14 degrees! On the tape of the investigation, you can clearly hear me announce: "Bob, I have 14 degrees on Charlie's back."

And if this was not strange enough, it was about to get stranger. After the investigation was over and the film from the television camera was being analyzed, it was discovered that the Night Vision scope had picked up something very strange at the exact same time that the cold chill moved across Charles' back. At the moment that I announced to Bob what was happening with the temperature device, the camera recorded a white, human-looking face that appeared just above his left shoulder! As I mentioned, this film was analyzed closely by the company that created the scope and they had absolutely no explanation for it.

In my opinion, something supernatural occurred that night in Anderson Cemetery. Were there ghosts among us? I don't know, but whatever it was, I have never forgotten it. To this day, the graveyard remains a peculiar and curiously haunted place. The strangeness of the haunting is rivaled only by the fact that it really seems to have no reason to be haunted, and yet it is.

Could this graveyard be a stopping point or "way station" between this world and the next? I have no idea --- but I suppose it is as good an answer as any.

4. HUNTING THE POLTERGEIST

One of the more intriguing aspects of "hauntings" to me has always been the possibility that some paranormal events are created by the human mind. I have been interested in this side of the unexplained for nearly as long as I have been interested in ghosts and spirits. In fact, as you might recall from the first chapter, one of the first actual cases of strange happenings that I followed (at the time it was actually taking place) was the infamous "Columbus Poltergeist" case in 1984. Ever since that time, I have tried to track down accounts of cases like this.

But what are these cases? And what makes them different from a haunting that involves an actual spirit? The word "poltergeist" actually means "noisy ghost" when translated from German and for many years, researchers believed that these noisy ghosts were causing the phenomena reported in cases of a violent and destructive nature. The variety of activity connected with poltergeist cases includes knocking and pounding sounds, disturbance of stationary objects, doors slamming shut and usually violent, physical actions by sometimes heavy objects. Despite what some believe, many cases like this have nothing to do with ghosts.

The most widely accepted theory in many "poltergeist-like" cases is that the activity is not caused by a ghost, but by a person in the household. This person is usually an adolescent girl, and normally one who is troubled emotionally. It is thought that she is unconsciously manipulating the items in the house by "psychokinesis", the power to move things using energy generated in the mind. It is unknown why this ability seems to appear in females around the age of puberty but it has been documented to occur. Most of these disturbances are short-lived because the conditions that cause them to occur often pass quickly. The living person, or "agent" as they are called, subconsciously vents their repressed anger or frustration in a way that science has yet to explain.

My interest with such cases began with the Columbus case but as my research continued, I found cases that were even closer to home and at least one of them went beyond the mere movement of objects. In at least one instance, the bizarre energy that was expended came in another form --- the creation of fire. And this was no ordinary series of fires. They obeyed a different set of physical laws that no one could comprehend at the time. The origin of these fires were not only bizarre --- but terrifying, as well.

The most disturbing poltergeist case that I discovered in my early reading took place in Illinois in 1948, galvanizing the residents of the small town of Macomb. This fire-starter case became so well-known that it appeared in almost every newspaper in the country, often on the front page. The case of the "Macomb Poltergeist" created a mystery that remains unsolved to this day.

In the summer of 1948, a disturbed teenager named Wanet McNeill was forced to live with her father after her parent's bitter divorce. They moved to a farm that belonged to an uncle, Charles Willey, located just south of town. The situation with her father and mother had plunged Wanet into a deep depression. She had been uprooted from her home, school and friends and didn't understand what had occurred between her parents in the divorce. She was very unhappy about being forced to live on the farm, which was very rural compared to her former home in Bloomington, and her emotions were running very high. Soon, those emotions took a dangerous turn and it is believed that, in the weeks that followed her arrival, Wanet somehow managed to start fires all over her uncle's farm. She didn't do those with a box of matches and some oily rags however; it is believed that the fires occurred due to a force from Wanet's mind. She had no idea that she was causing the phenomenon to take place. The kinetic energy in her body inexplicably caused an eruption of power that ignited combustible material all over the house and property.

The mysterious fires began on August 7. The farm where the events took place belonged to Charles Willey and the place was located about 12 miles outside of Macomb. The residents of the farm included Willey, his wife, his brother-in-law and Wanet's father, Arthur McNeil and McNeil's two children, Arthur Jr., 8, and Wanet, who had recently turned 13. As mentioned, McNeil and his wife had recently divorced and contrary to the standard of the day, he had received custody of the children. His former wife was living in Bloomington, where Wanet wanted to be. There is no information available as to what had caused the marriage to end or what may have occurred that would have given McNeil custody of the children. Whatever the situation had been, it had apparently been a volatile one and it had caused a horrible family situation, which the McNeil's brought with them to Macomb.

The first fire began not as a blaze, but as a small brown spot that appeared on the wallpaper in the living room of the Willey farm house. That first spot was followed by another and then another. The spots would appear, spread out several inches as they smoldered and then, when they became hot enough, the spots burst into flames. They occurred day after day, leaving the family confused and befuddled. They searched for some cause for the fires, thinking that perhaps wiring in the walls was going bad, but they could find no reason for them. Willey called on several of his neighbors to investigate but they were as mystified as he was. However, many of them stayed on the property, crowding into the house and even sleeping on the floor in an attempt to help keep watch over the situation. Pans and buckets were filled with water and placed all over the house and each time one of the small fires broke out, it was quickly dowsed.

In spite of this, fires materialized right in front of the startled witnesses. As word spread, more people came to see what was going on and to offer assistance, if possible. Volunteers stood by with hoses and with buckets of water to put out the blazes. They were quick to extinguish them but no one could come up with a reason as to why they were occurring at all. The fire chief from Macomb, Fred Wilson, was called in to investigate. He was just as perplexed as everyone else but he did have some ideas that he believed could help the situation. Wilson directed the family to strip the wallpaper from every wall in the house. Since the brown spots were burning on the wallpaper, he surmised that perhaps it was something in the paper or the glue that held it in place that might be causing the fires to appear. The paper was quickly torn down but then dozens of witnesses, including Chief Wilson, watched as the anomalous brown spots appeared on the bare plaster and again, burst into flames. And then, a new development occurred as small fires began to appear on the ceiling as well.

"The whole thing is so screwy and fantastic that I'm almost ashamed to talk about it," Wilson said. "Yet we have the word of at least a dozen reputable witnesses that say they saw mysterious brown spots smolder suddenly on the walls and ceilings of the home and then burst into flames."

In the days that followed, fires also appeared outside of the house on the front porch. Curtains were ignited in several of the rooms, an ironing board burst into flame and a cloth that was lying on a bed burned so hot that it turned into ash. In a bizarre turn though, the bed beneath the scorched cloth was untouched. According to witnesses, the quilt that covered the bed was not even warm. Later on though, the bed itself was completely engulfed by flames -- but the floor beneath it, as well as a nearby rug, was not burned at all.

Chief Wilson was still convinced that the wallpaper in the house was somehow to blame for the fires. He had never seen anything like what was happening on the Willey farm before and this small town firefighter was searching for some sort of explanation that made sense. He sent a sample of the paper to the National Fire Underwriters Laboratory and they reported that the wallpaper had been coated only with flour paste, which was a flame retardant, and that no flammable compound, such as an insect repellant that might contain phosphorus, was present in the material. They had no explanation for what could be causing the fires in the house.

Thanks to the damage that was being done in the house, Charles Willey, understandably, contacted his insurance company. After receiving the filed report, the company immediately sent investigators to the farm, looking for any evidence that Willey, or a member of the family, was starting the fires in an attempt to commit fraud. They could find nothing to suggest that the fires were caused by arson and could provide no explanation for the blazes.

The insurance investigators were not alone. Deputy State Fire Marshal, John Burgard, was contacted by Chief Wilson and he too came to the Willey farm. He was also confused by the strange events. "Nobody has ever heard anything like this," he announced to the press, "but I saw it with my own eyes".

In the week that followed, more than 200 fires broke out at the house, an average of nearly 20 each day. Finally, on Saturday, August 14, one of the blazes raged out of control and before the Macomb fire department could be summoned with trucks, the entire Willey farm house was consumed. Charles Willey drove posts into the ground and made a tent shelter for he and his wife, while McNeil and the children moved into the garage. The next day, while the Willey's were milking cows in the barnyard, the barn burst into flames and destroyed the building. Willey, already distraught, was now shattered. He had only $1,000 insurance on the house and $400 on the barn. Neither policy would come close to replacing the buildings. To make matters worse, at this point, the insurance company was still unwilling to pay even those small amounts. Their investigators were still perplexed about the cause of the fires but believed that further investigations might reveal the source.

Two days later, on Tuesday, several fires broke out on the walls of the milk house, which was being used as a kitchen and dining room for the family. On Thursday morning, there were two more fires and a box that was filled with newspapers was found burning in the chicken house. A few minutes later, Mrs. Willey opened a cupboard door in the milk house and discovered more newspapers smoldering on a shelf inside. There had been no one else in the building and the cabinet had not been opened. There was no logical reason for the newspapers to have caught fire.

Later that day, at about 6:00 p.m., the farm's second barn caught fire. The blaze burned so hot that the entire building was destroyed in less than a half hour. Firefighters who arrived on the scene were unable to get close to the inferno. A company that sold fire extinguishers was on hand with equipment, but it did little good. An employee of the company stated that "it was the most intense heat that I've ever felt."

Only six small outhouses remained on the farm, so the family escaped to a nearby vacant house. Regardless, the fires continued. The United States Air Force even got involved in the mystery. They suggested that the fires could be caused by some sort of directed radiation, presumably from the Russians, but could offer no further assistance. Lewis Gust, the chief technician at Wright Field, Ohio, sent an expert to the farm to test for "very high frequencies and short waves". He thought the fires might be related to several unsolved airplane fires in which radiation was suspected of playing a part. The Russians were believed to be the culprits. "We can't afford to take any chances," he told reporters. "We must test anything, even if it sounds a bit far-fetched. Suppose you had material that could be ignited by radio and wanted to test it for sabotage value. Wouldn't you pick some out of the way place like the Willey farm to make the test?"

Gust explained that scientists believed that powerful, high-frequency or extremely short radio waves could cause fires to start. For example, radar waves set off photographic flash bulbs inside of airplanes that were in flight. An interview with an unnamed scientist in Chicago confirmed these theories and agreed that radioactivity or radio waves could cause "such disturbances" but also added that it was "highly unlikely because there had been no other reactions in the area". If Russian spies were shooting radio waves at the Willey farm, it would have been impossible, the scientist noted, to direct them in such a way that no other homes or farms near Macomb would be affected.

By the end of the following week, the farm was swarming with spectators, curiosity-seekers, official and self-appointed investigators, and reporters. Over 1,000 people came to the farm on August 22 alone! Theorists and curiosity-seekers posed their own theories and explanations. They ran the gamut from fly spray to radio waves, underground gas pockets, flying saucers and more. The authorities had a more down-to-earth explanation in mind. They suspected arson. They realized that they could not solve the riddle as to how fires could appear before the eyes of reliable witnesses, but things were getting out of hand on the Willey farm. An explanation needed to be discovered, and quickly.

Two investigators noted that there seemed to be a difference between the fires in the house and the later blazes. Professor John J, Ahern, from the Illinois Institute of Technology, suggested that combustible gases inside of the walls might have caused the house fires, while those fires that destroyed the barns seemed to spring from "other causes". State Fire Marshal John Craig said that the burning of the house "looked like an accident" but that the barn fires might have been "touched off by an arsonist." This was enough for some of the officials involved. They overlooked the mysterious nature of the fires and heard only the fact that some of the fires might have been started by arson. There was no conclusive evidence of this but the case had to be closed as soon as possible.

On August 30, the mystery was publicly announced "solved". The arsonist, according to officials, was Wanet McNeil, the slight, red-haired niece of Charles Willey. They claimed that she was starting the fires with kitchen matches when no one was looking, ignoring the witness reports of fires that sprang up from nowhere, including on the ceiling. Apparently, this little girl possessed some pretty amazing skills, along with a seemingly endless supply of matches.

According to Deputy Fire Marshal Burgard, there had been a minor fire at the farm house where the family had moved after the other buildings had been destroyed. He had placed a box of matches in a certain position and the box had been moved. Wanet was nearby --- but she was never seen touching the box or holding a match. This didn't matter however. Burgard and State's Attorney Keith Scott had taken Wanet aside for an hour's worth of "intense questioning". After that, she had allegedly confessed. She stated that she was unhappy, didn't like the farm, wanted to see her mother and, most telling, that she didn't have pretty clothes. The mystery was solved! This was in spite of the fact that witnesses to the fires had seen them appear on walls, floors and furniture ---- all when Wanet was not even in the room.

This explanation pleased the authorities but not all of the reporters who were present seemed convinced. The hundreds of paranormal investigators who have examined the case over the years have not been reassured either. One columnist from a Peoria newspaper, who had covered the case from the beginning, stated quite frankly that he did not believe the so-called "confession". Neither did noted researcher of the unexplained Vincent Gaddis, who wrote about the case. He was convinced the case was a perfect example of poltergeist phenomena.

He noted that many poltergeist cases made it necessary to figuratively --- and sometimes actually --- slap little girls into "confession". In many cases, there is no doubt about the paranormal nature of these manifestations and yet there is a general prejudice against real mystery. Perhaps it is a fear of the unknown that demands explanation. And so, no matter how incredible the phenomena, no matter how impossible it would be for a person to produce the phenomena by trickery, we have "confessions". The agent, not realizing consciously that she is causing the phenomena, seems, at times, to have a sense of guilt or perhaps even some small awareness of their part in the matter. Such agents can be pressured into a confession, despite the fact that the events could not have been caused by normal means.

Irritated investigators and worried parents occasionally use force to get confessions and the history of poltergeist manifestations is riddled with examples of boys being whipped and girls slapped. In other cases, the agent may be told to reproduce the phenomena by paranormal means or confess that it was fraudulent. Frantic, some may resort to crude trickery, only to be caught, or may simply make a false confession. And these false confessions occur much more commonly than people outside the field of psychology realize, according to experts. Dr. Ian Stevenson, from the University of Virginia School of Medicine, stated that "a vague impression of guilt about something often suffices to motivate a false confession. Innocent persons have frequently confessed to serious crimes like murder, sometimes implicating innocent persons as accomplices..."

For just this reason, confessions in poltergeist cases are often worthless unless they can include an explanation for how the manifestations were accomplished that is reasonable, practical and fits the known facts. In the case of the "Macomb Fire Starter", the confession certainly didn't fit the facts but by the time it came, people were too worried, tired and traumatized to care.

What really happened on the Willey Farm? We will probably never know because the story just went away after that. Wanet was taken to Chicago for examination at the Illinois Juvenile Hospital but was found to be mentally normal by Dr. Sophie Schroeder, a psychiatrist. "She's a nice little kid caught in the middle of a broken home," she reported. She was later turned over to her grandmother and spent the rest of her teenage years untroubled by mysterious brown spots that appeared, spread and burst into flames.

The insurance company paid Willey for the damage done to his home and farm and the farm house was later rebuilt. Arthur McNeil and his son moved back in with the Willey's for a time before eventually moving out of state.

Fire officials abandoned the case after the "confession" cleared up the mystery for them but privately, many of those involved continued to question what really occurred on the Willey farm for years afterward. Fire Chief Fred Wilson talked about the case for quite some time and later retired from his position convinced that something unexplainable had taken place.

The reporters who descended on the Willey farm all received closure for the stories, whether they believed the conclusion or not, and the general public was given a solution that could not have possibly been the truth. Not surprisingly, the case is still listed as "unexplained" today.

The Alton Poltergeist & Others

My own personal experiences with poltergeist cases have been varied and often frustrating. As time passed, and I became more involved in paranormal investigations, I received many phone calls from people who believed their homes were haunted. It's quite possible that some of them may have been, although as any ghost researcher knows, not every house is active all the time. Despite the many false alarms and natural explanations that I investigated, there were also the cases where I truly believed the accounts of the witnesses, even though I experienced nothing at the location for myself. There were many cases where the occupants of the house simply had no reason to lie. They did not want publicity. They did not want their story to appear in a book with their names attached to it. They simply feared their house was haunted and called me to confirm --- or to debunk --- the activity they believed they were experiencing.

Many of the cases seemed to point toward poltergeist-like activity, but this was very hard to confirm and, as mentioned, frustrating as well. My frustration with these cases mostly stemmed from coming into such cases "after the fact". There has only been one case where I was actually present when the strange events were still occurring. At other times, I arrived as the outbreak was coming to an end.

In 1999, I was contacted about an apartment that was shared by four female college students at a small Illinois university. They explained to me that weird events had been occurring for several months but by the time I arrived, they had become less frequent. After interviewing the young women, we deduced that the height of the outbreak had occurred during the most stressful time of the year, which was semester exams, and had actually started at the same time that one of them was going through a bad breakup with a boyfriend. By the time we were finished talking, even the young women were theorizing that it had been their own stress that was responsible for the activity. This did not make the phenomena any less unnerving, though, as they told of breaking glasses, slamming doors and cabinets and shower items that were constantly flying around the bathroom. As with other cases of this type, though, it did not last long.

In 2001, I got involved in another memorable case, which I have dubbed the "Alton Poltergeist". Once again, I never really saw any of what was reported for myself --- but I did believe that what the witnesses claimed really did take place.

The activity began in August 2001, although I did not get involved in the case until August 20, about a week after the outbreak began. The family, who I will refer to as "Smith" for the sake of this narrative, lived in a nice home in a historic part of Alton, Illinois. The house, although it had little bearing on the case, was located on the river bluff, a number of blocks from where the old

Alton prison was once located. I received a telephone call from Mrs. Smith on August 18 and she explained to me that she believed her house was haunted.

According to her report, a number of strange events had occurred. Beginning on the night of August 14, Mrs. Smith, along with her husband and two children, began to hear knocking sounds that seemed to come from the walls of the house. They could find no source for the noises, even though they searched extensively for loose boards, an open door and even something outside blowing in the wind. The knocking sounds continued the next day and were accompanied by objects that moved under their own power.

The first incident of this occurred in the kitchen. The family was in the living room, watching television, when they heard a loud "clinking and jingling" noise in the other room. When Mrs. Smith went into the kitchen to see what it was, she discovered that a cabinet drawer had opened and silverware that was once inside had now been scattered on the counter. When she asked if someone had placed it there, the other members of the family denied it. A short time later, another sound was heard in the kitchen (more clinking, but this time a different type) and ended with the additional sound of breaking glass. This drew the attention of the entire family and when they entered the kitchen, they found an upper cabinet door standing open and a shattered glass on the floor. The other glasses that remained in the cabinet looked as though they had been shuffled around. The broken glass apparently slipped off the edge during the shuffling. Mrs. Smith stated emphatically that no one had been in the kitchen at the time and that the back door had been locked.

On August 15, the family was awakened in the early morning hours to the sounds of doors slamming. Mr. Smith immediately got out of bed to see if the house had been broken into, but the place was empty. The doors that had been slamming were apparently located on the second floor. The Smiths told me that they and the children had all been asleep at the time of the commotion. Later on that morning, lights in the living room began turning on and off by themselves. Mrs. Smith said that whenever she would turn a light off, it would immediately come back on again. Eventually, she unplugged the lamps but the overhead light continued to switch on and off for about 45 minutes. She eventually called her brother-in-law (who is an electrician) to come over to look at the problem. By the time he arrived, the lights were no longer behaving erratically and he could find no reason why they would have acted in the way that they did.

On August 16, they reported that the doors began opening and closing again and this time, lights in the dining room began to turn on and off. The overhead light in this room was attached to a ceiling fan and the fan itself also began to turn without being switched on. When Mr. Smith attempted to turn it off, it changed speeds instead and refused to stop moving. Later on that evening, a large cabinet in the dining room, which was filled with extra dishes, glassware and party silverware, apparently fell over by itself. A number of the items inside were destroyed. Mrs. Smith told me that no one else was in the room at the time.

On August 17, the activity seemed to peak with reports of more slamming doors, a number of items that vanished and then reappeared elsewhere a few hours later and an incident with the refrigerator. During lunch, Mrs. Smith and the two children were in the kitchen when they heard a loud "thumping" noise that came from the refrigerator. When they opened the door, a number of jars, plastic containers and loose food came spilling out onto the floor. The noise had apparently been the sound of all of these items as they flew forward against the closed door. When the door was opened, they fell onto the floor. I had to agree with Mrs. Smith when she told me that there was no way that anyone could have manipulated these items from inside of the closed refrigerator. Later on that evening, three drinking glasses that were sitting on the dining room table flew off onto the floor and two of them were shattered.

By the time that I received a call from the Smiths on August 18, the activity was much quieter. That morning, Mrs. Smith told me that the knocking sounds had been heard again, but that was all. Unfortunately, I was tied up that weekend and was not able to make it to the Smith house until Monday, August 20. At that point, I was able to meet the entire family (except for Mr. Smith, who was at work) and to view some of the wreckage from the reported events.

The Smiths' two children were "Danny" (age 9) and "Amanda" (14). Both seemed to be well adjusted and polite and took great pains to show me around the house and to take me into the dining room, where the remnants of the broken dishes from the cabinet had been stacked. The cabinet had been left on its side and most of the dishes remained where they had fallen. I took a look at the mess and while the cabinet was not so heavy that it could not have been moved, it was unlikely to have fallen over because of any vibrations or shifts in the house. I also examined the cabinets in the kitchen, where the silverware had been moved and where the drinking glass had fallen. I noted that the cabinet had no noticeable tilt to it and Mrs. Smith assured me that nothing like that had ever happened before. As for the refrigerator, it had already been cleaned up, although stains from jelly and other food items could be seen on the small rug that had been placed in front of the appliance. The rug appeared to have been laundered, but some stains still remained.

The family also took me upstairs and showed me the doors that had been opening and closing on their own. I looked for possible window drafts and tried swinging the doors back and forth to see if they would slam or not. I didn't have any luck. Checking a hunch, I also used a carpenter's level to see if there was any pitch to the floor of the old house. As far as I could tell, the floor did not lean in such a way that it would have caused the doors to act in a way that the Smith's reported. I asked them if there had been any further activity after the knocking sounds on August 18, but they told me that there had been nothing. Whatever had been causing the strange events was now apparently quiet.

Since the activity had no real pattern as to when it occurred, I couldn't really plan a time to return to the house to try and observe it. However, I promised to come back that night and visit with the family some more and hopefully have a chance to see what had been occurring for myself. In the meantime, I went down to the library to see if I could track down any history about the house. If it was haunted, there might be some clue in the past as to why the weird events were taking place. This search turned up nothing, though.

Later on that evening, I returned to the house to hear that nothing further had occurred. They asked me if I thought the house might be haunted. Having no way to answer that for sure, but suspecting that poltergeist-like activity might be involved, I asked if I might speak to everyone in the household individually so that I could get their personal take on the odd outbreak. The family quickly agreed.

I spoke to Mr. And Mrs. Smith first and they went back over the happenings that had started the week before. As I stated earlier, I had no reason to believe that they were lying. I had seen the evidence of the events in the house and I did not feel that the Smiths had any reason to stage the broken china and glasses for me to find. Their account was convincing and it was obvious that they were upset by what had happened. Mrs. Smith in particular was convinced that the house was haunted by a ghost, even though they had been living there for nearly three years and had never experienced anything like this before.

My interviews with the children turned out to be more revealing, especially my interview with Amanda. I spoke to Danny first and asked him point blank if he believed the house was haunted and if not, what did he think was going on? I had already gotten the impression that he was a smart kid, especially for being nine years-old, and had not ruled out the idea that he could (in some way) have been behind the activity. I had a feeling that he could be mischievous when he wanted to be but even so, I was hard pressed to figure out how he could have been behind what was going on. Danny told me that he also believed there might be a ghost in the house because he had no other way to explain the weird things that were happening. Was he scared by it? No, he told me, he was not scared but he did think that it was awfully strange.

After that, I sat down with Amanda and asked her for her thoughts on the happenings in the house. Like her brother and her mother, she also felt that perhaps a ghost was causing the events to take place but it was the other comments that she made to me that seemed to shed more light on the mystery. She said that the slamming doors, and the general nervousness caused by the other events, was making her lose sleep at night. She explained that she was having enough trouble sleeping already because she was getting ready to start high school in just a few days. She was very worried about the adjustment that she had to make going from middle school to high school and having these events occurring in the house was making her even more upset than she already was.

I wasn't sure how to explain to her that I believed that her stress was causing the events to occur in the first place! The more upset that she got about it, the worse the events became until they finally peaked at the end of the previous week. That was my theory in the case anyway, although I was unable to gather any real evidence of it since the events had come to an end before I was closely involved. The best that I could really do was to gather the materials that I already had and make the best suppositions possible.

Regardless, the activity had come to an end by this time and I mentioned what could have been the reason behind it to the Smiths as I wrapped things up. Surprisingly (and this is not always the case!), they were open to the idea and seemed relieved that I did not think the house was "haunted" in the traditional sense. It was only a theory, created after the fact, I told them, but it was certainly a possibility. And perhaps it was right. I kept in touch with the Smiths for several years after the events and there was no repeat of the weird happenings --- and yes, Amanda continued to do quite well in school.

The Christine M. Poltergeist Case

During the years that I have been hunting and investigating poltergeists, there has only been one case where I have been present when the weird activity occurred. Even in this case, though, I found myself wishing that I had done things differently than I did.

In 1997, I got involved in the case of a young woman that I have since referred to as "Christine M.". The home where she and her mother lived became the first, and possibly most active, human agent poltergeist case that I ever got involved with. In the case of "Christine M.", I believe that the outbreak in the home was genuine, not only because of the eyewitness accounts of the witnesses but because I saw some of it myself. To this day, I cannot explain what I saw and heard in that house.

This case could almost be described as "textbook" when compared to many of the other cases that I had read about. Remember that, at the time, my only knowledge of cases like this were from what I had been able to glean from the writings of researchers like Dr. William Roll, Loyd Auerbach and D. Scott Rogo. My information was all second-hand but I went into the case with my eyes wide open. I discovered then what I would find repeated in cases in the future --- that human agents in the case usually suspect their house is haunted before they suspect that they might be the cause of the activity they experienced.

This is what occurred in Christine's case. She contacted me because she believed her house was haunted. She told me of a wide variety of weird phenomena that was taking place like knocking sounds, lights turning on and off, doors slamming, cabinets opening and closing, windows breaking and other destructive happenings. Because she was under 18 at the time, I contacted her mother about the location and she assured me that the events described were actually taking place. She also agreed that an investigation might be in order.

During this initial interview, I asked her about the history of the location and if she had any thoughts on why the phenomena was taking place. I also asked how long it had been going on. Her answer surprised me. She explained the phenomena had started just two years before, when Christine had gotten pregnant at age 15. She was very upset at the time and became so depressed, and so anxious, that her mother had taken her to see a therapist. She stopped going, however, and the weird activity began a short time later. While Christine believed that the house was haunted, her mother (who had no experience or interest in the paranormal) believed that her daughter was somehow causing the things to happen.

With the home owner's permission, I began a series of five in-depth investigations of the house. These investigations were the first that I had ever conducted of this sort of activity but I feel that I learned a lot from it, including what not to do! In the *Ghost Hunter's Guidebook*, I put together an entire section on "ghost watching" during a poltergeist investigation. Much of what went into that article came from what I learned during this case.

My interviews with Christine and her mother collected numerous accounts of the activity that was taking place. The events began one night when Christine was laying on the living room floor watching television. The living room was the largest room on the first floor and when I visited the house, it contained a couch, some chairs, a table and a large piano. There were three doors leading into the room. They led to a spare room, a screened porch and to the kitchen. As she and her mother were watching television, the piano began to loudly play by itself.

Not long after that, things began to escalate. Soon, doors began to open and close by themselves, windows broke inside of empty rooms and the sounds of knocking and footsteps began to be heard, usually on the upper floor of the house when no one was present. Lights turned on and off, radios turned on and off and the volume of the television would often raise and lower without assistance. The footsteps and noises from upstairs became so bad that Christine insisted that her mother put a padlock on the door leading to the second floor. She remained convinced, even after my initial visit and after her mother's insistence otherwise, that the house was haunted by ghosts.

Not surprisingly, the events in the house did not convince her that she was wrong. The strangest event that reportedly occurred (and I did not witness this for myself) was when Christine's sister ended up with a horrible bite mark on the back side of her upper arm. There were no pets in the house and no way that the girl could have managed to bite herself in such an area of her body. I don't think that it was any coincidence that the bite mark appeared just shortly after Christine and her sister had an argument. It should be noted that the argument was not a violent one. Christine did not bite her sister. During the conflict, though, the mysterious bite somehow appeared.

As you can imagine, I was having some reservations about the house being infested by spirits at this point, especially since her mother again told me that she was convinced that the activity centered around Christine. However, the young woman insisted that the house *was* haunted and would only agree to the investigations that I had planned if we would proceed as if ghosts were actually in the house. I reluctantly agreed and the five investigations began.

Most of the time, things were fairly quiet, including the two uneventful investigations that were conducted when Christine was removed from the house. When she was not present, there was absolutely no sign of any activity at all. However, on two occasions, I was present when violent phenomena occurred and I was also present when one of the other investigators snapped a photograph of a bright ball of light in the downstairs hallway. According to his account, the light was actually coming down the hallway, literally following Christine's little boy, who was two years-old at the time. I was in the kitchen with Christine when this occurred but I did see the resulting photograph, which shows a glowing light (apparently in motion), just a foot or two behind the boy as he is running into the living room.

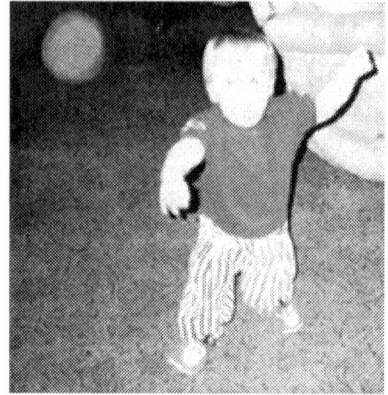

(Right) The photograph taken by one of the investigators in the Christine M. Case. He actually observed this light following the little boy down the hallway and managed to snap this photo of it.

One evening, Christine, her mother, three other investigators and myself clearly heard what seemed to be someone banging loudly on the walls of the second floor of the house. There was no one else present at the time but the sounds really seemed to be made by a person upstairs, walking down the hallway and hitting the walls with his fists. Christine's mother told me that these were exactly the sorts of sounds that they had become used to over the past number of months. Unsure of what else to do, I ran up the stairs to see if anyone else was there. I was certain that we were alone in the house --- but I had to make sure. The downstairs door, as mentioned, had been padlocked, so Mrs. M. had to open it for me and I hurried up the staircase with another one of the investigators in tow. The pounding noises had stopped by the time we reached the upper floor, but if anyone had been there, we would have found them. Instead, we discovered the hallway and the rooms to be dark, quiet and empty.

During another investigation, on a separate night, I saw two cabinet doors actually shut under their own power. The incident occurred while I was in the living room with Christine, her mother and one other investigator. As we were sitting and talking, we began to hear a repeated rapping sound coming from the kitchen. It began to increase in volume until it started to sound like someone rapidly hammering on a wooden surface. The first sound was joined by a second and then a third. Each of the sounds was identical and my first thought was that it sounded just like someone slamming a cabinet door closed. Since it was coming from the kitchen, this was not a far-fetched idea, expect for the fact that no one was in the other room!

Just as I had done when we heard mysterious sounds upstairs, I ran for the kitchen as quickly as possible. The two rooms were separated by an open doorway, a little wider than usual, and curved into an arch. Hurrying from the carpeted floor and onto the linoleum floor of the kitchen, I slipped just as I was going under the archway. I stumbled but didn't fall and was able to look up quickly enough to see two of the cabinet doors waving back and forth and cracking against the wooden frame. The movement ceased almost immediately as I came into the room but it was certainly the first time that I had ever seen "paranormal movement" during an investigation.

Over the next several weeks, the activity in the house continued but it did begin to decrease after two months. Thanks to the relentless and intrusive interviews that I conducted with Christine, and the fact that we conducted the two completely uneventful investigations with the girl removed from the house, I felt that we could determine that the cause of the haunting was indeed Christine.

Eventually, her mother and I were able to get her to agree with these findings and she returned to the therapist. Not surprisingly, the phenomena ceased completely soon after and to this date, nothing else has occurred at her home. She is now happily married and no longer bothered by any strange activity.

5. "HAUNTED" HALLWAYS, "MYSTERIOUS" FOOTSTEPS AND WHEN THE LIVING ARE SCARIER THAN THE DEAD

Although no one has ever asked me this, I am sure that there are those readers out there who question how I am qualified to produce books like the *Ghost Hunter's Guidebook* and to school others in the best ways to conduct paranormal investigations. I can only reply to that by saying that I have based my writings and instructions on past experiences and have learned many things the hard way --- as you have already seen in this book and will learn more about in the pages that follow. It's been a strange trip from ghost enthusiast to ghost hunter and there have been many weird stops along the way.

In spite of all of that, though, I continue to maintain that there are no "experts" when it comes to the paranormal. I certainly do not claim to be one myself. I simply pass along the information that I have learned to other enthusiasts and investigators and hope that all of these readers might be able to learn something from the successes and failures that I have taken part in.

The pages that follow will provide anecdotes from not only some of my "questionable" experiences but some of my early dealings with the media, as well. Even so, they only scratch the surface of all of the places that I have gone to over the last decade or so. I have been fortunate enough to conduct literally dozens and dozens of investigations over the years but as mentioned before, so many of them were uneventful that there is no reason for their inclusion here. Instead of page after page of sitting around waiting for something to happen, I thought this chapter was best served by including some of my favorite "disasters".

As you will soon see, whoever first said that "if something can go wrong, it will" must have been talking about investigating the supernatural!

The Living Can Sometimes Be Scarier than the Dead

One of the things that I have been stressing for a long time is to suggest to those who contact you about their "haunted house" that there might be a natural explanation for their "ghost". When I am speaking to someone who has called me, I like to suggest some non-paranormal reasons for what might be occurring and then wait to see how the witness replies. In one case, I actually had someone suddenly realize what was causing the "strange sounds" after I made one such suggestion. Everyone laughs a little in embarrassment but it saves you from going out on a "wild ghost chase".

Once again, I learned to do this the hard way. The anecdote that I am about to relate to you will seem silly to experienced ghost hunters, but keep in mind that I really didn't have any sort of pattern to base my early investigations on. There was no blueprint to follow. I was so excited that someone had actually called me that I would literally go out and investigate anything.

I received a call from a woman one day who was convinced that her house was haunted. She wanted me to come there and do an investigation and if possible, suggest someone who might be able to get rid of the ghost. I told her that I would come but, of course, I had no interest in getting rid of any ghosts before I got there! I told her that if the house was indeed haunted, we would see what we could do to help from there.

What was going on that led her to believe the house was haunted? She explained that she and her husband had been experiencing lights turning on and off by themselves, appliances that would suddenly stop running, a television set that would immediately switch off under its own power and more. Well, that certainly sounded like a ghost to me in those days and I made plans with her to come and do an investigation the next week. Did I mention that this woman lived about four hours away from me?

Anyway, I packed up all of my gear the following Monday and drove up north to the woman's home. I found it on the edge of a small town in northern Illinois and was warmly greeted by the caller at the door. We went into the house and I took a quick look around. I estimated that the house had been built some time in the late 1930s or early 1940s, giving it ample time to have gathered a dark history of death, murder or suicide to explain why it was so haunted today!

I was taken on a brief tour of the house, which ended in the basement. It was here that I realized my first mistake. While looking in the utility room, I glimpsed the electrical box that was mounted on the wall. The dented metal door hung open at an angle so it was easy for me to blow off some dust and push the door open a little wider with my finger. The fuse box had obviously been installed at the time the house was built and had never been replaced or updated. The wiring was stripped and so old that they don't even make that kind of insulation anymore. Gee, I wonder why the lights would turn on and off by themselves?

It was shortly after we went upstairs to the kitchen that I realized my fatal mistake, though, and I have never again traveled to do an investigation without talking in-depth to the witness before agreeing to make the trip --- even if it's just across town. We sat down at the kitchen table and I took my tape recorder from my pack, prepared to document all of the activity that the witness had already hinted at. I confess that I did have some doubts about the happenings after seeing the electrical box but I was willing to put aside my doubts and listen.

That ended after my first question though.

I asked the witness: "So, what makes you feel that the house is haunted?"

She explained: "Well, after the lights starting turning on and off, I decided to call a telephone psychic and ask why it was happening. He told me that he sensed a presence in the house and so I decided to call you."

And that was the end of that.

Many readers may be surprised to learn that it isn't always necessary to immediately visit even an active site. I often get calls from people whose "ghost" is easily solved over the telephone as a natural event, or perhaps the activity they are describing occurred only one time and has never been seen or heard since. In a situation like this, it is best for you to suggest that the witness keep a "journal" or a "logbook" of any activity. Then, leave it up to them to call you back and keep you updated about any new activity.

I learned this after making several visits to allegedly haunted houses and finding out that the haunting was limited to either a few times a month or worse, once or twice a year. As you can imagine, this makes it awfully hard to check out anything unusual that might be going on!

Perhaps my hardest lesson of this type learned occurred several years ago when I was traveling in Maryland. In addition to visiting a number of historical haunted sites, a friend also made arrangements for me to visit a house that was currently active. I had spoken to the owner on the telephone prior to the trip and she gave me the rundown on the activity that was occurring. According to the ongoing history of the house, there was a woman in white who often appeared in the formal dining room, doors refused to remain locked, beds unmade themselves and occasionally, the voices of children could be heard coming from the grounds outside of the house. Please note that I reported that the woman in white appeared "often", or so I was told. I only wish that the owner of the house had told me in advance what she meant by "often". There had been repeated sightings of the woman and she actually had a list of 25 of them. The problem was that the 25 sightings had occurred over a period of 152 years!

Another important thing to try and determine with the initial interview is whether or not the witness is (and how do I say this delicately?) "stable" or not. Believe me when I say that I am not trying to be cruel or humorous with this warning because I can speak from painful experience when it comes to this. Nearly every experienced investigator has run into a situation of being contacted by someone is not in complete control of their mental faculties. In fact, at one time I was being repeatedly contacted by someone who claimed that a "giant ghost with teeth the size of a shark's" was flying about his house and "biting the heads off other ghosts". Who was I to say this wasn't actually happening, but let's just that I had some serious doubts!

It can happen that your witness may be mentally unstable. This does occur, and more frequently than most researchers would care to admit. I have been called to houses where the residents are just plain "nuts". Obviously, we are not health care workers, so there is little we can do in this situation but try to extricate ourselves from the predicament as politely as possible.

I once went on an investigation for a man who lived alone in a small house in central Illinois. I would love to come up with a polite way of describing the place, but honestly, I can't. The house was absolutely filthy and smelled so bad that my eyes started to water when I walked in the door. There was clothing, newspapers and magazines scattered all over the front room, along with pizza boxes, take-out containers and worse. The carpeting had likely not been vacuumed in years and if possible, the kitchen was even worse than the rest of the place. Imagine your worst housekeeping nightmares --- then multiply them by 10! The sink was filled with dirty dishes, garbage overflowed onto the floor and there were dead cockroaches all over the place. It was as if things were so bad in the house that even they could not survive!

The owner of the house was a large, overweight, unkempt (obviously!) man who had called me several times to explain that his basement was haunted. He reported that he often heard footsteps going up and down the stairs that descended from the kitchen and that a shower in the basement would often turn on by itself. (If the house really was haunted, perhaps the ghost was trying to tell him something!)

It didn't take much for me to realize that the home owner was not mentally stable. The house in general was enough for me to see that, but his rambling speech and unnerving manner bothered me even more. He had actually sounded pretty convincing on the phone, but I had apparently needed to talk with him for a little while longer. This was one lesson that I learned from this outing but the second lesson reinforced the idea that I should never go out on an investigation alone! I am not a small person and am not easily intimidated by others, but this guy gave me the creeps!

When he began to insist that I go down to the basement with him and look for the ghost, I hastily explained that I had not brought enough equipment with me to do the investigation. I had forgotten one of my bags, I told him, and would have to go and get it. As he continued to try and get me to "just come down and take a look", I began to get a little more nervous and imagine that I made a less than graceful exit from the house.

I'm sure that it won't come as a surprise to the reader to learn that I made it a point not to return to that "haunted house".

A witness may deliberately fabricate events too and not because of any mental problems. This is a two-fold problem. On one hand you have a person who has made the whole thing up and on the other, a person who actually had a real experience, but can't recall all of the details, so they have "filled in the blanks" with less honest information.

In 1997, I got involved in the investigation of a private residence that had been converted over from a small country church. It was a little strange to arrive there and enter the sanctuary doors to find that someone's living room was located in the space were parishioners used to sit, with a big-screen television in place of a pulpit. Some would say that it should have been no surprise to discover that a former church was haunted in some way. I have run across a number of churches that have become residually haunted over the years, mostly thanks to the amount of energy expended in these locations. According to the owner of this former church, this was apparently occurring in his new home. But in addition to the sounds of voices, music, bells and whispers that would filter through the building after dark, he also claimed that he had seen figures in black and had felt ice cold hands touch him while in bed. One night, his fiancée became so frightened by an image that she saw that she ran out of the house in the early morning hours!

The place certainly seemed promising and while the initial investigations didn't turn up much as far as evidence went, we were able to document some pretty bizarre accounts. One investigator also snapped an infrared photo of a bright white light that zipped along the outer wall of the building. It would be this photo that would lead to confusion with the case.

Apparently, the home owner (who seemed to have a vested interest in the house being haunted --- he later turned up on the local television news) became concerned that we would lose interest in his house if the activity that we were able to record was outside, instead of inside. This led to him informing us that he had been told by the church officials, from whom he had purchased the building, that a cemetery had once also been located on the grounds. He said that local rumor had it that the gravestones had been removed when the church left but the bodies had been left behind. He explained that this was what he believed led the church and the grounds to become haunted.

As the reader might imagine, this new piece of information sparked our interest and we began to consider the idea that we might have an active, full-blown haunting on our hands. For the next two weeks, I spent quite a few hours at libraries in the area looking for information about this church. What I discovered was that there had been no cemetery on the grounds and I also spoke with one of the former church officials, who assured me that even if there had been, they certainly would not have left the deceased behind. When I took the information to the home owner and confronted him with what I had found out, he admitted that he had lied about "that part of the story". He was worried that since our first investigation hadn't really turned up anything concrete that we might become disinterested in the spot and not return.

In the end, it turned out that he was right. We did not return, but it was not because we were not interested in the case. It was because we now had no idea what part of his story was truth --- and what part was fiction.

"Mysterious" Footsteps in a "Haunted House"

Another thing that I have learned is that you should always try to be open-minded, but optimistically skeptical with dealing with witnesses and locations. Depending on the person, they may be looking for reassurance that they are not "crazy" and that their experience has a logical explanation, even a strange one. You must start out by trying to prove that the situation is not a ghost. You don't want to listen to their story and jump to the conclusion that it is! People who are scared might misinterpret natural events as supernatural ones and you have to be careful not to encourage the witness until you have actually investigated the location.

Even worse, you have to be careful not to get too involved in their story that you start believing it yourself!

One of the most embarrassing incidents of the time that I have been hunting ghosts happened in the summer of 1998. I had recently moved from Decatur to Alton, Illinois and I was contacted about a possible haunted house in Missouri. According to the home owner, she and her daughter regularly witnessed a phenomenon that occurred on the second floor of their house. It seemed that, on an almost nightly basis, a ghost walked down the upstairs hallway! Needless to say, there was no way that I wanted to pass up an opportunity like this and even though she related to me that they had never seen the ghost, they always heard its footsteps as it paced the length of the hallway and disappeared. It's rare for a ghost hunter to ever have an almost *guaranteed* opportunity to experience a haunting, so I immediately made plans to come over to her house the following night.

I arrived late in the evening since she told me that the ghost usually took its nightly walk around 9:30 p.m. or so. The home was located just outside of the city of St. Louis and was a narrow, older home with two stories and rather small rooms inside. The owner let me in through the front door, which opened into the living room. Beyond that was a kitchen, a small bathroom, a utility room and pantry and a small bedroom at the back of the house that was used by the owner's daughter. Upstairs was another bathroom, the master bedroom and a smaller bedroom that had been converted into a home office. A staircase led upstairs from a short hall that was located between the living room and the kitchen. There was a blank wall at the top of the staircase and the hallway was accessed by turning left and then right again. There were three doorways and a closet that opened off the corridor. The master bedroom was to the left side and the doors to the bathroom and the office were on the right. The hallway was lit only by a wall sconce but it was bright enough to see a hardwood floor that was covered by a long and narrow decorative rug. It was along this hallway, starting at the top of the stairs and running to the window at the end, where the phantom footsteps were always heard.

Behind where we were standing at the head of the hallway, and next to the staircase, was a small couch that had been tucked into the corner. It was here where we sat and waited for the performance to come. Keep in mind that at this point in the evening, I was still more than a little skeptical about the "walking ghost". It ran against everything that I had already learned to think that a specter would be so easily found. Regardless, I kept an eye on my watch and moments later, my previous doubts went right out the window.

At exactly 9:37 p.m., the sound of what seemed to be a hard-soled shoe tapped against the wooden floor just a few inches from where we were sitting. I jumped a little in my seat --- that's how precise and clear the sound was. The first tapping sound was quickly followed by another and then another, tracing a line all of the way down the corridor. When they reached the end, the sounds stopped. Previously skeptical or not, I couldn't believe what I had just experienced! There seemed to be no mistaking the fact that what I heard had clearly been the sound of heavy footsteps as they traveled down the hall. All that I could think of at this point was to come back again the following evening --- and to bring equipment and other investigators with me this time!

I returned again the following evening with cameras, recorders, motion detectors and EMF meters, as well as with two other investigators and their own gear. We arrived much earlier this time, around 7:30 p.m., and proceeded to "wire" the hallway for anything that might happen. Infrared motion detectors were placed at intervals in the corridor, as well as EMF meters, and we placed a video camera at either end of the hall. Just shortly after 9:00 p.m., we turned everything on and got ready to record another journey by the phantom footsteps.

Again, we were not disappointed. At 9:35 p.m., the rap of the footsteps began near the top of the staircase and sounded one after another as they moved down the corridor. I was just as excited as I had been the night before and the other investigators were even more delighted. We quickly checked our Polaroid photos and the video tape that we had recorded, although the EMF meters and the motion detectors had remained completely silent. As I played back the video, I could hear the faint tapping of the footsteps but any hope that I might have had that the infrared video would have recorded something otherworldly was quickly dashed. We had recorded the sounds of the footsteps --- but nothing else.

So, now what? We wondered how to proceed and what would be the best way to document the activity in some other way. After some discussion, we finally fixed on the idea of some additional cameras and perhaps some more old-fashioned methods of tracking the phantom walker. I spoke with the home owner and she agreed that we could sprinkle powder in the hallway, as long as we agreed to vacuum it up afterwards. It was an old method of doing things, hearkening back to the days of Harry Price, but I thought it might be worthwhile since nothing else seemed to be working. The plan was to position cameras directly in line with the powder, hoping that the footsteps might appear in the dust.

We returned once again the next night and set all of the equipment back up again. We replaced the motion detectors and EMF meters, still hoping that they might pick up some disturbance, and spread a thin layer of powder along the corridor. It was now 9:20 p.m. and we prepared for the arrival of the footsteps. I took a position at the head of the stairs and the other investigators waited just inside of two doorways along the corridor. They had turned on the monitoring equipment in the hall, careful not to disturb the powder that had been spread along the walkway.

As I stood near the small couch at the end of the corridor, I reached down for my camera and found that it was missing. I shook my head in disgust and realized that I had left my camera bag sitting on the table downstairs in the kitchen. I spoke quietly to the other investigators and told them that I would be right back upstairs. I hurried down to the kitchen and found my bag sitting on the table. I snatched it up by the handle and headed back for the staircase. As I was heading for the steps, I turned and saw the owner's daughter as she was leaving the bathroom that was located just beyond the kitchen.

She waved at me. "Good night," she said and went on down the hall to her bedroom, which, again, was located to the back of the house.

"Good night." I smiled at her and dashed back up the stairs. When I arrived on the second floor, I found my fellow investigators standing anxiously at the edges of the corridor. I asked what was going on.

"You missed it!" one of them told me. "While you were downstairs, they came again. But they never made a mark in the powder." He pointed down to the floor and I saw that the dust was as undisturbed as our equipment had been. What could we do to actually document that this was taking place? Could we ….?

And then suddenly, it hit me.

"Stay right there," I told the other two, "and tell me what happens while I am gone."

I left my camera bag on the small couch at the top of the steps and quickly descended the staircase again. When I reached the first floor, I went down the hallway to the small bathroom. I switched on the light and pointedly flushed the toilet. With that done, I turned and went back upstairs again.

My friends greeted me when I came back up. "It happened again!" they told me and then one of them, perhaps seeing the look on my face, finally asked. "What's going on?"

I let out a breath and began to explain my theory behind the "ghostly" footsteps, which later turned out to be correct, thanks to an investigation by an acquaintance who is a building contractor. Apparently, each night at around 9:30 p.m., the owner's daughter got ready to go to bed and as she did so, she made one last trip to the bathroom. When the toilet downstairs flushed, a banging would occur in the pipes that sounded just like footsteps going down the corridor. The reason that the sounds were not heard every night, and were sometimes experienced by the young woman, was that she was not always downstairs to use that particular bathroom.

You can imagine my embarrassment when I had to explain all of this to the home owner --- and how acute that embarrassment was while I was vacuuming the rug in the upstairs hallway. She took it quite well, though. In fact, she was even a little relieved when she realized that her home was not haunted after all.

The "Haunted" Attic

Hard lessons were still being learned....

I was contacted one day, about a year after the last incident, by a family who lived in a small town not far from Alton. They were convinced when they called me that the attic of their home was haunted. And I had to admit, from the history of the place that they recounted to me, I could understand why there might be a ghost lingering behind.

Old newspaper reports had it that the original builder of the house had been a farmer who was ruined by the Great Depression. One day, he went up to the attic of the house and hanged himself from one of the overhead rafters. His body was not discovered until friends came to look for him about a week later and smelled his decaying from the upper floor. Pretty gruesome, huh? Not surprisingly, the family who resided in the house had come to believe that the strange noises, the bumpings and thuds, coming from the attic, were the sounds of the farmer's restless ghost.

I had high hopes when I traveled to the house but having learned my lesson about expecting too much, I began searching for an alternate explanation for what was occurring. I sat down with the family and began documenting their stories and have to admit that they made a good case for a haunting. One of the things that I also noticed about their accounts was that all of the weird sounds came at night. With that in mind, the entire group of us went up to the second floor as the sun began going down, hoping to hear the ghostly noises from the attic. We gathered in the master bedroom, which had a closet that offered access to the attic rooms. A trap door in its ceiling could be pulled down to release a collapsible staircase that led upwards into the dark.

We waited for an hour or so, talking softly, before we first heard the sounds. The muffled scrapes and thuds sounded as though someone was walking around and I imagined the old farmer's boots as they shuffled across the attic floor ---- or worse yet, the bumping of his heels as he dangled from the end of that rope! Of course, that was my imagination hard at work and I made a quick decision to try and ignore it and find out what was going on for myself instead.

The home owner quickly pulled down the trap door latch for me and he and I unfolded the stairs. I had a flashlight gripped in my hands and I hustled up the stairs, switching it on as I climbed. I peered over the edge of the attic floor and turned my wrist to shine the light around. A bright reflection caught my eye and I swung the beam of the light back in the direction where I had seen it.

For a moment, I caught my breath --- and that's when I saw the ghost!

Okay, not exactly. I saw the so-called "ghost" all right and in fact, I saw three of them! They were low to the floor, covered in grayish fur, had long ringed tails and black masks around their eyes. That's right --- the ghosts in the house were a family of raccoons that had taken up residence in the attic! Apparently, as they began to stir each evening, the family had mistaken the sounds of their rustling as the ghostly footsteps of the former owner.

Media Messes & The "Cursed" Location Shoot

Over the years, I have been unable to avoid the media, seeing myself misquoted and badly portrayed in newspapers, new programs, television shows and documentaries. In many cases, though, working with the media can be very beneficial to a ghost hunter. A good newspaper article or an appearance on a television news program may help you to get established in your area --- but there are definitely downsides to dealing with the media as well. I can't count the number of newspapers articles that have been written about me with headlines like "Who Ya Gonna Call?" and "He Ain't Afraid of No Ghosts!". It's imperative that you keep a sense of humor about the publicity that you get and make the best of it.

Sometimes, that may be harder than you think, though. For example, back in 2001, I had the misfortune to work with what was then a popular television show about haunted places in America. Thankfully, the show is now defunct and even when they contacted me, they were already gaining a bad reputation for not exactly portraying their stories and locations with accuracy and also for hiring actors to pretend to be local folklorists or worse yet, eyewitnesses to hauntings. When I was first contacted by one of the producers, I declined to work with them. However, they informed me that they were going to do a story about Alton, Illinois --- whether I was part of it or not. So, I agreed to set a day aside for them in hopes that I could at least portray the town in an accurate light. Unfortunately though, anything accurate that ended up being filmed was apparently edited out of the final product!

One of the things that they chose to focus on was the fact that Alton was so haunted because bricks from the old state prison (which had a reputation for being haunted) were used to build many of the other haunted locations in the city, including the McPike Mansion, the First Unitarian Church and the old Mineral Springs Hotel. Sadly, this was totally untrue!

When I informed them that there was absolutely no validity to the story, they replied that they didn't care. This was the story that they were going with and I could be a part of it or not. I shot an introduction about Alton for them but I refused to say that the "story" they had concocted was true. Because of this, I was relegated to the opening 30 seconds of the segment and did not make another appearance. Believe me, I was happy about this! The rest of the segment turned out to be one blatant misrepresentation after another with phony video footage, fake investigations and completely inaccurate history.

It turned out better for me to not be a part of this story but for years afterward, I would get calls and messages from people who believed the story that was done for the show was true. Even though I bowed out of the ridiculous segment, it's now become my responsibility to explain to people why it was inaccurate.

But not all of the experiences that I have had with media companies have been completely negative. Some have been great, but those stories aren't nearly as amusing as some of the others --- especially the show that I did that I am convinced was "cursed"! To say that things started off all wrong with that whole "adventure" would be an understatement.

A staff member from what can best be described as a "tabloid television show" first contacted me a week or so before I would begin what turned out to be a strange trip to West Virginia. When she asked me if I might be interested in doing a segment on ghosts for the show, I immediately answered that I wouldn't be interested, at all! In fact, I had once stated that I would never work with this program again! Just a year and a half before, the show had filmed a segment about our annual American Ghost Society Conference and to say that they presented us in a bad light would be yet another of my colossal understatements.

Despite my initial misgivings, I did listen to what the researcher had to say and once more told her "no". I explained my bad feelings and she assured me that she could understand my concerns. After a few more minutes of small talk, we bid each other a pleasant goodbye and hung up. Thinking that I had heard the last from them, I immediately forgot all about it. But they would not go away that easily!

A short time later, I heard from the same staff member who wanted to try once more. She gave it another valiant effort and told me that she had gone back and watched the 1998 segment. She could understand why I had been upset and if it was any consolation, the original reporter for the piece had been fired. It had not been because of that particular segment, but he had been sent packing anyway. Once more, I thought about it and this time, reluctantly agreed to listen to her pitch. I asked what she had in mind for me to do.

According to the researcher, they had contacted the owner of an allegedly haunted antebellum mansion in West Virginia called Solitude Farm and he agreed to let a ghost hunter and a reporter spend the night in the house. Would be willing to do this --- with all expenses paid, of course?

She promised me that it would be a well-done segment and would hopefully make up for the last piece that I had done with them. The reporter assigned to the piece handled all of the paranormal-related segments they did on the show and was known for having an open mind. Would I do it?

To be honest, it sounded like fun and I was in the midst of the winter dry spell for ghost investigations anyway, so I agreed. I would be limited to only the amount of equipment I could take on an airline, but it sounded like just the sort of old-fashioned adventure I loved. I would really be able to get back to basics with the investigation and would bring along only my camera, a flashlight, notebooks, video camera, IR thermal meter, geo-magnetic field detector and of course, my laptop computer. All of the equipment, save for the laptop, would have to be shipped in my checked luggage, for obvious reasons. Can you imagine trying to explain the uses of a thermal scanner to an airport security guard? No sir, I would say, it only *looks* like a gun!

I told her that it sounded like fun and that I would be glad to do the show.

She told me that she would get back to me with details and so I envisioned the trip coming on some distant date, several weeks away. About five minutes later, the phone rang and this time it was the segment's producer. "So, I understand that you've agreed to spend the night in our haunted house?" she asked me.

I told her that I had and added that I really hadn't been given too many details yet, nor did I know when this would all be happening. To my surprise, she told me that I would be flying to West Virginia in just five days!

We soon got to work on travel arrangements and the first glitch in our adventure occurred. I should have had some sense of foreboding, but it seemed a simple enough mistake at the time. The fax machine rang and my travel itinerary began printing from the machine. As I picked up the first page and read it, I saw that my flight was scheduled to leave O'Hare Airport in the early morning hours of February 16. The problem was that this particular airport was about a four-hour drive from my home! The travel department, upon hearing that I was based in Illinois, automatically assumed that I must be near Chicago!

As you can imagine, airfare that is booked only five days in advance is far from affordable, but somehow, the flight problem was corrected and I was booked out of St. Louis instead. One possible disaster had been averted, but there were more to come!

Wednesday morning came and I was able to smoothly catch my flight out of Lambert International Airport. My first stop was Pittsburgh and then I would catch a connecting flight to Charleston, West Virginia. This was the closest airport to Solitude Farm and even then it was still a two-hour drive from our final destination.

Shortly after arriving in Pittsburgh, I heard my name being called over the airport intercom. I had a message and could I call the segment producer in New York? I soon got her on the line and learned that I was still supposed to catch my flight to Charleston, although I would not be joined there by the reporter who had been supposed to meet me. Apparently, he had taken ill the night before and was now so sick that he had been admitted to the hospital! The source of his illness was a mystery.

While this was bad (and apparently was nearly fatal for the segment), they wanted me to continue on and possibly do most of the on-camera work that was supposed to have been shared with the reporter. All that I had to do now was to wait for his replacement to arrive in Charleston, which would prove to be a mind-numbing seven-hour wait at the tiny airport.

"We're really sorry about this," the producer assured me, "but the show is still going to work out fine." What else could go wrong?

So, I grumpily boarded the plane that would take me on the next leg of my journey. It was a crowded flight on board a fairly dirty and very uncomfortable plane. After arriving in Charleston, I headed for the baggage claim area. It was a short walk as this was a very small airport. The buzzer sounded and the luggage carousel began to spin, unloading the various pieces of baggage from my flight. The rotating bags drifted past me for several minutes and I waited patiently for my suitcase to appear --- my suitcase with a couple of thousand dollar's worth of electronic equipment inside.

You may have already guessed where this is going, but if you haven't --- they lost my bag! Somewhere between Pittsburgh, Pennsylvania and Charleston, West Virginia, my case vanished into the ether! No one had any explanation for what had happened to it but they promised they were on the lookout for it. The (very nice) people in the luggage claims office assured me that if it didn't turn up on this day, they would deliver it tomorrow to Solitude Farm. I appreciated the thought, although that would make it hard to use the equipment during the overnight investigation we had planned.

What else could go wrong? That was a good question --- and I hadn't even gotten to the house yet! Luckily though, another disaster was narrowly averted when my suitcase showed up at the Charleston airport three hours later. Apparently, someone had forgotten to load it back in Pittsburgh.

So, after the producer finally arrived, we were off for the tiny town of Cashmere, West Virginia. The hamlet was located just a short distance from the Virginia border and not far from Greenbrier County, which was once home to the Greenbrier ghost.

On the way to Cashmere, I made it a point to learn more about Solitude Farm. The house had been built in the early 1840's by a man named William Peck, the designer of a place called the old Red Sulphur Hotel. The house had been constructed using slave labor. All of the wood flooring and joists had been cut on the property and the bricks used for the walls and foundation had been made at the small creek that passes through the farm. The stories vary as to who exactly designed the house, although it is believed that Peck sent one of his slaves to England to study architecture and brick-laying. Upon his return, the house was then built.

Originally, the house had been an L-shaped structure, two stories high, but a dining room was added with original bricks in the late 1880s. Sometime after the turn-of-the-century, a more modern wood edition was tacked onto the back of the house. The house had only seen five different owners during its existence, including the Peck family. It was later purchased by a Mrs. Lowe, who owned the house for a number of years. Her family started the Lowe's hardware company, which is now a national chain. After that, it was purchased by the Mann family, who lived in the house from 1967-1998. They later sold it at auction to a cattle rancher, who never lived in the place, and then in 1999, it was purchased as an investment by Bill Gadd, the owner at the time of the visit.

Stories of ghosts had plagued the house for years and, shortly after moving in, Bill Gadd had the first of his many unsettling experiences in the place. One night while he was working on his computer, he heard four sharp footsteps cross a room in the older portion of the house. The sound was followed by the slamming of a door, more footsteps and then another door, which opened and closed. Gadd told me: "If it had only been one door, I would have dismissed it as just the wind --- but two doors, and the footsteps? Well, I didn't have an explanation for that."

And this was only a small sampling of the many tales of Solitude Farm, as I was soon to discover.

When the producer and I arrived at the house, the camera crew was there waiting for us. They had spent the last hour or so setting up gear and getting ready for interviews with Bill Gadd and the son of one of the former owners of the house. This young man had grown up in the house and had agreed to come and talk about some of the occurrences he and his family had experienced during their three decades on the farm.

Shortly after we arrived, Bill gave us a tour of the place and I learned about the many strange happenings, ghost sightings and inexplicable events in the mansion.

We entered the house through the back door, which opened into the newer addition of the house. This was the only section of the place that was heated and it had never been bothered by the ghosts. They seemed determined to continue their existence in the older, original part of the home. I soon discovered that the old part of the house was empty and had been literally stripped of the decades of antiques that had once been there. They had been sold during the auction several years before, leaving the house bare and empty.

To be honest, this actually added to the eeriness of the house. The rooms were now only filled with shadows and each footstep echoed as we crossed the hardwood floors. The curtains had been removed from the windows, leaving them open to the black night beyond them. The farm was located in a remote and secluded valley. There were no lights visible from neighboring houses and this only added to the feeling of seclusion and isolation. I could understand why some people might be attracted to such a place, but for me, it was a little off the beaten path.

The downstairs portion of the house was shown to us first. To the right of the huge front door was the former music room. It was here that a piano was once located that had the unnerving habit of playing by itself. To the left of the door, and across a narrow foyer, was the front parlor. A staircase curved lazily up from the foyer, connecting to the upper floor of the house. It was on this staircase where witnesses in the past have claimed to experience one of the many phantoms of the mansion.

This particular ghost was that of a Confederate military officer, complete with a gray uniform, sash, saber and a large plumed hat, which he had the habit of removing in a graceful flourish to women he encountered in the house. A number of ladies had reported the officer in the past, including one of the former owners and her sister. Shortly after Bill Gadd moved into the mansion, he was visited by an old friend. On the very day she arrived, she told Bill that she saw the officer, peering through a window located near the top of the staircase. This window, which had once looked outside, now only displayed the new portion of the house. The officer had looked directly at her, she explained to Bill, then had bowed and removed his hat, which had a large feather in it. Moments later, he vanished.

Many of the strange sounds in the house seem to radiate from the staircase landing where Gadd's friend had reported the officer. There had been many reported episodes of "phantom footsteps" pacing up and down the stairs and roaming the second floor bedrooms. Doors opened and closed and inexplicably slammed shut. Voices, whispers and moaning sounds were commonplace, as was the chilling sound of a crying infant. This tiny spirit was another of the mansion's famous ghosts.

Legend had it that, many years ago, the mistress of the house became pregnant. This would not be so out of the ordinary except for the fact that when the baby was born, it was obviously racially mixed. At this time, such a birth was not acceptable. The man of the house went searching among the slaves for the most likely culprit and when the young man was found, he was hanged from a tall oak tree on the property. The lore of the house does not mention the woman's fate, but the baby was allowed to live on the house --- at least for the next year or so. At some point, a short time later, the child fell (or some say was pushed) down the main staircase and he died. His piercing cries have filled the night at Solitude Farm ever since.

Another ghost of the house is believed to also be connected to this same incident. Directly on the left side of the upper staircase landing is the door to the unfinished attic of the house. According to former owners, this door has had a habit of opening on its own for many years. Family members and friends often reported the sounds of footsteps on the landing and then the sound of the door opening. Even though it was locked tight the night before, it would be found standing open the following morning. In addition, witnesses in the house have also claimed to see the apparition of a black man, likely a slave, standing on the narrow attic stairs. It is said that he is always clutching a red brick in his hand. He is believed to be one of the architects who were sent to England to learn the craft --- and the man who seduced the mistress of the house. Although he was murdered many years before, he still does not rest in peace.

Just off the staircase landing is what is called the "Big Bedroom", so named for its large size and for the antique set of bed furniture that had once been located there. The bed, dresser and bureau set had been so big that it had to be dismantled to get it out of the room after the auction.

This was the room where Bill Gadd heard the first unexplained footsteps in the house. They had crossed this room and had opened and closed the two doors on the opposite sides of it. The haunting in this room was notable because of a mass sighting that took place here in the middle 1980s. Several sons of the former owners had invited a number of friends out to the house one evening and were sitting around in the "Big Bedroom" talking and sharing experiences of the house. Suddenly, as one of the boys was speaking, everyone in the room jumped to his or her feet and with a collective scream ran out of the room --- and all of the way out of the house! All of them refused to go back inside. Apparently, as the young man had been talking, a large, white misty shape had appeared directly behind him. That was more than enough excitement for the young people for one evening!

It would be in this room where I would experience my only unexplained incident in the house --- and where I would choose to bed down for the night!

After our tour of the house, we all returned downstairs to join the camera and sound technicians, for the interview with Bill Gadd. The interview and various film set-ups lasted for a number of hours, until finally it was almost 1:00 a.m. At that point, the crew planned to follow me as I took them on my own tour of the house, one involving temperature equipment, an IR camera and my geo-magnetic field detector. It was time to look past the legends and search for a scientific explanation for the strange activity in the house. Unfortunately, science would provide us with no plausible explanations -- just more strangeness.

The tour began in the downstairs portion of the old house. With my trusty EM Meter in hand, I scanned each room carefully, followed by the camera crew and the producer. However, despite my searching, the meter remained very quiet. I was able to detect no activity downstairs and even the staircase, where the Confederate officer had been seen, was silent and empty of unusual energy.

We then went upstairs and I found that all of the rooms were just as quiet as those on the lower floor. Finally, we crossed the landing to the "Big Bedroom" and it was here that all of the equipment began to suddenly react. The EM readings began to spike nearly off the scale! There was something in this room causing a disruption of the natural electro-magnetic field and it was apparently of massive proportions. As I scanned the room, I noticed changes in the field, as though whatever energy source was present was not stationary. It was moving back and forth and about the room. The device I was using was designed to pick up natural radiation disruptions, not electrical outlets or fixtures. Besides that, this room was not fitted with electrical conduit or fixtures, save for the overhead light and one plug that had been wired into the doorframe! When the house had been built, electricity was still decades away and the little wiring that had been done had been added later.

There was simply no explanation for the bizarre energy that I detected. I searched for a possible explanation and even inspected the outlet that was present, but I could come up with no logical to explain it. Of course, I am the first to admit that it *may* not have been a ghost but whatever the source of the energy, it was completely unexplainable. The mystery would continue later that night, and the next morning, when I checked the room again. Whatever the energy had been that night, it had now completely vanished!

So, would I consider Solitude Farm to be a haunted place? I would have to answer that with a "maybe". No, I didn't experience anything ghostly there, save for the unexplained energy, but the testimony provided by reliable witnesses was compelling, to say the least. My night in the haunted bedroom was uneventful, as well, but that does not lead me to believe that "something" was present in that house and might only be active on certain occasions.

Oh, and one last thing --- whatever happened with the "curse"?

I would have been willing to pass that all off as coincidence, and perhaps so will you. Regardless, I will let you judge those incidents for yourself. Just keep this last piece of information in mind as you do so....

On my way home, my flight was cancelled two times and delayed once. I was originally supposed to arrive back in St. Louis at 7:55 p.m. I made it instead just a little after 1:00 a.m.! Was it the curse? I don't know, but it sure seemed like it to me!

The St. Francisville Experiment

My "cursed" investigation turned out to be quite a bit of fun, in spite of my initial misgivings about it --- and in spite of the numerous things that went wrong. When the segment actually aired, I have to confess that it really did present both the house, and my investigation, in a positive light. Final products that do not do this (as you may have noticed from my first anecdote about working with the media) can often turn out to be the bane of your existence.

And that's exactly what happened to me when I got the chance to make my feature film debut back in 1999. I guess that I can say that I should be happy about the chance to be in a movie, as I don't know too many people personally who have been, but it was the movie itself that changed my mind about being overly happy to be involved.

The film, which was called *The St. Francisville Experiment*, was produced in September 1999 and it was originally scheduled to be released in theaters in October of the following year. As it turned out, though, it was dumped into a straight-to-video release in December 2000. Some would say that this might have been for the best although, surprisingly, there are many people who have actually enjoyed the film. I can tell you that some critics have called me the "best actor in the film" but that's not saying much since I am playing myself.

But to start at the beginning....

When I was first contacted about the project, it sounded very promising. The idea behind the "experiment" was to send four strangers into a haunted mansion and to have them film whatever strange things they experienced. My role was to train these strangers on how to conduct a paranormal investigation and to appear in the film as a consultant to the project. This was going to be, I was promised, an actual documentary about a very real investigation. With that in mind, I agreed to work with the producers and to appear in the film.

I was first contacted by film director / producer / writer Paul Salamoff and a producer who would soon no longer be involved with the film. The call came in August 1999 and I was asked to consult for a film that was designed to be, as they put it "the *Blair Witch* - except for real". The premise, as they explained it, would be to send this group of people into a genuine haunted house and to have them spend the night and to film everything that happened. At that point, the production of the film was a convoluted mess and involved not only the production company who later sold it to a Hollywood studio, but another small company that was famous for its low-budget but highly profitable horror films. The involvement of the latter company was not exactly a comforting thought for what was then a "documentary-style" film, but I admit the premise sounded like fun. After I was assured that it would still be a documentary, not a horror film, I again agreed to be involved.

The search began for a location for the film and since one of the other producers had been raised in Louisiana, she wanted to find a location that was based in South. Perhaps the most terrifying ghost story that I had ever heard was based in New Orleans and involved the terrible deeds committed by Madame LaLaurie. It's a great story, but unfortunately, her former home in New Orleans had been turned into condos --- so we would have to look somewhere else for the film's location.

From there, I suggested the St. Francisville region, which I was already familiar with thanks to it being the home of the Myrtles Plantation and other haunted spots. Soon, I was to hear that St. Francisville could be tied into the LaLaurie story, as well. Although I am convinced that some dramatic license was taken, there was a story that said that one plantation house in the area had allegedly been owned by relatives of Madame LaLaurie. Those familiar with the gruesome LaLaurie story will recall that after having her slaves taken away from her on charges of cruelty, they were purchased by relatives and then sold back to the family again. According to the source, some of these relatives had resided in St. Francisville. Local legend also had it that when the LaLauries escaped from New Orleans, they came here to hide. Do I really think that the mansion in St. Francisville was really a hiding place for the LaLaurie family --- or in any way connected to the legend at all?

To be honest, it's really, really doubtful but regardless, according to local stories, the house actually *was* haunted. For the purposes of the film, though, the plantation became the last hiding place of Madame LaLaurie. There were ghosts here, the stories said, and since the main thing (to me) was sending the participants into a haunted house, it didn't really matter whose ghosts they were. Perhaps they were another collection of ghosts, still haunting the house because of the tragedies of the past, which ranged from slavery to the Civil War, floods, disease, and even the classic unfinished business from the past. So, an agreement was reached with the current owners of the plantation and soon we had a location where the participants in the paranormal experiment would come (hopefully) face to face with the resident spirits. As I said, it didn't matter that much to me if the ghosts in the house were Madame LaLaurie or her victims. What seemed important to me was the chance to capture some real paranormal events on film. But could the producers (outside of Paul Salamoff) be trusted not to "stage" some ghostly activity if nothing extraordinary actually happened? Well, believe me, you'll get the answer to that if you see the finished version of the film. And yes, you'll be right when you surmise that I didn't trust them!

You see, somewhere along the line, the original vision for *The St. Francisville Experiment* became lost in a mix of special effects, comedy sight gags and improvisational acting. The "documentary" went wildly off track somewhere after I was finished with my portion of the film. But first, back to the actual making of the movie...

The premise of the "experiment" was to send four people with various backgrounds into the house --- an aspiring filmmaker, a student historian, a psychic and an amateur ghost hunter. My role was to meet with these people and offer them a crash course in conducting paranormal investigations. In September, we all flew to St. Francisville, where our first meetings took place and the majority of the filming would be done.

Having familiarized themselves with the story of Madame LaLaurie and my own *Ghost Hunter's Guidebook*, the participants then began trying to get comfortable with the various pieces of equipment and cameras that were provided for the investigation. This equipment included EMF detectors, motion sensors and temperature gauges, all of which was supposed to help them to discover the authenticity of whatever they experienced in the house. You'll get a chance to see segments of my crash course in the film. This was the longest segment that I did in the movie, aside from a dinner segment, where I am apparently trying to frighten the investigators (or so it was edited). A few people commented after seeing the film that it appeared that I seemed uncomfortable during the "training session". It seemed, they told me, that I was giving some children some very expensive toys to play with --- and I didn't really trust them to have them!

Once my "crash course" was completed, the cast was given some time to prepare and then, with a box of food, were sent into the house. Dramatically, an ambulance waited outside --- just in case. I rode along as the cast was taken to the house and there is no question that they were nervous. One thing that you won't see in the film (because, unbelievably, no one thought to film it!) is Ryan literally hyperventilating as we drove up the long road to the plantation house. It was probably the only genuine reaction of the whole film and none of the cast members even bothered to turn on their cameras.

Once the cast entered the house, my participation in the film came to an end. That was at the point where my suspicions began to surface, though. While I was outside the house, I learned that a trailer had been set up in the back from which the producers could monitor what was going on inside of the mansion. This would not have seemed to strange, if not for the fact that I (and later, Paul Salamoff) was banned from the trailer and from the property. My questions about this, and the extent to which the house was monitored and wired, went unanswered.

I would later find out that the entire house had been rigged with "special effects" so that the cast would actually think they were experiencing something. These "effects" would create a couple of the only worthwhile segments of the film, when the chair flew across the attic and when a door closed in an upstairs bedroom. These incidents managed to make the final cut of the film --- and so did a lot of other horrible material that never occurred at all! What most viewers don't know is that not all of the film was shot in Louisiana. There were a number of re-shoots that were done in a house (that looked uncannily like the mansion in St. Francisville) in California. But more about that in a moment...

After the film was completed and I returned home, things went into a spin with the movie. The situation had already been confusing while on the set. When I had arrived in St. Francisville, I discovered that the original movie company was no longer involved in the making of the film. All of the producers and everyone that I had been in touch with, with the exception of Paul, had been fired or removed from the set. Once the movie was in the can, it was sold off by the second company for distribution to a third. This new company decided that they didn't like the fact that nothing really "horrific" occurred during the filming, so they decided to abandon the "documentary" aspect and create a "pseudo-documentary" instead. They left in most of the intro information (although not all of it) that I was a part of and a portion of the original footage that was shot in the Louisiana mansion. The new company then decided to re-shoot a new ending, and quite a lot of phony footage, in California. It was during this re-shoot that the infamous scenes were created with the "bug in the sandwich", the falling chains, the cat in the armoire, people falling through the floor, the basement torture chamber and of course, the horrible "ghost" in the mirror. If the movie wasn't bad enough already, it had now gotten even worse!

Then, to make matters even more convoluted, the new film company was bought out and taken over by yet another studio. This led to many of the people who were working to bring the movie to theaters being fired and also led to many of the company's current projects being shelved, shuffled around or canceled altogether. As luck would have it, I ended up becoming acquainted with one of the disgruntled employees who was losing his job with the company. One of the last things that he did during his employment was to send me three *different* cuts of the movie (none of which turned out to be the final cut) and a collection of t-shirts and posters, which were never used for publicity. The movie had originally been planned for release in theaters and in September 2000 was shown in a handful of theaters around the country as test screenings. Predictably, audiences hated it and the movie vanished, only to be released on video in December of that same year.

One thing that I can say in the film's favor was that the trailer for it was great. In fact, it was much better than the movie itself! Many were excited when they saw it, only to shake their heads (and laugh uproariously) when they finally got the chance to see the finished product. Luckily for me, it faded quickly and while I received scores of questions about the movie when it was first released, the flood of queries soon faded. Occasionally, I am still questioned about my part in it, and just how much of the movie was real. Luckily, as time has passed, I can laugh about it now.

With the passage of that time, I can look back on the movie with a little more fondness than I did when it was released. My feelings of being tricked and conned into appearing in the movie have passed and it all just sort of seems fun now. As I asked earlier, how many people can say they have been in a movie? It may not be one of my proudest moments but I have stopped thinking that it's something to be embarrassed about. Instead, it's become just one more bump on the highway of my education.

BIBLIOGRAPHY and RECOMMENDED READING

Auerbach, Loyd - ESP, Hauntings and Poltergeists (1986)
Gaddis, Vincent - Mysterious Fires and Lights (1967)
Ghost Report Newsletter (edited by Troy Taylor)
Guiley, Rosemary Ellen - Encyclopedia of Ghosts and Spirits (1992 / 2000)
Haining, Peter - Ghosts: The Illustrated History (1987)
Hauck, Dennis William - Haunted Places: A National Directory (1996)
Hope, Valerie & Maurice Townsend - Paranormal Investigator's Handbook (1999)
Ogden, Tom - Complete Idiot's Guide to Ghosts & Hauntings (2000)
Price, Harry - Confessions of a Ghost Hunter (1936)
Price, Harry - End of Borley Rectory (1946)
Price, Harry - Poltergeist over England (1945)
Price, Harry - The Most Haunted House in England (1940)
Rawcliffe, D.H. - The Psychology of the Occult (1952)
Reader's Digest Books - Into the Unknown (1981)
Rogo, D. Scott - An Experience of Phantoms (1974)
Rogo, D. Scott - The Haunted House Handbook (1978)
Rogo, D. Scott - The Haunted Universe (1977)
Spencer, John and Tony Wells - Ghost Watching (1994)
Taylor, Troy - Beyond the Grave (2001)
Taylor, Troy - The Ghost Hunter's Handbook (1998)
Taylor, Troy - The Ghost Hunter's Guidebook (1999)
Taylor, Troy - Ghosts of Millikin (1996 / 2001)
Underwood, Peter - Ghosts and How to See Them (1993)
Underwood, Peter - The Ghost Hunter's Guide (1986)
Wilson, Colin - Poltergeist: Study in Destructive Haunting (1993)
Wilson, Ian - In Search of Ghosts (1995)

Personal Interviews, Correspondence & Investigations
Special thanks to all of those investigators, researchers, home owners and witnesses who gladly shared their hauntings with me.

Also, thanks to:
Nancy Napier
John Winterbauer
Len Adams
Bill Alsing
Luke Naliborski
Dale Kaczmarek
Tom & Michelle Bonadurer
Rob Johnson
And Haven Taylor

ABOUT THE AUTHOR:
TROY TAYLOR

Troy Taylor is the author of 49 books about history, hauntings and the unexplained in America for Whitechapel Press and Barnes & Noble Press respectively. He is the founder and president of the "American Ghost Society", a national network of ghost hunters that collects stories of ghost sightings and haunted houses and uses investigative techniques to track down evidence of the supernatural.

Taylor was born on September 24, 1966 in Decatur, Illinois, a Midwestern city that is steeped in legend and lore. Even the hospital in which he was born is allegedly haunted by a phantom nun! He grew up fascinated with "things that go bump in the night", as well as the writings of haunted travel writer Richard Winer and legendary ghost hunter, Harry Price. In school, Taylor was well-known for his interest in the paranormal and often took friends on informal ghost tours of haunted places all over downstate Illinois. He would later turn this interest into his full-time career.

In 1989, Taylor started working in a bookstore and a few years later, he wrote his first book on ghosts. It was called Haunted Decatur and delved into the ghosts and hauntings of the city where he grew up. He also created a tour that took guests to places that he had written about in the book. The book became an immediate success and its popularity, along with his previous experiences with ghost hunting, established Taylor as an authority on the supernatural. The book and tour led to media and public appearances and numerous requests to investigate ghostly phenomena.

In 1996, Taylor organized a group of ghost enthusiasts into an investigation team and the American Ghost Society was launched, gained over 600 members in the years that followed. The organization continues today as one of America's largest and most honored research groups.

In 1998, Taylor moved his operations, which now included the American Ghost Society, a history and hauntings bookstore and a publishing company called Whitechapel Press, to Alton, Illinois, near St. Louis. In Alton, Taylor started his second tour company, Alton Hauntings, which took guests to local haunted places in the small Mississippi River town. He would go on to put the place on the map as "one of the most haunted small towns in America."

Taylor remained in Alton until 2005, when he returned to Decatur. By then, he had also established two more tour companies, in Springfield, Illinois and another company that arranges overnight stays in haunted places called American Hauntings. These tours, including those in Decatur and Alton, were organized under the heading of the Illinois Hauntings Ghost Tours. Taylor also continued the operation of Whitechapel Press, which specializes in ghost-related titles and has more than a dozen authors working under its banner.

In 2006, Taylor also launched the Weird Chicago Tours, which are based on his book, Weird Illinois, which was published by Barnes & Noble Press. In 2007, Illinois Hauntings also launched ghost tours in Lebanon, Illinois and in Jacksonville.

In 2007, Taylor incorporated as Dark Haven Entertainment, Inc., a parent company for Whitechapel Press, the Illinois Hauntings Tours and for the Ghosts of the Prairie Website and Magazine. The new company also handles the film rights to Troy's ghost books and stories. Currently, there are three of his works optioned for possible film and television production.

Along with writing about the unusual and hosting tours, Taylor is also a public speaker on the subject of ghosts and hauntings and has spoken to literally hundreds of private and public groups on a variety of paranormal subjects. He has appeared in newspaper and magazine articles about ghosts and has also been fortunate enough to be interviewed hundreds of times for radio and television broadcasts about the supernatural. He has also appeared in a number of documentary films, several television series and in one feature film about the paranormal.

He currently resides in Central Illinois with his wife, Haven, in a decidedly non-haunted house.

☠ WHITECHAPEL PRESS ☠

Whitechapel Productions Press is a division of Dark Haven Entertainment and a small publisher, specializing in books about ghosts and hauntings. Since 1993, the company has been one of America's leading publishers of supernatural books and has produced such best-selling titles as Haunted Illinois, The Ghost Hunters Guidebook and many others. With nearly a dozen different authors producing high quality books on all aspects of ghosts, hauntings and the paranormal, Whitechapel Press has made its mark with America's ghost enthusiasts.

You can visit Whitechapel Productions Press online and browse through our selection of ghostly titles, plus get information on ghosts and hauntings, haunted history, spirit photographs, information on ghost hunting and much more. by visiting the internet website at:

WWW.PRAIRIEGHOSTS.COM

Dark Haven Entertainment & Whitechapel Press is the headquarters for the Illinois Hauntings Tour Co, offering the following ghost tours:

Weird Chicago Tours / Chicago, Illinois
Created by Troy Taylor and based on his book Weird Illinois from Barnes & Noble Press, this is an alternative tour of Chicago, offering visitors the chance to see the other side of the city. Visit Chicago's most haunted sites, most notorious crime spots, most unusual places and much more! Available all year round!

WWW.WEIRDCHICAGO.COM

Haunted Decatur Ghost Tours / Decatur, Illinois
Created by Troy Taylor in 1994, these are the third longest running ghost tours in the state of Illinois! Visit the city's most haunted spots and take a nightime stroll through Greenwood Cemetery! Available April - October!

WWW.HAUNTEDDECATUR.COM

Alton Hauntings Ghost Tours / Alton, Illinois
Created by Troy Taylor, these tours are an interactive experience that allow readers to visit the historically haunted locations of the city and can be booked every year from April through October. Hosted by Len Adams, Luke Naliborski & Troy Taylor ---

WWW.ALTONHAUNTINGS.COM

American Hauntings Ghost Tours
Created by author Troy Taylor these tours offer Haunted Overnight Excursions to ghostly places around the Midwest and throughout the country. Available all year round!

WWW.ILLINOISHAUNTINGS.COM

Springfield Hauntings Ghost Tours / Springfield, Illinois
Join us in the Prairie State's haunted Capital City for Springfield's only authentic ghost tours. Experience the hauntings of Abraham Lincoln, the Springfield Theater Center and much more! Available April through October and hosted by John Winterbauer ----

WWW.SPRINGFIELDHAUNTINGS.COM

www.ingramcontent.com/pod-product-compliance
Lightning Source LLC
Chambersburg PA
CBHW030016290326
41934CB00005B/360